TAJ MAHAL

AUTOBIOGRAPHY OF A BLUESMAN

Also available by Stephen Foehr from Sanctuary Publishing:

Jamaican Warriors – Reggae, Roots & Culture
Dancing With Fidel (US)/*Waking Up In Cuba* (UK)

Printed in the United Kingdom by Biddles Ltd, Surrey

Published by Sanctuary Publishing Limited, Sanctuary House, 45-53 Sinclair Road, London W14 0NS, United Kingdom

www.sanctuarypublishing.com

ISBN: 1-86074-247-5

TAJ MAHAL

AUTOBIOGRAPHY OF A BLUESMAN
TAJ MAHAL WITH STEPHEN FOEHR

Acknowledgements

First, to Taj Mahal's immediate family – people who live by the code of goodwill, sincerity, honesty and integrity – and to Lynwood Perry, who died in April 2001. Also to Emily Hunter, touchstone for all that is wise and compassionate; Richard Haight, mentor and renaissance mind, who prevents me from looking foolish in print; and Mary Horrocks, who applied her sharp eye and mind to this book.

And a special thanks to my son, Lucian, for keeping the pure heart of love beating in my life.

Stephen Foehr, March 2001

Contents

Introduction

Taj Mahal is not a front-porch, guitar-strummin' blues guy goin' on about cottonfields and suffering. He has always defied that image of a bluesman, yet he is considered to be the most authentic living link to the old feeling of the blues, while he continually expands the language of the blues idiom. He makes the music new by recombining the many colors of the blues taken from disparate cultures: 13th-century West African, South African, Caribbean, Hawaiian, Delta USA. Taj's music carries the knowledge of late-19th- and early-20th-century blues, today's blues, jazz, folk, R&B, zydeco, gospel, reggae, rock 'n' roll, ragtime, slack-key guitar, and calypso. Musicians who have played with Taj include, among many others, John Lee Hooker, Big Mama Thornton, "Sleepy" John Estes, Yank Rachel, Mance Lipscomb, Eric Clapton, The Rolling Stones, Miles Davis, The Chambers Brothers, Jimi Hendrix, Bob Dylan, Bonnie Raitt, BB King, Linda Ronstadt, Bob Marley, The Neville Brothers, Billy Joel, Sheryl Crow, Dr John, and Howard Johnson.

To the casual ear, his music can be deceptively simple, while the educated ear delights in his music's complexity and range. In one song, he can weave together West African, Caribbean and Delta blues so seamlessly that the boundaries can't be differentiated. To think of Taj as simply a bluesman is to know only one shade of blue.

He became a professional musician in the early 1960s, when the music of the times was tribal, a driving backbeat for the ideals of a generation determined to restructure society on the principles of Love and Peace. From folk to rock 'n' roll, the music was the equivalent of an "underground newspaper of the air, prophetically criticizing society's moral failures and standing up for the hopes and dreams of American youth," according to *Time* magazine. Free love. Drugs. Hippies. The Vietnam War. The civil rights movement. Black Power. The Great Society. The war on poverty. The Peace Corps. A man on the moon. The '60s were charged with revolutionary zeal that made everything seem possible.

Taj's music gave the tribe of the '60s generation a grounding that extended beyond their own moment in history. His tribe stretches back to his African and Caribbean roots, and reaches to future generations. The underlying chorus of Taj's music is that "you don't know where you're going unless you know where you came from." That, without the guiding wisdom of your ancestors, you're lost. Music is the universal voice of wisdom for Taj, the ineffable rhythmic connection of life that spans distance and time.

Throughout his career, Taj has remained true to the sources of his music, a fidelity that at times cost him dearly. He is respected and honored as much for his role as the "roots champion" as for his original music. He is a self-taught scholar of ethnic music, a virtual encyclopedia of the blues lineage, as well as a get-on-your-feet-and-stomp performer. He's also recorded more than 37 albums – in 1998, his album *Señor Blues*, recorded with The Phantom Blues Band, won the Best Contemporary Blues Grammy award, and in 2001 Taj and the band won another Grammy for the album *Shoutin' In Key*. People who listened to his 'Fishin' Blues' as children play it for their own children. Taj is such a legend that many people think he's dead, but he's only 58 years old.

1 Showtime

We're at Seattle's Jazz Alley in the bland, modernistic glass-and-steel United Airlines Building. The club's entrance is on the rear side, in the alley, perhaps to evoke some jazz/blues back-alley, alley-cat ambience. Inside the small dinner club, the balcony hangs over the downstairs bar. Tables with white tablecloths pack the main floor, leaving only thigh-squeezing space for people to slip past. We're sitting right next to the stage, with our elbows nearly on Taj's feet.

Taj is onstage wearing wraparound sunglasses, a bright shirt of colorful tropical fish, an island's grass-woven hat, and blue pants. He strums, checking that his guitar is right for his ear, and then says, "As a consumer, you ask, 'How come I can't go out and buy or listen to the artists I like?'" He leans forward, hips jutted back, shoulders thrust forward, his thumb keeping a steady walking beat on the bass string. "How come I hear only this narrow band of music on the radio, when I know there's so much more music out there?" He strums a high, sharp chord, as if to call attention. "Well, that's because the record companies sign twelve groups and hope they get one hit out of the bunch. If they get that hit then they ride it, promote it as far as they can drive it. They're driving that hit toward their bottom line, not toward the music's line. An artist gets twelve cents per record. The record company gets 88¢ per record. That's human nature behaving badly."

The audience waits, expecting a shot of hard cynicism, but Taj's voice is gentle, wry with can-you-believe-that-foolishness humor. Human beings behave badly, that's all right. You don't have to behave badly back.

"Blame it on the white man!" someone calls out.

"Everyone has responsibility, if you're breathing," Taj shoots back without a hitch in the rhythm. "It's all crazy, but sometimes it's good. It gives us an opportunity to take responsibility to change things. You want to survive, it takes all of us."

"Thank you, man," comes a response.

Taj runs a couple chords and tells a story about how his schoolteacher mother was always after him to enunciate his words clearly, in proper English. "'No des, does, dems, dats,' she'd say. But I'd go spend some time with my Caribbean grandmother" – he breaks into a perfect lilting Caribbean dialect – "and come back talking like dis. My grandmother had some serious grandmother rights with me."

He starts finger-picking the beginning of 'Freight Train.' "There's two women who had a pickin' style for which we owe a great deal: Elizabeth Cotton and Mrs Etta Baker. I met Elizabeth Cotton about 1963. She'd say," – he does her aged, cracked voice pitch-perfect – "'Will you bring me that guitar, Taj? I've got something you'll like.'" The audience laughs. "You can't deny a woman with a voice like that." He plays a few more bars of 'Freight Train.' Each note is clearly accented, so in the cascade of music you hear each note drop. "Make the music tumble from the guitar," Taj says. "That's what those two ladies did. Mrs Etta Baker was from Morganton, North Carolina. Out back of her house, she had an orchard with lots of birdhouses. We'd go walking through the trees and those birds came swooshing low. They knew they were safe. If Mrs Etta Baker was out there with you, those birds knew they had nothing to worry about.

"Both those women had a special pickin' style, very light. Finger-pickin' originated in West Africa and came over here on the slave ships. It eventually got mixed into Celtic, Scottish and Irish styles strong in the Appalachians." Taj goes into an extended medley of 'Freight Train' and 'Railroad Bill.' He quietens the music and says, "You can hear the style and rhythm in the blues, down-in-the-Delta blues." This reminds him of Mississippi. "You ever watched little girls skipping Double-Dutch rope? They're out there with ribbons in their hair and penny-shiny faces and dresses that stick out above their knees and red knee-high socks and patent-leather shoes, and they're chanting, 'Humpback, humpback, I, cricket letter, cricket letter, I, cricket letter, cricket letter, ippi.'" Taj and the audience break up. "Cricket letter means 'crooked letter,' as in s, but the pronunciation is an echo back to the African dialect of the slaves." This leads him to a story about Mississippi John Hurt. "He told me that he got a lot of practice time in when his job was to watch the cows so they don't stray from the field. Can you imagine that? That was the only job he could get then."

He runs some heavy blues chords. The cows remind him of Hawaii and slack-key guitar. "Cows originally came to Hawaii from Mexico, as part of a cultural exchange. When the United States annexed the Hawaiian territory, the US suddenly had itself a royal family, which countries like Mexico recognized. As a matter of protocol, the Mexican government offered King Kahmehameha some long-horn cattle. The king placed a taboo on the animals so people wouldn't butcher them. Eventually, some of those cows were allowed to range free and went feral, causing injury and death to people out in the bush foraging for medicinal plants in the highlands. King Kahmehameha requested aid from the Mexican government on how to deal with the cattle. The Mexican government sent over Mexican cowboys to round up the wild cows and teach the Hawaiians cowboy skills. The cowboys brought their guitars and the Hawaiians picked up on it, but they didn't know how to tune a guitar, because stringed instruments were foreign in their culture. So they experimented and developed open tuning."

He starts a song based on three harmonic chimes and plays the chords repeatedly, adding subtle variations. "This is based on the three-note whistle my father sent up the stairs to my mother every night when he got home from the late shift. She answered with a three-note trill. Up in my room, I'd half wake up when I heard their whistles, then snuggle back down in the blankets, knowing all was all right." His strumming becomes so soft that the audience leans forward to catch the barest of vibrations coming off his guitar. He learned to play so softly as a boy, up in the attic of the family house late at night, when he practiced this nearly inaudible music, so as not to wake his siblings.

The audience is mesmerized, silent, as if listening to childhood memories they'd forgotten. Carey Williams, Taj's tour manager, musician, and friend since 1979, leans against the wall behind the soundboard. He's a tall, slim, handsome man with broad shoulders, a dapper mustache, and close-cropped dark hair.

"The blues, it's like wine – it gets better with age," Carey stage-whispers. "People don't acknowledge that until it gets past a certain age. I think that's what's happening with Taj. More and more people are starting to acknowledge him. Age has matured his blues. His voice has matured, too. His voice has a lot of different dimensions to it that didn't show earlier in his career. He may not be that technical a singer, but he has an emotional quality that brings forth what he's trying to convey. People identify with the emotion and the quality that he sings. Even when he's surly and doesn't want to talk directly with people, he talks through the music. It's a gift he has.

"Taj has never been a flashy guitar player, but he's an incredible picker. You can hear so clearly the technique and the notes. He uses the dynamics of the whole range of the note – the sound, the volume, the timing. Not many people can entertain like that, and he's an excellent entertainer. I'm amazed how he can do this year after year and people never get tired of seeing him."

Onstage, Taj is going through his song 'Little Red Hen Blues,' a sly song about lovers, using the traditional metaphorical double-speak favored by the blues.

"He's a musician's musician. A lot of musicians respect him and want to play with him, open the show for him, because they know that his audience appreciates good music," Carey says. "A lot of musicians who once opened for Taj, and are now big stars, have come back to say, 'Hi.' Like Billy Joel – he opened for Taj in the early 1970s. Then a few years back, after he was a star, he sat in with Taj. He was acting all nervous, like it was his first time playing. Robert Cray opened for Taj. Stevie Ray Vaughan opened for Taj.

"Taj does a whole scope of music from all sorts of different styles and traditions, so it's bad form to try to pigeonhole him into one style of music. If you do that, you miss out on all the other things he does and who he is. His solo shows, like tonight, are different from his band shows. His solo shows are mostly Delta blues. The band shows are more wide open. He has more than one band at the moment, so the sound changes even within the bands. The Phantom Blues Band is more R&B retro. The Hula Blues Band is more Hawaiian-Caribbean.

"His music is right in our face, but [it] has subtleties. He wants you to hear it, but he wants you to *listen* to it. He doesn't want to just bang it against your head. That's why musicians, as well as non-musicians, appreciate him. They're getting taught, not banged against the head."

The audience laughs with Taj's clever song about the hen pointing out to the rooster that he doesn't come around her hen house as much anymore. Taj makes the hen's observation sound like a complaint and an invitation at the same time.

"He allows the feminine side of the music to come out, and a lot of women identify with that," continues Carey. "They sense that he is sympathetic and understanding. Also, he brings out a lot of the feminine qualities of a male in his music. That's why men don't feel threatened if the woman they're with – like here at the club – gets into his music. The men can get into the masculine side of the music and the women into the feminine side.

"Taj has a presence that, for women, is really exciting. It's not in an overt sexual way, but in a musically sexual way that excites. He's sexy. It's his whole aura – the presentation, not just the package."

A woman standing in front of Carey leans forward, bending to Taj and his music. Given the opportunity, she'd be up onstage in a flash and wrapped around Taj, but the smile on her face is one of delight, rather than the leer of lust. She turns and whispers, "He's so funny and intelligent and smart and riveting." Carey cocks an I-told-you-so eyebrow.

For the encore, Taj calls his 20-year-old son, Ahmen, up onstage. "We've been trying to arrange this for three years," Taj says. Tall, lanky Ahmen – also wearing a festive Hawaiian shirt, and with close-cropped, aqua-green hair – straps on his bass guitar. He has studied at the Berkeley School of Music, but this is like no classroom he's ever been in. He's a little nervous, but he hides it behind cool. No doubt it's like father like son, up there. They start with a song from Taj's *Sacred Island* album, a paean to island cultures ranging from Hawaii to Fiji to the Caribbean. Taj leans forward to the audience; Ahmen slouches back toward the monitor. Taj swings his guitar around to Ahmen, who flashes a starburst grin. They're in the groove, riding the music, the most intimate language they share.

2 Blended Roots

We're standing at an outlook in Tilden Park, above Berkeley, not far from the first house that Taj ever owned. The two-storey, white-frame house represented his recovery from near financial ruin. Four years before he bought the place, in 1974, he'd returned from a six-month, self-administered burn-out recovery program in Spain. His career was on a do-or-die edge. He was sleeping on his manager's couch in the office, was deep in debt, and had fallen behind in child-support payments. He didn't even have a driver's license. As we look out over the sun-baked golden hills, Taj starts the story about his music, life, and family.

"I didn't come on island-culture music in some jump-on, opportunistic way. Among the first songs I heard as a child were from the Caribbean, like 'Sly Mongoose,' 'Matilda,' and many others. I was born Henry St Clair Fredericks Jr in New York City's Harlem Hospital, May 17, 1942. My mother and I lived with my father's mother and father, who were both from St Kitts. My grandparents lived in the Brownville section of Brooklyn, where there was a big community of immigrants from the Caribbean, the Mediterranean, and Eastern and Western Europe. My father commuted by thumb from his job in Springfield, four hours away in Western Massachusetts.

"My grandmother, Clara Eldrina Carey, was the one who tuned me up to the whole West Indian side of the family. She had 17 kids, and she lost most of them. She only had five live. My father was one of them, and I was the first male grandchild. She could see through me that the generation was going to move on. She had certain grandmother rights, even though she and my mother didn't get along all that well. Even so, my mother never got in the way, so I had a full-throttled West Indian energy directly from my grandmother and grandfather – uncut, unadulterated. I didn't have that much straight-on experience with my grandfather, although I did get some input. He was from the older, stricter, British/Caribbean kind of thing. My grandmother was from the same thing, but there was a woman in that, so she had mothering instincts – the tone of voice, the asking of questions that the men don't usually ask in that kind of situation.

"I also spent a lot of time with my mom's stepmother, Ethel. She was really nice. I just loved Ethel. She was really soft and had a melodic type of voice. She came from a traditional South Carolina Southern background, and was a very powerful woman in her family.

"I spent a lot of time with Clara. I was really excited about her and liked her a lot. With her, I grew up hearing Caribbean music from the old-time players, the people who really played it, and not through any mainstream filter. She was a country woman from a far-out place I was connected to. She was funny, had a great sense of humor, as did my grandfather, Samuel, who was a very direct, correct, brusque, powerful man. He had gone up as far as he could in St Kitts and couldn't go any further. The best thing for him to do was to go to the United States, where he could turn on all jets and go full out and make sure that his kids had the best possible things they could have in the 20th century. My childhood was infused with all those ideas, from every kind of way. World culture was part of my childhood – not the armpit of world culture, but the possibilities of it.

"My grandfather came to this country after the turn of the century and did the typical immigrant thing – work, work, work, save money, save money, save money, send for the wife – although he met my grandmother here in the States. She, too, had immigrated, looking for a better life. My grandparents were intense people; you knew they were there. My brother, Richard, he describes our grandmother as being so *thick* – like, when you look at the pictures of the old people and you know that they carry their native land in their very being. He says that our grandmother had West Indian and African fire coming out of her eyes, and he's right. He says that Grandma and Grandpa scared him because they were so fierce looking, but she was beautiful, and he's right.

"I wrote the song 'Clara (St Kitts Woman)' on the *Mo' Roots* album [Columbia, 1974] for my grandmother. In the song, I tell how, when she'd come visit us in Springfield, she'd make peppermint patties on the stove. She'd send me and my brothers to the drug store to get a tiny green bottle of peppermint extract. She'd mix that with sugar and water and some other kinds of flavor. Then she'd drop dollops on the hot stove top, one of those wood-burning stoves with solid cast-iron lids over the cooking holes. The heat would instantly draw out the water. That was an old-country thing. Like the song says, 'She'd love you, hold you, scold you, making sure she told you what you need to know.'

"My father, Henry St Clair Frederick Sr, was born in Harlem. The *s* on our last name was added later. We added the *s* because there were too many Frederick, so the mail kept getting mixed up. We clarified that. He grew up in Brooklyn, in a very ethnic, heavily immigrant community: Puerto Rican, Cuban, and a lot of Eastern and Western European people – the woman who lived upstairs was from Barbados; the night watchman down at the corner was from St Lucia. My father grew up in that rich cultural mix, and that was an important influence on me, later on.

"Father was a jazz musician who also had some training as a classical musician. He could read and write music. His oldest brother was also a musician – violin and drums – who had a combo that played for years in the hotels at Lake Placid in upstate New York. Another of my uncles was a reverend, and my Uncle Joe – the only one of the brothers still living – worked as a troubleshooter for Con Edison in New York City. Uncle Joe said my dad had music in his bones. Father composed jazz for the piano and collaborated with my godfather, Buddy Johnson. Buddy was a jazz musician, and had a big band with his sister, Ella. According to Uncle Joe, my dad wrote the lyrics for 'Jammin' In Georgia' and 'Swamplands,' both for Earl 'Fatha' Hines.

"My grandmother wanted my father to marry a Caribbean woman, but in 1938 he met Mildred Constancer Shields, who had come to New York in 1936 or '37 from the Cheraw-Bennettsville area of South Carolina, along the PeeDee River. General William T Sherman captured Bennettsville – which has about 5,500 people – during the Civil War, on his march to the sea, on which he burned everything in his way – crops, houses, the whole lot. He scorched the earth. My mother was raised in the tradition of very strict, black Southern roots. Her mother was half Cherokee, but looked like a full blood. She passed away when my mother was 13 or so. My mother, her father, stepmother and stepsisters and stepbrother all migrated to New York City. She was a college graduate from South Carolina State, with a degree in early childhood education. She had taught in the South, but came north to find a better job. Like many people from the South, she had the idea that things were going to be so much better up north."

Taj stands stock still while reciting the early history of his family, baseball cap pulled low over his eyes. It's a hot, bright California day. He looks out over the parched hills of Tilden Park, which look like golden dumplings – no trees, just long, yellow grass. He speaks in a low voice, slipping from a college-educated cadence to rural folk-talk, often in the same sentence. As he starts into the next part of the story, he shifts a few steps this way, pauses, a few steps that way, as if picking up a beat. These little rhythmic patterns of movement often accompany Taj when he starts to speak about – or play – music.

"This whole migration thing to the North was important in spreading the blues. With the people came the music. Rural blues of the Mississippi Delta were taken north up the Mississippi River to Chicago. The first stop for the rural blues guys was Memphis, and from there a train ride to Chicago. Blind Lemon Jefferson made that trip. He had a hit, 'That Black Snake Moan,' in 1926 in the rural South and among blacks of the northern cities. Charley Patton, Robert Johnson, Son House, and other early blues singers came up on the blues train. Memphis Minnie, Jimmy Yancey, Big Mama Thornton, Big Joe Turner, T-Bone Walker, Muddy Waters, Big Bill Broonzy and other blues legends made the trip in the 1940s, and along the way rural blues evolved into urban blues. But it's all the blues.

"That same blues migration happened up the East Coast – actually, all the states above the Mason Dixon Line. Western Massachusetts, the Boston area, all around there, was abolitionist country, and played an important role in the underground railroad, bringing slaves up from the South. So there was a lot of Southern blues and gospel in the culture I grew up in.

"My parents got together around music, which was swing and the beginning of bebop. That is significant, in terms of what kind of music I heard from them. My mother – very beautiful, in an Ella Fitzgerald way – wanted to be a singer. Supposedly, she sang in the Fox and Apollo Theaters in New York, but church music was her main thing. She had a real diverse sense and love of music. She even sang in a couple of local opera productions when we lived in Springfield.

"After I was born, my father basically quit playing music and started working as a day laborer. In those days, it was pretty much impossible for a musician – especially a black or a Latin musician – to really make money, in terms of the larger scheme of things. It was like the black baseball players – they played for the love of the game.

"At that time, you'd hear from black families about towns and cities that were real cool to move to, where work was available, with decent wages, decent housing, not a lot of racism. Springfield, Massachusetts, was one such town. My father hitchhiked up there, got a room in a rooming house, then found a job in a brass foundry, Chapman Valve. On Friday nights, he'd hitchhike back to spend time with my mom, then on Sunday afternoon hitchhike back about 175 miles to Springfield.

"When I was six months old, the family moved to Springfield, in 1942, just before Christmas. There were perhaps 1,400 black people living in the town. That included the so-called Black Yankees, who had been living there since the Civil War or before. It was a positive town, pretty well settled in its racial attitudes. Folks worked together, knew each other, generations grew up together, so there wasn't a kind of Southern division. There were places where, because of your color, you couldn't get a house. But there was so much more good stuff for you that living in a white neighborhood was way on the outside of your concerns.

"Springfield developed with waves of immigrants. Each ethnic group initially settled into a neighborhood – Eastern European Jews, Latins from the Caribbean, blacks from the South and the Caribbean. As people made their lives better with economics, they'd sell their place in the city and move out to the newly developing suburbs, the Greater Springfield area. Back when I was growing up there, the suburbs were mostly woods. A lot of the Caribbean, European, and Mediterranean people had gardens and fruit trees. All us neighborhood kids knew where the fruit trees were, even the mulberry trees. Berry bushes were all over. In one of the houses where we lived, I could lean out the second-storey window and pick apples off the tree. A lot of my love for nature came from our family weekend picnics in the country.

"At least 50 percent of our neighborhood was black, maybe 60 percent. It wasn't all Southern people; there were a lot of Caribbean people. I didn't have the attitude of a lot of kids who came up from the South, that attitude that 'The white people have been bad to us, we've been beaten, we've been shackled in slavery, so therefore we're never going to get a chance.' The Caribbean element of the community was important for me. I was hearing music and a way of life coming out of the culture. In those days, islands music wasn't carried by the radio or on the jukebox. The closest to Caribbean music carried would be Harry Belafonte. In areas where lots of West Indians lived, you might hear The Mighty Sparrows, Calypso Rose, or The Duke Of Iron.

"Because of the close-knitness of the Caribbean community – and our family was part of that – I was always hearing and communicating with people of that background. I took on some of the philosophy and understanding of life from a Caribbean 'can-do' perspective. For example, as a boy, I spent a good deal of time looking at fishing reels in the hardware-store window. I studied how they worked. I had an old broken reel without a spool to wrap the line around. I took one of my mother's sewing spools and a wing nut and fixed that reel so it'd work. It didn't work as well as store-bought, but it got the line out and the fish in.

"We were working class when I was growing up. My parents were typical Caribbean in that, as soon as possible, those people get their own place and space. My parents rented, moved several times – Union Street, Lilian, Hancock – and bought a house on Monroe Street in 1947 or '48. They raised us five kids in that house – myself, Samuel, Richard, Connie, and Carole. After my father died, my mother married Hughan Williams, who had three kids. Then Osborne came along.

"Now Samuel – known in the family as Eddie – owns an art gallery. Richard, aka Seabreeze, or Rick, is a technical service supervisor for an electronics firm and has his own sound company, Seabreeze Audio. Connie is married to Dr James Malone, a college dean, and has a little cottage industry of searching fleamarkets for antique lace and linen. She's also on the board of directors of the Huntington Arts Council on Long Island, where they live. Carole is a popular singer in Paris, where she has lived for the past 20 years. She had the Top Three songs in France in 1998. Osborne, or Ozzie, who toured with me as a drummer, manages a home for people with disabilities and co-ordinates a work program for them.

"The neighborhood on Monroe Street was a good 1950s community. Everybody knew everybody. My father was working and Mom was mostly staying home baking cookies and looking after the kids. My mom was also involved in the local musical scene. If there was a big do, she'd be asked to sing. She attended night school at Springfield College to get her master's degree in education. Even though she had a teaching degree, and had taught in the South, she couldn't teach in Massachusetts without a master's degree. Later, she became the first black teacher in West Springfield. She taught at the Main Street School for 25 years before she retired.

"My parents had the respect of the community, and as children we all knew that. They were responsible and caring. They never exchanged a harsh word in front of each kids, never fought in front of us. We all felt their love for each other. It was a strong bond that we all felt. We really didn't clearly know, as kids, the depth of their love. When we were whining, they'd say, 'Look, it's not like this for all kids – parents who love you, parents who love each other. You have a roof over your heads, clothes on your back, and food in your belly. You're smart, intelligent, and you can do anything you set your mind to.' They were always supportive. My father would say, 'I don't care if you're a garbage man or whatever, but whatever you do, you do the best you can possibly do with what you got.' That was it. It was, like, okay, cool. All the flak that came from people in the street never cut through that support and love. How you going to get over that?

"A lot of our close friends were families from the South, the West Indies, East and West Europe, and Africa. People in our circle were getting their education, teaching school, being doctors, lawyers, ministers, independent business people, successful entrepreneurs. People from all walks of life stopped in at our house. There were also white folks who enjoyed being around a group of black people who were progressive.

"Buddy Johnson, my godfather, who was a great bandleader, on the level of Billy Eckstine; Trummie Young, a real good friend of my dad's; the bandleader Jack Teagarden – these people my parents knew personally. They came to town or to play in Holyoke, about nine miles away from my home, at the Valley Arena. That's where all the big bands played. Back in the '40s, being on the road for black musicians was a problem about where to eat. One time, my mother set up to cook for this big band. Some odd hour in the morning, this big band bus pulls up in front of the house, and in comes all these musicians. They're clapping my father on the back and hugging Mom, because she put out all this real Southern cooking. These guys were just knocked out.

"All us kids got woke up and we came down. It was one of the most exciting times a kid could have, with all these musicians. I remember being excited about that for years later. Real musicians came by our house and really knew my dad. Once, in Hawaii, I had a chance to speak with Ella Fitzgerald. I told her that my parents spoke highly of her, especially my dad, and went on a bit about him. She looked at me, and it dawned on her that, oh my god, this is that man's son. 'Oh, yeah. Genius,' she said. 'I knew him really well.' My mother had talked about them meeting.

"So, as a child, I was aware of this mix of peoples and languages and cultures. I grew up in an eclectic melting pot of music and all kinds of people and accents in and out of the house. High energy all the time. All kinds of music – not just black music, but Mario Lanza, Kate Smith, classical, jazz, blues, all the Christmas carols, Bing Crosby. My mother used to sing us German lullabies. She brought her Southern gospel music with her, so I was hearing those sounds as I grew up. Instruments were regarded as magical things. As a kid, you just didn't go put your hands on one unless you knew what the hell you were doing. To pick up an instrument was a serious commitment."

Taj stops ambling across the small prow of the overlook where we stand. He looks at the yellow-land/blue-sky pretty picture and falls silent. Taj can talk a very entertaining streak, but in the more private moments the words slow down to a thoughtful pace. Now, as he continues the story, the tone shifts, with more bottom notes and fewer bright accents.

"My dad was known as Harry or Henry St Clair. He had a reputation for preaching on the stump to people, and was heavy into the Garveyite doctrine of black self-determination, as were most of the Caribbean people we knew, being Garvey was Jamaican. Marcus Garvey was, after World War One, this country's leading black nationalist. His African Zionist Movement had 500,000 members at one time, and back around 1921 he founded a steamship line, the Black Star Line, with the idea to link black peoples around the world in commercial enterprise. He purchased a freighter and ran trade between New York and Jamaica. Garveyites had an independent 'can-do' attitude, rather than just waiting around for everybody to get together or be given what you needed. Garvey was one of the ideological forebears of Elijah Muhammad, founder of the Black Muslims, so Garvey's influence has continued from my father's time to my time.

"My father thought about going back to Africa, but mostly that was to give us kids a full circle of connection to our ancient culture. As kids, we always talked about going back to Africa. In 1979, I did a tour of West Africa with my brother Seabreeze. The State Department sponsored the tour as part of a cultural exchange program during the Carter administration. I did then – and do now – [feel] that Carter had an exceptional foreign policy that sent a lot of people around to represent the United States. And he had great respect from world leaders.

"I totally understand the music from that part of the world. There are things on the inside of such music that you have to understand as it goes along, like the historical perspective. The music is an accompaniment to a narrative of how people live in those particular areas. Often, the narrative is about a great person or events. It tells the exploits of the man, that he is wonderful and generous, so that smoothes the way for him to come into town. There is something in that music that resonates in me beyond the guitar.

"On Fridays, my mother would prepare food to take for our Saturday picnic in the country. We'd never do a picnic on Sunday, because my mother was churchgoing. She was the religion in the house, a born Baptist, with all that gospel stuff going for her. But we were never pressured to join any particular church. It was a free choice, in terms of what church I went to and how often, so I went to church with a lot of different people.

"My father was totally the other way about religion, but he didn't discourage her from encouraging us kids to attend church. The reverend was always coming around trying to talk to him – 'We know you are a very strong-minded man, Mr Fredericks, and you have ideals,' and so forth. Dad would say, 'I can't get past this. I can't get past that.' The reverend could never give him a reason to really go for it. Dad was too independent in thought. A lot of my father has rubbed off on me.

"I didn't care for the hypocrisy that I saw connected to religion. What I saw was that some people did whatever the heck they wanted to for six days without regard for the Good Book and on the seventh day talked about those things they shouldn't be doing. Then, on Monday, go back out and do everything – from dipping in the till to not communicating – all over again.

"I learned certain songs from church, but I was ambivalent about church music, [although] it was probably a bigger influence than I acknowledged at the time. Singing in a choir didn't make me want to sing music or use my talent that way; it was only about the music. I didn't worry about the philosophy or dogma behind it. The music encompassed all the best of what the words were trying to say. That was one of reasons I recorded 'You're Gonna Need Somebody On Your Bond' on the *Giant Step* album.

"As a boy I took clarinet lessons, but the clarinet was a difficult thing. Trombone was a little more fun. The piano teacher said I'd never learn to play music. She was right, if that meant I wouldn't learn to regurgitate what was put in front of me and I wasn't supposed to look anywhere else. The harmonica was fun, but I never understood how you got that sound out of it. What were the players doing to get music out of it? Playing a special kind of harmonica? Did they make them anymore? I could not figure it out. It was a confusing instrument. The harmonica doesn't give its music up right away. With a piano, you can sit down and get a melody out of it.

"I could hear that there were different kinds of harmonica players. There were the popular players, who didn't have too much soul, and then there were other guys who played like there was something going on that was totally connected, so I always listened for that. I heard early on the difference between just playing music and *music*. Now I know there are certain cliché ways of playing, or somebody's particular way to playing, or the way the piece was arranged. But as a boy, it was all music for me."

3 First Hard Lessons

"I suppose I've got to talk about my father's death." It's a subject that Taj clearly wants to avoid. "Come on, I've got some errands to run." We leave Tilden Park and drive to his travel agency in Berkeley, where he books flights for gigs on the East Coast. Taj is talkative, jiving with everyone, doing business in a very personable way. We go to a grocery store stocked with all the good stuff – 16 different kinds of olives, more cheeses than you can name, select wines, foods from nearly every country in the United Nations. This is a place where chefs shop. Taj, knowledgable about cooking, spends a long time selecting slabs of filleted fresh fish.

Then we find an obscure coffeehouse and sit in a far corner with a couple of tall, skinny lattes. "I only want to talk about this once," Taj says. "My father's death has been a painful thing, and still is, to an extent. I may have resolved it, but I still have trouble." His voice drops to the private tone, low and soft, not meant for an audience.

"We lived on Monroe Street. My dad borrowed $1,500 from his dad to buy the house. Our property had a couple houses and a long drive that led to the back yard, with six garages. My father had gotten into a labor dispute with his employer, Fisk Rubber. While waiting for arbitration between the union and the company, he did independent contracting with a dump truck and a tractor with a big scoop on the front. He was in the back yard trying to drive the tractor up onto the truck bed. He tried twice to get that tractor up on the bed but couldn't get it right. My mother went out and told him that food was on the table, and he said, 'All right, I'll be right in. I want to try this one more time.' That's when the accident happened. September 1954. I was twelve years old."

Hughan Williams, a good friend of the Fredericks, and who later became Taj's second father, witnessed what happened next: "Normally, Harry had a place where he could drive the tractor right onto the truck, but this day he was loading the tractor onto the truck in his back yard. I was right there, that day. He put two planks on the back of the truck and drove the tractor up onto the truck. The planks were not secured, and the tractor's rear wheels kicked the planks off. The tractor was not completely on the bed of the truck and tipped over. He fell first and the tractor fell on top of him. Busted his head right open right there. What could we do? Nothing. Just sit and watch it."

Taj ran out of the house. He saw his father's crushed skull, the brains on the ground, the blood mixed with motor oil. "I was so stimulated by the situation I don't think I slept for three days – I was awake for everything, watching to see what was happening with my mother, watching where my brothers and sisters were. They had to give me some liquor to bring me down, to make me sleep. At other times, my father had said to me, 'If anything happens to me, you look after your mother and brothers and sisters.' I kept thinking, why is he saying that to me? Then, one day, *kaboom* – that was it. It wasn't a slow change over years. You go forward from there.

"Coming from a culture that is not a whining culture – like, we don't air our laundry on the street, we don't whine about the bad – death happens. That's the way life is. Things change, and you have to pick up and make it work. I never saw myself as not being able to survive my father's death, but it made me very careful as an individual in later life.

"My father's death made me realize that I had to be doing the work that I needed to be doing. It made me more serious about doing my stuff, not being frivolous. Instead of lounging around, waiting for stuff to happen, I got busy. I started working as soon as I could, because that was the responsibility of the eldest. From 14 and 15 years old, I was a pretty busy guy, working on tobacco farms and, at age 16, a dairy farm. By 19, I could handle anything. I had had five years of work in already, on weekends, school vacations, summers. I never took vacation."

The tragedy devastated the family. Taj's brother Richard remembers, "My mother lost it. She was a beautiful, educated Southern woman whose husband thinks the world of her, encourages her to complete her formal education, who says, 'I'll do the grunt work here on the ground, drive the tractor and truck to make sure you get your master's degree.' Then he dies. I remember her wailing and moaning. The older ladies would not let us younger kids go into the room where she was. We wanted to be with Mommy, but Mommy was just freaking out. The ladies gave her some whiskey in a little brown bottle, because nothing would stop her from crying. That's the first time I saw alcohol in my house."

"That one event altered all of us," says Connie, the eldest daughter. "We were changed completely as a result of my father's death. My mother was extraordinarily happy with my dad. They had a strong, black love together. They had a really solid relationship that was the core of us. It was destroyed when he died. I think from that pain of his death came a whole myriad of pains that affected our family and our lives, especially in relationships. I know Taj carries a lot of pain around Dad's death. He is Harry Fredericks' son. Harry adored his son. He really did. He was very proud of him. Taj's first memories are with his dad."

After Harry's funeral, the distraught Mildred took her two young daughters to New York and stayed with her family. Taj and his two brothers spent two months at the Buckingham Street Home, connected to St Peter's Church. "I didn't have an opinion one way or the other about being left there," he says. "I was the eldest, so I had to look out for the situation. I didn't think, 'How is this impacting me? Oh, gee, I'm really resentful,' or any of that kind of stupid stuff. That didn't even compute."

Mildred wrote from New York and asked Hughan Williams to stay and look after the house. "She told me that she'd need a man around the house," Mr Williams recalls. "After she got back, I stayed keeping the house and everything."

Mr Williams, in his late 70s, is a small man with a bald dome fringed with gray hair and a vigorous voice that carries the lilt of his native Jamaica. Osborne (Ozzie), born to Hughan and Mildred, describes his father as "a very quiet man, unless you get him in the right mood. He talks when he needs to talk. He says a lot with his non-verbals – just his mannerisms, and his uniqueness in the way he moves about, and his facial expressions. From the nose up, you can see a lot what's on his mind, tell what he's thinking, what you're doing right, what you're doing wrong. He could just look at me when I was doing the wrong thing and I'd get it – he didn't have to open his mouth. I think that's a West Indian trait, the facial expressions and non-verbals. Often we communicate that way. He has that formality and reserve of the islands, of someone who has a great respect for work. He was a very hard-working man."

Mr Williams came to the United States from Jamaica in 1943 as a contract worker to harvest crops, given the labor shortage due to World

War Two. He first worked on a farm in Saginaw, Michigan, and then, when his six-month contract was up, he went to Florida to cut sugar cane – dangerous, back-breaking work. He followed the crop planting up to Connecticut, where he got a job picking tobacco in summer and, in the winter, worked the tobacco warehouse in Hartford. He and other Jamaicans often spent their weekends in Springfield, where they had made friends.

He met a woman named Viola Baisden, and they took a liking to each other. One day, in 1949, all of the contract-labor Jamaicans were ordered home. Mr Williams didn't want to return to the island. There was no work, and he didn't want to leave Viola. She was an American, so if they married then Mr Williams would be eligible to return. The ceremony was performed on the day before he took the bus south on the first leg of his homeward journey. He returned to Springfield on April 1, 1950.

"Viola and I had three sons: Robert, Winston, and Hughan Jr." Mr Williams tells the story in the living room of the same house in Springfield, where the Williams and the Fredericks became a family. "Viola died suddenly from an aneurysm when our youngest boy was ten months old. During that period, I was working for Monsanto, in the kettle room, where they melted down plastic to mold into a product. I rotated shifts – 7am to 3pm; 3 to 11; 11 to 7. Six days on, two days off. I wanted my sister in Jamaica to come care for the kids, but I had difficulty getting her up here. A friend of mine knew of the Fredericks family. She let them know that I was looking for someone to care for my three boys. I took the boys to the Fredericks' on Monroe Street for the six days I worked, then would take them back on my days off. Mildred was at home caring for her five kids.

"I didn't know Harry or Mildred before that. During the days, when I was working nights, or when I was off, I generally walked up to Monroe Street and helped Mildred with the eight kids. We'd all do it together. Harry and I were close friends. Very close friends.

"After Harry's death, the city took the Monroe Street property by eminent domain for a parking lot. That's when I bought the present house, at 163 Marion Street, and we moved there. Mildred and I got married there two years after Harry died. About a year after, we had Osborne. In our house, there was never stepbrothers or stepsisters. You couldn't tell the Williams from the Fredericks."

Connie recalls, "My mother told me many times that Harry had said to her, 'If anything ever happens to me, Mr Williams would be a good person for you to be with.' That's what happened. He died and my mother married the man, just like her husband had told her to."

Mr Williams also bought the house next door on Marion Street. "There wasn't much back yard with just one house for the kids to play," he recalls. "I bought the other house and removed the fence between them and used that fence to fence in the whole yard. I said, 'You can all play in that back yard there, but I don't want you out in the street. You can bring your friends in, but your friends have to behave.' Even today I can walk the streets and people say, 'Hi, Mr Williams, don't you remember me? I used to come play at your house.'"

Initially, it took some time for the Fredericks children to adjust to Mr Williams and his thick Jamaican accent, which they could hardly understand. Taj recalls, "It was a pretty big step for a man to walk in there and realize, 'You know, I can't really step into Harry's shoes; I've got to make my own shoeprints.' He didn't come the other way and be namby-pamby and try overly hard to reach out. He was just himself, all the way along the way. I remember people saying, 'You're really nice to your stepfather.' I'd say, 'Yeah.' They'd say, 'Well, I don't know if I could be that.' See, if I ever had a beef with him, we wouldn't just have an attitude; we'd talk to communicate. As the oldest, I was more of the communicator with the adults. I never had any beef with him just because he was my stepfather. He always treated me decently."

"With Hughan," Connie says, "we tried very much to embrace him. However, he had the daunting task of living up to the memory of our dad, and that was hard. Harry's memory was so alive in our house that I don't know how easy it would be for any man to survive in there without feeling threatened or intimidated. I'd think it would be very hard for Taj, Eddie, and Rick to embrace another man as a father figure. They might try to have a respectful relationship. It was easier for me and Carole – we were six and four – to accept him as a father." Nevertheless, the families blended successfully. Mr Williams became "Poppo" and Mildred was "Moms" to the nine children.

"When the two families came together, the artistic things started coming out from day one," recalls Winston, one of Mr Williams' sons. "Our biological mother, Viola, was a good singer in the Baptist church choir, and she did crafts, like crocheting, all sorts of things with her hands. Me and my brothers also did a lot of artistic stuff with our hands –

drawing, painting, sculpture, batik, woodcraft. In the third and fourth grades, we were drawing portraits and people were paying for them.

"There was lots of music around the house when the families joined. Our parents had 78rpm records of the blues and jazz. The youngest six kids, we were the Motown generation. By the time we hit sixth and seventh grades, we were forming trios and quartets with each other. We'd harmonize, do group singing, imitate The Supremes, The Temptations, The Marvelettes. Then each of us took a solo. And we were into dancing, could do all the steps. Ozzie, at two years old, still wearing diapers, was putting a little suit jacket over his shoulders, wearing shades, and using a fork for a microphone to do Jackie Wilson – every lick, every word. He'd throw that jacket off his shoulders and get down with the fork mic, and we'd cheer and clap him on.

"I remember we had this old Firestone radio. Taj knew what hours blues programs would come on from stations far away, so there was a lot of static, but he'd concentrate through that noise to hear the licks and notes. Then he'd play those licks over and over, often late at night upstairs in our room or up in the attic playroom, careful not to wake us up.

"Our parents didn't know what to make of all this artistic stuff, or what to do with it. They wanted us to be lawyers and doctors and teachers, and here we were trying to be artists. They thought that, if they ignored it, it would go away. Eventually, they went with the flow. They sent my brother Hugh – now deceased – to art class, from elementary all the way up to art college. Carole was given singing lessons. Ozzie was encouraged on the drums."

Winston himself became a sculptor, singer, artist and actor, founding his own acting company, Williams Productions. Currently, he teaches in the Alameda school system, in California, and is pursuing his drawing and acting careers. He formed a jazz band to perform in the schools. "I want kids to know there is something besides hip-hop, so I sing ballads – Big Joe Williams, Lou Rawls type of stuff."

During a late-night talk from his home, Winston says, "We got to be performers in the family. Mom would have all the godparents over, a good 30 or 40 people, and she'd cook up these parties. Us kids were all great cooks, and we'd entertain. Taj would play the guitar and the rest of us would do our thing. By then, he was going off to college, and soon to California, to turn professional; but whenever he came in the area to perform, he'd bring his whole band to stay at the house. We'd all get up, no matter if it was two or three in the morning and there was school the next day. Mom would cook up Southern fried chicken.

"A few times on those visits home, when us younger kids were in junior high and high school, Taj would round us up and take us way out in the boonies to some big house where he'd be having a big bash with live bands. Taj would say, 'Okay, you guys sing back-up for me. Give me a little shoop-te-do.' We'd get onstage and start snapping our fingers and singing – mainly me, Carole, Robert, and Connie. We'd fall right in and turn the house out.

"In that one-horse town we were in [Springfield], people would say, 'Oh, your brother is a professional musician. Who is he?' We'd say, 'Taj Mahal.' And they'd go, 'Ain't never heard of him.' But we were proud of Taj as a musician. We always hoped that he could be in the Top 40, or Number One, so we could say, 'That's who my brother is.' When the movie *Sounder* came out [in 1973], in which Taj did the music and acted some, that was the first time people said, 'I saw your brother in that film.'

"We wanted him to go for fortune and fame, but that wasn't what he was about. Most of us siblings worked for him when we were in our 20s, and we tried to push him toward fame and fortune. All we got was a lot of growling from him. Taj sings to the healing spirit, that's what he's about. He sings to put you at ease, to relax you, to make you feel comfortable, to make you happy, to forget about the trials and tribulations, because that's what singing does for him."

The artistic charge in the household didn't give the kids license to be wild or bohemian, however. Their mother was a stickler for manners, politeness, and solid middle-class respectability, and Hughan – being from a former British colony – brought with him a British sense of politeness and the proper way of carrying yourself. "I was a strict disciplinarian, as was Mildred," confirms Mr Williams. Physical punishment in the form of spankings – often with objects other than the hand – was accepted. In the 1950s, spankings with a wooden paddle were administered in schools, with the approval of parents, as an accepted form of child discipline.

"We were taught how to answer the door and announce people," says Taj. "You just didn't let anyone in the house. If it was a friend of the family then you'd announce them as 'Uncle James is here' or 'Aunt Alice is here.' We had a very formal relationship with the people around us. We never called an adult person by their first name. It was Miss, or Mrs, or Mister, or Uncle, or Aunt. I used to think it was really terrible that kids called adults by their first name. Our attitude was to give the elders their due. My mother, for a lot of women in that town, was a champion of being able to have her creative energies used at home and pursuing a career. She was very respected, and wanted to protect her position in the community.

"My father also emphasized our dignity and respect. I remember one time, when I was eight or nine, he gave me a whuppin' because I stole a can of Red Devil ham. I was found out. Dad was not happy, to say the least. I was crying and ashamed. My dad had a point to make. He said, 'What you did tells the whole town that our family doesn't have sense enough to know better than to steal; that we are so without, our kids have to resort to stealing. Don't you *ever* do that again.' He was telling me that, if you become the stereotype of a poor, thieving black, the others have won. You can't do that to your family, or to yourself – you're worth more than that. That was a good lesson, one I passed onto my kids.

"That was the only time I got a severe lashing by my father. While it was harsh in the eyes of today, that punishment was not out of place when I grew up. I grew up in the older generation, especially in a small West Indian community, where stealing was very serious and trust was very important. I understood that. I never felt abused by such punishment for violating those rules. Believe me, it cleared up the problem. Our parents tried other methods of teaching us kids, but when things gave out they went [back] to the old method.

"My childhood home was not violent, not volatile and not abusive. My parents loved each other, respected each other and expressed their love. We were a close family, a hard-working family. In many ways, my parents were traditional and held traditional roles. My father was formal in his personal style, very strong as a person – he had great strength of character. But my parents balanced out. They had a clear balance in their roles in the family. Us kids couldn't go to Mom and say something that Dad didn't know, or go to Dad without him consulting with Mom. They didn't like [it] if you even thought about using one parent against another. They told us that that was a terrible thing to do, because you were putting your parents in a difficult place by trying to divide them.

"So many kids actually get away with that divide-and-conquer because of the traditional power-struggle relationship that the parents have. The dad is gone all the time, so he doesn't quite know what is going on, [and] so the kids can soft-soap the mom. She figures, 'Okay, once I get the dad into a close, intimate situation, I can say, "Janie is thinking this or that."' The husband is more or less at sea. Part of the American culture goes back to Western culture, in the divide-and-conquer scene, whether the kids know it or not. That message is slipped in there.

"It helped a lot, not having the desolate Southern American family with no more than slavery in the background. We weren't running from that experience – we just didn't have that. We had more range of emotional and cultural imprint – from Africa, from the Latin Caribbean, from the French and English-speaking Caribbean.

"It was very important for me to realize the lines of [descent] of my family. A tremendous amount of Americans in general don't have information past their parents' generation. I got a clear understanding of how my mom was raised, of what value system and upbringing my dad came out of. Both my parents talked about how they were raised. Us kids asked them a lot of questions, because we knew that we weren't raised in the South but we were being raised Southern/Caribbean style. Other people who came up from the South always related to our family. When you came to our house, my mother wasn't making New England boiled dinner; she was still cooking like she was in South Carolina.

"My family was culturally a mix of West Indian and Southern. The males – whether they knew it or not – received a tremendous amount of energy from the West Indian side, because we didn't fall into the category of American men, particularly black men, who thought that they couldn't do anything, or that there were no alternatives to the way things were done, or they couldn't put their mind to doing anything. We may not be accepted by the mainstream line, but the information that came in from my parents was that this country is independent, and everybody was included.

"When I grew up, my father made it clear to me that I should go for what I believed in. I'd reach my goals by hard work. I wasn't expected to make excuses. Oh no, no, no, nonononono. That was out of the question. That was a Caribbean way to viewing life – you're on an island. But here, in this country, I didn't recognize that I was thinking island style in the midst of this larger group of people in the United States, where there is so much and the media is controlled in such a way that you can't have the independent thought. It's not that there isn't stuff – laws and institutions and opinions –

that keep people from going too far off the edge, but the fact of it is, in order for people to have a personality, they need the freedom of their own style.

"Jamaicans have a different personality from people from Antigua...from Trinidad...from Puerto Rico...from Cuba, although there may be overlay in music, the tropics, how people dress. The people in the Caribbean are really strong about their national identity. In our family, we were strong about our own personal identity without having to trumpet it in the face of the people.

"In the '60s, I was absolutely confused that black people didn't understand that we came from an African root, but it didn't occur to me that a lot of people were brainwashed, in that we had no information about what happened before we came alone. We didn't know about our ancestors. The older generation – and, to some degree, my mother – refused to talk about the South, because they didn't want the kids to know about the pain they went through, so they didn't talk about it at all. Yet it was different in my grandparents' case, when they were living in what was a very civilized country in the islands and had a long history of dignity. Because the center of British colonial operations was in St Kitts, the level of education in St Kitts was always high. If you could leap over the bar they set up for your education then you had to be given the job. It was your education, not the color of your skin, that mattered.

"As kids, we were taught to respect other people's culture on the basis of their humanity, not their color; not their creed. We didn't grow up with a whole lot of aggravation other people have because they have never been taught anything different. That's a reason I don't feel competitive. I just do what I can, to the best of my ability, with the gifts that I've been given."

The Fredericks-Williams family stood out in Springfield, even in the black community. "We were different in that town," recalls Winston. "I don't know what Taj went through, but us younger kids can tell horror stories about going to school in that town – being artistic, having a West Indian background. Often, we were treated very negatively. At that time, nobody knew anything about West Indians or Jamaicans. I don't think race entered into Taj's consciousness very much. Those who were racists, he'd let them go on and be, but he wouldn't go down that road with them. We were all raised that way. We carry ourselves like we don't see color. If you see yourself as a black person then everybody else will see you as a black person. We saw ourselves as people."

4 The Fateful Guitar

We're riding in the car, with Taj driving, on a dark, rainy night. A tape that Taj and The Phantom Blues Band recorded live in an LA club is playing. The tape is unedited, unmixed, missing the horn sections. Something about the music reminds Taj of the mysterious guitar lying in the corner of the front-hall closet of his childhood house on Marion Street. That guitar, and next-door neighbor Lynwood Perry, were a powerful influence on Taj. He turns the music down and tells the story.

"I had been listening to guitar since about 1945 on the radio, and all that great guitar playing on my father's Nat King Cole records – that was one kind of guitar playing. Then the country people played another style, and then there was another style, of the Caribbean. I was listening to all that as a kid. Then the '50s came, with the folk energy and hootenannies, so I started hearing more commercial groups playing guitar. Plus, culturally, there was a lot of guitar playing in the neighborhood, like in the barbershops. Barbers were always guitar players. In the slack time between haircuts, they'd sit up in the chair and work out their little parts. They were good with their hands, so they were good with the guitar. A lot of times, the guitar player is the barber for the band on the road. Anyway, the local barbers, they played on the music circuit, so lots of people knew them and people came to their shops, as did the traveling musicians.

"One day, I was rambling in the hall closet at home and felt this shape. I pulled it out and opened the case. What?! A guitar! That was what I needed at that moment. I was completely beyond caution with this. I took it across the hall to the cellar steps and sat in the stairwell and tried to pick out notes. I didn't know how to tune it. I didn't there was such a thing as a pick. My mother had combs with big, wide teeth, and I used to break the teeth out of the combs to use as guitar picks.

"I tried to hear songs in my head and figure them out on that guitar, but nothing happened. So I kept doing this back and forth, putting the guitar back in the closet, then sneaking it out to play. One day, I was sitting on the stairs, playing, and the door opened behind me and all Hughan said was, 'Well, I see you found it.' No more. No, 'You can't have it, you can't use it, you don't touch it.' Just, 'Well, I see you found it.' Stop. After that, I assumed from my relationship with him, the way we communicated, that it was okay. He never ever hassled me about it. I took the guitar with me everywhere.

"On the heels of that, next door moves in a boy about my age, Lynwood Perry, from North Carolina. One of the first questions he asked me was, 'Do you play guitar?' I said, 'I have a guitar.' 'You have a guitar? Let me see your guitar.' So I bring the guitar out, and he knows how to tune it and how to play it. Oh my god, what a gift! Now I'm really flipped out. Here's a guy that's my own age who can play what Robert Johnson and Blind Boy Fuller were playing. He was that good. Myself, Samuel, and Rick took turns, with Lyn teaching us on Hughan's guitar, but it only stuck with me – I just went out with it. Lyn and our other neighbors, the Nichols brothers, didn't put the music out of reach for me. They were important to me because they played the stuff they knew, and from those basics they played everything else.

"When I finally came up to Robert Johnson, when I was somewhere between the ages of 19 to 21, I wasn't that impressed with him. Not that he didn't play good; it was just that there were lots of guys – like Lynwood Perry – who played that good. It's just that Robert Johnson got recorded at an exceptional time in his life, so he became well known. You go back and listen to Skip James, or the Reverend Gary Davis when he was 27 years old. That stuff is incredible."

Later, Mr Williams shed some light on the mysterious guitar: "When I was working at the tobacco farm, my roommate, he was a very good guitar player, but he didn't have a guitar. I said to myself, 'I'd love to play the guitar.' I went and bought a guitar, but I couldn't get anywhere with it. I had difficulties just learnin' it. But I kept it with me, moved it around with me, and I had it in the house on Marion Street. Taj knew it was there. He didn't ask for it; he just took it. He was the only one of all the kids who took to it. When I see Taj, I say, 'Where is that guitar now? I bet you don't know where to find it now.' That guitar, I'm sure I'd get some money for it. That would be worth some money now. That guitar really turned him into music. He got into music right there."

The next-door neighbors, the Perrys, were Southern, *very* Southern, with very Southern ways, and they talked Southern. Leonard "Lynwood" Perry, along with the Nichols brothers – from a family who were also from the Deep South, who lived around the block – introduced Taj to Southern blues, direct from the Deep South. Taj had the music in him, and Lynwood showed him how to get it out. A year older than Taj, Lyn lived in Springfield until his death in 2001, working for the City until a mild stroke put him into retirement. "Thank God," he said when I spoke to him at his house on Page Boulevard. "Thank God almighty it didn't leave me messed up in any kind of way."

Lyn taught himself how to play the guitar when he was still a nine-year-old boy by watching his older brother, who, like his father, played the old Southern songs. "I used to watch every place he put his fingers. I'd take my hand like I had a guitar and put my fingers there." Lyn spoke lively and laughed often as he talked, recalling those early days. "I'd memorize where his fingers went, the keys, what fret the key was in. One night, my brother was going to the movies with our cousin. They were in hurry. My brother usually put his guitar up in the closet so nobody could mess with it, but this time he left it laying out on the bed. I said, 'Oh, man, this is my chance.'

"Everyone was in the kitchen, so I had the living room all to myself. I tried to remember how my brother had his fingers when I was watching him. I put my fingers like he had his. The guitar was bigger than I was. I put my fingers like I had seen my brother, and I strummed and I made a chord. Oh, man, I was grinning from ear to ear. I was grinning and grinning. I called my mother – 'Mom! Mom, I can play the guitar. Listen! Listen!' So I did it for her.

"Before we came to Springfield, we had our own farm down near Louisburg, North Carolina. We'd grow fruit, vegetables, tobacco, cotton. My father was also a bootlegger, made his own wine and home brew, a little bit of moonshine. People would come over to party. Nobody would get slammed, no fights, just dancing and clowning around and everything. It was all having a good time. People would request that I play the song I had learned. They poked nickels, dimes, and quarters into the hole in the middle of the guitar. It was like a guitar piggy bank. They'd poke dollars in there. I had to stop playing and clear the dollars out between the strings. That guitar got a little heavy with all that money.

"One year, our farm went bad, making no money. The farm just went dead. Almost everyone around there was having a hard time with farming that year. We got in a hole we couldn't get out of, so we got in touch with my brother living in Springfield. We left one brother on the farm to look after the animals and the rest of the crops. My brother was living on Marion Street, next door to Henry's family. I met Henry and his brothers, Eddie and Ricky, out in the yard, and we got talking and became friends.

"The Nichols family lived around the corner. They were another Southern family, and the brothers, Ernie and Billy, played music. They had a full drum set out on the front porch, and ran a cord through the kitchen for the guitars, the microphone, and the amp. So we got together and played. We were just a home band – a drum, two guitars, and a bass. We'd sit out on the porch and play 'Little Darling.' There was a lot of group singing, harmonizing, and the band would get behind them. We saw a chance to play little parties. We started getting paid, like, ten dollars a night. Ten dollars would last me a whole week. Henry wasn't playing with us; he was still learning how to play.

"One day, I went over to Henry's house. He said, 'Come on upstairs. I want you to show me something on the guitar.' We went up in the attic, where the kids played. That was their play room. Ricky had his Lionel choo-choo train up there. I liked to watch that little train go around the track. Ricky had a little pill you put in the smokestack to make smoke. You could make the whistle blow. I loved that train. Up there in the attic is where Henry first learned the guitar.

"The first song I taught Henry was 'O, Baby,' and then 'Come On Down To My House.' It's a three-change song. I played it first and told him to watch my fingers, just like I learned with my brother. I gave the guitar to him. I told him, 'Take your time. Make it as slow as you want, as long as you make it sound like that.' He started doing it. I showed him how to drop down from G to the next key. He kept doing that and doing that. Then I showed him how to play 'Tequila.' Just simple stuff. Then he started to learn some stuff himself, just like I did. I learned by ear, and that's how Henry started. When Henry got better, he'd come over to the Nichols' and play with us on the porch. When Henry learned 'Honky-Tonk,' he liked it so much that he'd play [it] all the time. He played it so much we gave him the nickname Honky-Tonk.

"My dad played the real down-home blues, the *real* down-home blues, blues you don't hear today. Us Southern guys, me and the Nichols, we had those blues in our blood, in our roots. When we came up north, the people up here, when they first heard us, it seemed that they had never heard any real-live blues. Henry heard the first authentic blues live from me and the Nichols.

"Later, I taught Henry some of the Southern blues. The Northern honky-tonk blues is a blues you can dance by; the Southern down-home blues, that is a blues that tells of the troubles you had, of the troubles the player heard, of the troubles about people they love and hate. All the blues songs have a meaning of problems, like, 'I left my baby and my baby left me.' The blues have come from a long way, if you go back to our people coming from Africa. Blues is here today, and blues is here to stay, you know what I'm sayin'?

"I remember sitting on the porch and Henry going by the house heading for Winchester Square a couple blocks down, where the stores were. He had a string tied to the guitar so he could carry it across his back. Back then, he was big and bulky, with a big, high rear end and big thighs, a big guy full of energy. When he walked, he had a bounce. He'd bounce up and down the street with that guitar bouncing on his back. Wherever he was going, he wasn't losing no time. Henry didn't hang out with anybody, not even a walk group, you know, just walking down the street together.

"We went through high school together, and then I lost track of Henry. When I first heard of Taj Mahal, I didn't know he was Henry. Then, when I knew, I was amazed. There was a grin on my face that you couldn't unzip. I was very proud of him. Here was a guy who hounded me to teach him the guitar, and now he can show me something."

Billy Nichols smiles as he remembers those front-porch band days with Taj. He's at his desk in his workroom on Manhattan's West Side. Around the desk is a mixing board, six guitars, two bass guitars, a computer, and a video camera. He is now an R&B musician, producer, and songwriter.

"Have you heard 'Do It Till You're Satisfied,' a big hit in the 1970s, recorded by BT Express? Recently it was used on a Burger King commercial. That's my song. Or 'Give Your Body Up To The Music,' a 1979 disco song featured on a new Rhino Records three-set CD, *Give Your Body Up To The Music*?

"When I first met Henry, my family had moved up from our home near Stovall – where Muddy Waters grew up, in the Mississippi Delta – to

Springfield and settled in around the corner from Henry's family. There were five boys and four girls in our family, so right off Henry and I had something in common, coming from a big family. My father was a blues guitar player and taught my brothers. I learned from them.

"Down South, we just had an acoustic guitar, but when we moved into Henry's neighborhood my brother got an amplifier. My brothers, Ernest and Junior, and I would sit out on the porch and play. We'd play loud, and the cops would come by and say, 'Hey, turn that music down.' As soon as they left, we'd turn that amp back up. Henry and Lyn Perry, they'd hear and come around. Henry would bring his guitar over in a burlap sack. Our house became like a meeting place for the musicians and singers.

"The rest of us were fooling around a lot, making noise, but Henry, he took the blues seriously. I don't know why, seeing as he was a Northerner. He wanted to be a farmer, and we could never figure that out. 'What is this?' In high school, we all played in a doowop band together and did gigs around at teens clubs and the local air force base. After school, we'd go down the Dunbar Recreation Center – which had big halls, so the voice would echo – and blow some harmony.

"To me, Henry never seemed a girlkiller type of guy. He was a regular guy. He wouldn't be voted the most likely to succeed. As far as his personality and demeanor, he was a calm guy – I never saw him get into any fights, or even get angry. None of us would say that Henry, as he was as a kid, would be what he is today. He didn't seem like the type. He was always a loner, a stand-outside guy. I'd see him every day, but he never would hang out with us, like *hang* hang. Only when we were playing music. Not that he was unsociable; he just seemed in another place. He knew everybody in the schools, and all the happenings, but he was just alone.

"During that time, in the 1950s, I never thought Henry was a great guitar player. Then one day, after he had gone to college – that would be in 1961 – Henry came home to visit. He came by the house with his guitar, 'William, I want you to hear this,' and he started to play for me. I couldn't believe how far he had advanced. It just blew me away. It was amazing, just amazing."

When Taj started getting together with Lyn and Billy, he heard about the twelve-year-old Aretha Franklin from his mother, who frequently commented about new talent on the gospel circuit. The young singer traveled with her dad, the Reverend CL Franklin, singing in different churches around the circuit, where she got her first recognition. Newsletters went from church to church about her, and her records were sold through the churches. Like other singers – Marion Anderson, Mahalia Jackson, Rosetta Thorpe, The Clara Ward Singers – Aretha was known in the black church community first before she came to the attention of the general public.

For Taj, this first exposure of how musicians were recognized and given value set him up for a long-running conflict with the music industry. He still recalls this liminal epiphany: "On the gospel circuit, somebody was recognized as good not because they sold lots of records; it was because you recognized their talent. Mahalia Jackson was first recognized as a great voice, not because she sold records. You wanted to go hear her because of her talent. The Afro-American community is highly critical of singers, of any talented person, so you have to come up with something, come up to a certain level of song or communication, before people even mention you. And even then you need some luck.

"As I grew up, musicians were everywhere, all the time, playing. Most people just took music as part of normal life – you'd go to church and the choir was smoking up there – but they don't make a big issue out of it. Singing in church can be competitive, but more on the human values of competition rather than [the] competitive that you get in the music business. When someone sings and moves the whole church, there's nothing you can do about it but go with the fact that it has happened, whereas the popular music business can create someone who really can't do anything, but the record company says, 'That person is happening, a hit, selling a lot.' It's about how much money one is making, and not so much on how well one sings. The record companies create excitement around something and help create the illusion of value. When I was growing up, because of the situation with the record companies, the opportunities for a black musician to make it were not all that great. You might make it on a local level because you were playing in a club and people responded immediately to you. They'd dance, they'd come to hear you regularly, but as soon as you get into the music business then it's the early stage of going corporate. Then, to be a success, you got to make a lot of different people feel good about what's going on.

"I always thought that popular music was a plastic, propped-up kind of situation. It was popular by virtue of what was going on in rock 'n' roll at the time, and because of young kids trying to approximate the sound of black music. The real music was in the church. You didn't have to have an education to understand it. The people knew it from an emotional source. It got to you in all kinds of ways.

"By the time I was in junior high, people figured out that I had talent. I played around with musicians, some who were highly schooled in music, but I was interested in the idea of playing music that wasn't the sterile, note-reading kind. I never did accept that first you had to play that kind of music – learned, schooled music – and then eventually you'd get to play the type of music you really wanted. I said, 'Well, why not start out playing what you want to do?'

"In junior high, every time I opened my mouth to sing, the songs were somebody else's music. It was fun doing other people's music, but it occurred to me that I was always somebody else's personality. When was I going to find my own? I would have loved to create something that would be popular, that people would be interested in, but the really most important thing for me was to know and to play what the real music was about.

"I read a lot about Ray Charles, who when I started out was covering other people's songs – he tried to sound like Charles Brown and Nat King Cole. I first heard him when he was just starting to break away from that and find his own voice, just before 'What'd I Say' came out. By then, he clearly had his own voice and way to do things. That was really exciting for me, how he used the black voice and the very black musical tone, and created it in such a universal way to touch everybody. That was a very important thing for me.

"I didn't go to music school. I didn't do that to figure out what music was about, what the tone theory was and all that. I was just going on instinct. The musical industry basically said that, if you didn't learn to read and write music, didn't go to school to learn it, then you basically couldn't play music. I listened to the guys who went that route, and their music sounded cold and canned.

"Then I'd hear some itinerants, who maybe had never been past the third grade, playing music. I asked them how they learned it. 'Well, I just picked it up.' That confirmed what I felt about how to come to music. Count Basie, before he learned to read and write music, played in big bands. The music came before the paper – that's a human experience. It was important for me to make that connection, that connection with people through music.

"Music is in culture, so it's not a real big thing. It's not seen as extraordinary so as to draw special attention or comment; it's just an extension of life. By the time I was 13, in the first year of high school, I started to have a good idea about that connection, the importance of it, in the purpose of music for me.

"In the sixth through ninth grades, at Buckingham Junior High, I played guitar and hung out with buddies – Jimmy Shafer, Lew Holly, Lyn Perry, Garland Edwards, Ernest and Billy Nichols. Then I went to West Springfield High. It was one of two schools that offered agriculture courses, which I was interested in. In the mornings, we'd have an assembly, and students were encouraged to bring music from home, so I brought Hughan's guitar and the music I was learning to play, plus other popular R&B and rock 'n' roll of the day.

"I was in a little doowop band from the ages 13 to 15. We'd play out at Westover air force base, near town, and at school dances, but there was no organization, no rhyme or reason to it, no management. We just played gigs as they came along – talent shows, impromptus. There was a lot of music going around the area, but it wasn't like a Memphis or Nashville or Chicago blues scene. In Springfield, it was just what kids did.

"I liked being onstage. I didn't get all nervous and flip out; I'd get very focused, because the music was something I was specifically trying to get across. I didn't want my energy to go so crazy that I couldn't get to that focus. I wasn't trying to control the audience with crazy energy. I didn't – and don't – think about trying to control the audience. That's impossible. If you have the music happening, then the focus happens, and that's why people come to hear you.

"I wanted to have the strength and ability to get up as a solo artist and play music. I wanted to gain the ability to make the music come off comfortable and relaxed, and that took a long time. In the early days, I wasn't confident in myself or in the material. I had to find ways to write the right material and find my way to the right spaces.

"I also discovered, while in high school, that black music was about four years ahead of popular music. How I discovered this was 'The Twist,' by Hank Ballard. To me, that song sounded like it was as loud as the sky. That record was targeted to our community. It had come and gone in the community when Chubby Checker came out with 'The Twist' four years later. His version was given national treatment. I thought we had already seen the twist craze, but we hadn't seen it go through the national craze. It's like rap. Early rap probably sold 150,000 records, but once it was a national thing we're talking about millions of records sold.

"I saw there was a distortion in music and, in particular, in the sources of the music. I didn't get that there were forces at work in the record industry trying to control the musicians and the market. Those forces were trying to make sure that the record companies were the recipients of the money.

"The music was supposed to be absolutely black music, but the blacks were not controlling it. Black musicians and groups would come and disappear, often without getting much money for their hits. White businesses were the ones primarily behind the movement. In the 1950s, Afro-Americans were fighting toward what the '60s turned out to be, more of a level playing field, yet it was clear that black music was a big influencing power on the youth of the day. Elvis Presley is a fine example. His music came out of the blues, basically black music he listened to when he was a truck driver in Memphis.

"Another thing I saw was that a tremendous amount of black musicians were learning to sound more European and less African – or even Afro-American – in their music. They did this to convince the public at large that black music wasn't all these unintelligible polyrhythms they couldn't figure out. All the indigenous sound of the music was being left behind. I was going, 'What are you doing that for?' My interest became to really deal with the older sounds and ultimately try to find my way back into where those sounds connected into older African music."

For all his detailed thoughts on music, at the time it was only a diversion for the young Taj. His future, professionally speaking, lay in farming. "At this time, I wasn't thinking that music was going to be my life. I was interested in farming and agriculture, and spoke my mind about going to an agricultural school. I wanted to become a farmer. My whole idea was to be a service to humanity. People who raise crops, and musicians, artists, poets, painters – I saw them as people who created and always added something to the community. I liked both agriculture and music.

"I went to West Springfield High School for the tenth grade and to Westfield High for eleventh and twelfth grades, where I studied vocational agriculture. That's how I came to work on Langevin's Dairy Farm."

5 The Farm

The Langevin Dairy Farm is still there on Route 20, near Palmer, reduced in size and hedged in by development. The sign out front is faded, and the cows are gone, but the land still produces hay. Herman Langevin and wife still live in the farmhouse where, one afternoon, Herman sat in the living room. He recalls the days when Taj was his farmhand: "Us dairy farmers were always looking for help. We'd go to the agricultural schools or vocational schools looking for people interested in learning first hand how to farm, to do plumbing, wiring, mechanics, planting. Farmers do everything.

"The teacher at West Springfield High School sent two boys, Henry and a friend, looking for work. I still can't get out of the habit of calling Taj 'Henry.' The other boy didn't work out too well, but Henry was really interested in farming. He came back to work for us whenever he had spare time – on weekends, school vacations, and summers – until he was 19 and started college. Sometimes he'd come unexpectedly, if he had time off from school.

"When he first came, his mother and father brought him out on weekends, after school. He'd stay for the whole weekend – Friday night, Saturday and Sunday, on a normal weekend. My wife and I always brought him home to Springfield on Sunday evening. We did that for years. I don't think that any of the time Henry worked here he had his own vehicle.

"During the summer vacations, he lived full time with us – lived in our house, left his belongings here in his own room. I had two younger boys, Kenneth and Wayne. He got along good with my boys. They really think a lot of him, as a friend. Nowadays, whenever Henry plays in the area, Kenneth and his gang go see him. We had a big family here. There was my wife and I, our two boys, my mother and father, and two grandmothers. He just lived here as a member of the family. My grandmother – 96 when she died – she was a friend of Henry's. She'd talk French to him. She'd holler at Henry just like he was her son. They were good friends.

46

"Henry did everything a dairy farmer does – milked cows, operated tractors, painted buildings, built fences, tilled, plowed and harrowed the land, helped seed the crops down. I would give him the dickens at times, when he first came here – he just wasn't a worker – but he learned how to work as time went by. He was a big, strong boy. Every time he sees me personally, he shakes my hand and thanks me and my wife for what we did for him.

"We had 85 milkers at that time and 45 young stock. I remember when I had animals outside the barn all winter long and they had to be fed in feed bunks. Henry would go out and feed them in the cold and mud. When we'd be working out in the field, Henry would say, 'It's time to do chores.' We'd let him go home and get the cows in. He had a lot of patience for cows. He sure liked his cows.

"Most farmers milk cows only twice a day, at morning and night. One year, Henry had an idea that it would be better to milk three times a day. That's what we did. It made more milk, but that's one-third as much work. We ended up with less time out in the fields to do the important work of keeping the cows fed. So we milked three times a day for that one year, but I did it with his help. It was his idea.

"While he was doing the morning milking, Henry would clean out the stalls, so as to free his time later in the morning to be in our machine shop. He loved to tear down tractor engines, bore out the cylinders and fix the machinery. He was good at it.

"We grew hay and corn silage to feed the cows. I had 60 acres of corn. Henry was always around, chopping the corn and blowing it into the silos. I had 136 acres when Henry was here, and still have 100 left. Now Kenneth has taken over the farm, and six others. We just make hay now. No cows.

"I had this old John Deere B putt-putt tractor, a two-cylinder. It'd run down the road going *putt-putt-putt*. You could spit inbetween the cylinders firing. The first summer Henry and the other fellow were here – I can't recall his name – I sent them out on a job in a field just up the road. Henry was driving the tractor, with a mounted plow on the back, and the other fellow was riding.

"They went out the driveway, and to this day I don't know what happened. I suspect that, when they made the right turn from the driveway to go to the fields, the other boy lost his balance and grabbed the steering wheel so he wouldn't fall off. That yanked the front of the tractor around, and it just nosed right over, fell on its side and hit the guard rail, which is just two cables mounted to cement posts. When they hit the cable, that flipped the tractor back into the road onto its side. They didn't get hurt, other than a bruised knee or something like that. They dinged up the front of the hood on the tractor, but it kept right on running. It ran for years after that. I'm so thankful that they didn't get hurt.

"I bought a piano at an auction and put it in the grain room of the horse barn. There was an old pump organ in there, too, the kind you push and pull the buttons. Henry played the organ and just about learned to play the piano on that old thing. After he learned to play the piano pretty good, he got himself a guitar. He sat out behind the barn at nights on a rock, or in the hayloft, and practiced and practiced, just by himself. He'd go down by the Quaboag River, which borders our land by a mile, and he'd talk to the birds and fishes and sing.

"Henry didn't mind being alone. I'd send him out to do a job in the field and he'd stay there until it was time to come home to milk or eat. He just enjoyed himself. But when he was around people, he was very talkative. You can't keep him quiet. He liked to talk about agriculture and languages. He'd sit and talk to anybody about anything.

"He still calls me, and we talk about agriculture in the rest of the world. It's interesting to me. He likes to know what is happening in the States, whether the milk prices are getting better, or how the farmers are doing. I like to know how people in other countries are doing. I've worked seven days a week and never had the chance to travel, never had the money to travel. I've learned a lot from him about the world and its agriculture. A couple of months ago, he was calling me once a day for a week. He said, 'I'm home and I'm just taking it easy.'

"Henry and my father would talk all the time. They'd go out picking stones out of a field that was plowed and harrowed. They cut brush in the winter along the edges of the fields. Henry says that my father taught him a lot about life. My father taught him some French. Henry says that's what helps him today in his world travels. My father got him started on the language, and Henry just kept picking it up better and better. He's a man who will learn by himself.

"On Friday nights, unless there was something that kept Henry from coming here, he always came out. All of his brothers and sisters would run around the yard. We'd always have some kind of barbecue. It was fun, living back then. I'm 69 now, and life seems to be getting miserable. I'm in good health, I work – I'm basically retired. I still do a lot of the farm work, help my son bale hay, mow and rake. I sold my cattle eleven years ago and went driving a truck. I was badly in debt, because of the cows and agricultural situation. I got a teamsters job. I paid off all my bills and retired a little over a year ago."

Kenneth Langevin, Herman's oldest boy, was two years old when Taj came to work on the farm. He lives just down the road from his dad and grows hay on the land and on several other farms. "I called my business Hay-Hay-Hay Farms, a name I got from Henry," Kenneth says. "Henry wanted to do a hay business and sell hay all over the country. I'm doing it for him. When I was a kid, Henry always treated me and my younger brother like pals. He was our friend.

"On summer evenings, about 8.30 – bedtime – we'd get in our pajamas and go out to the horse barn and listen to Henry play and sing. He'd sit at the door to the grain room and play for hours. He knew lots of songs, and my favorite then was 'Goin' Fishing.' Often, after the evening milking, he and I would go fishing in the Quaboag for trout or bullheads or pumpkin seeds, a bony trash fish that we didn't bother to throw back. It was okay if we didn't catch anything. The point was to relax. He'd take me hunting, too, for woodchucks and rabbits. He was an excellent shot with the .22 rifle. When we got rabbits, he'd skin them and prepare the skins.

"I remember once I drank some battery acid by mistake. Henry grabbed that jug away from me and washed my mouth out good. Henry taught that the grass may look greener on the other side, but where you are is the best place to be. Now, whenever he plays around here or Boston, I go see him. I shout out, 'Let's go fishing in the Quaboag,' and his eyes light up. 'Ah, I see the Langevins are here tonight,' he'll say, and then play 'Goin' Fishing.'"

Taj recalls his farm days with pleasure. In those early teen years, he learned lessons that have stood him in good stead in sustaining his musical career. Working hard was the main lesson. "I was still just a kid, and kids need summer jobs. In my family, first you'll have a job. You'll have a bank account, save, buy things you thought you wanted, be able to help out with the family, contribute. The parents will be proud of you. You didn't think, 'All this money is going to be all mine,' with no consideration for those who raised you, invested in you. As soon as you got an opportunity to give back something, you did. It represented that you had grown into the level of the big boys. You're starting to get on your own feet and go where you want. You had the confidence that you could start taking care of yourself.

"I figured that, if I could do anything to help in getting financially out from under my parents, that would be a help to them from worrying about me, financially. It was never a complaint on my part that they couldn't afford to send me to college. It never occurred to me to quit school. 'What are you talking about?' I was definitely going to finish high school, and college was definitely on the boards. Even if my parents couldn't have afforded to send me to college, which at that time they couldn't, I was still setting myself up for that. A lot of kids said, 'My parents can't afford to send me to college, so I'll just get a job.' My attitude was, yeah, get a job, and also save for college.

"When I was 14, I started working in the summer on the tobacco farms around Springfield. That was a big summer job for kids primarily from Southern or West Indian families. I was just waiting until I was old enough to get a job picking tobacco. I didn't want to work in a store in town; I wanted to be out in nature. Part of my dealing with my dad's death was to glom onto nature. The sky, the wind – that was much more powerful than the urban drama around me. His death was a heavier blow than I was ever able to deal with. I needed to be somewhere that was bigger than me. All I did was go to school and work on the farm. I think that kept me sane.

"And I could make some serious money. We were making $900, $1,000 a summer. That was a lot of money back then. I could come home and give my mother $200 or more during the summer and put some money away for school clothes in the fall. That made me one less person for her to worry about. The years when I was 14 and 15, I worked on tobacco.

"The tobacco, called Connecticut Shade-grown, was raised in the rich alluvial soil brought down by the floods in the Connecticut Valley area. Farmers grew it as a secondary cash crop, because if a farmer had only 30 dairy cows it was a hard route to go, if you had a family to raise. So the farmer might have 50 acres of tobacco. He could make some serious money with that.

"Connecticut Shade-grown tobacco is one of the premier wrappers for cigars. Basically, you got a tobacco leaf with a spine down the middle and veins branch out. They dry the leaf and take out the part of the leaf between the veins. That's the wrapper. In a cigar, you have the filler, the binder, and the wrapper.

"When I was 16, I started working for Herman Langevin on his dairy farm out on Route 20, near Palmer. That was an important place for me, as was Herman and his family. I got a fair wage, although my mom didn't think it was all that much. It was my decision to be there. The people were good to me.

"Being on the farm helped me know about people who did hard work, labored for a living. I think the most important thing people need to know is how to work. That's real important. I wasn't going to crop cotton for anyone, or work in a sawmill down South. I had some options of what type of work I wanted to do. Work is work, no matter what you're doing.

"There's a lot of work to being a musician. Being a musician may look romantic to people on the outside, but to musicians on the inside, they know how hard I work. The object is to make it look easy to the audience. That's one of the reasons the audience likes what I do. I make it look easy when I'm onstage. For me to do as much as I want during a show, I have to put myself in a relaxed state. There is a lot of energy going on that has to be channeled, smooth and easy. When I finish for the night, I – *whew!* – realize that's a tremendous amount of energy. It's like anything else: if you want to get good at it, you've got to work at it."

The farm served as a refuge for Taj, at least according to his brother Winston: "A lot happened on that farm. Taj got peace with himself. He was happy. Happy for him is not necessarily doing a whole lot of smiling and grinning and being around a lot of people drinking up. When he was really happy, he could go off and sit in the corner by himself and pick his guitar, even with a roomful of people around him.

"When the family would go out to the farm for a barbecue, in our big green Chevy '57 Bel Aire station wagon, he'd hang out for a little while; but soon after, he'd disappear. The happier times were the ones where he disappeared for the longest. I used to go look for him and find him in the hayloft playing his guitar. He never made me feel like I intruded on his space, like he wanted to be alone. I would sit for a long time and listen to him pick.

"When Taj's father died, he took on a lot of responsibilities for the kids, and his mother heaped that responsibility on him. He was disgruntled about being the babysitter, especially as he moved into the teenage years.

He had other things he wanted to do, like fishing. He was gone a lot. He and Mom would get into battles, and things could get intense around the house. They are both Taurus, and Taurus people are headstrong. Those two really bucked heads when they bucked. I think moving out to the farm full time in the summers was a way to escape the tension. [Taj's mother passed away in 1995.] That was when he started to rebel and seek his own independence. He had a taste of freedom. My mother would let him go from home, at an early age, from early in the morning and stay out until midnight. She'd never worry where he was. He'd be hours away from home, fishing, because fishing was also a place to seek solace. He had a freedom that showed him there was another side when he needed to get out there, so he fought for it.

"When Taj branched out, that's when the rest of us started going hog-wild, supporting each other in our creativity. That kind of independence inspired the rest of us kids. I remember we'd be around the kitchen table, trying to work out some musical riffs, and Taj would say, 'Write your own stuff. Write your own stuff.' Once he got on the farm, the rest of us, one by one, fought for our independence and started going into the direction of what we enjoyed – that is, being artistic."

6 How Henry Became Taj

How did Henry St Clair Fredericks Jr become Taj Mahal? Taj's brother, Richard, tells this story with the glee of a younger brother spilling the beans: "In the family, Taj was Harry Jr, or Juney, for Harry Jr. He also had the nickname Post, given to him by his teenage pal, Lew Holly. That's what most of the people in town called him, because he was built big and solid and straight up and down, like a telephone post. Some people in Springfield still call him Post. Those were his names when he went off to U-Mass Amherst for his freshman year. I rode up there with Pops and Taj, and we took him to the Middlesex dorm. Thirty days or so after Taj had been at the university, he came home to visit. We say, 'Hey, Juney, how you doin'?' He says, 'My name's not Juney. My name is Henri. From now on, my name is Henri.'" Richard says *Henri* with a deep guttural French accent bordering on sarcasm, a kid enjoying telling on his older brother. "Roll forward 30 or 40 days and Henri comes home for another visit. We say, 'Hey, Henri, how ya doin'?' He says, 'No, my name is not Henri. It's Taj Mahal.'"

But for Taj, the changing of his name came over a long period of reflection, starting when he was a boy. A series of dreams, a childhood television program, the influence of men he admired – Mahatma Gandhi, Julius Nyerere, Kwame Nkrumah (former president of Ghana) and Albert Einstein – all played into his choice. The name Taj Mahal had a deeper significance than just a showbiz handle; it reflected the positive forces in the world with which he chose to identify.

There is a rich tradition for blues performers to take on a signature name. The legendary bluesman Howlin' Wolf came into the world as Chester Arthur Burnett, named after the 21st US president. (His original nickname was Big Foots Chester, or Foots, in reference to his size-16 shoes.) He gave several different explanations over the years about how he was nicknamed Howlin' Wolf: a grandfather's scary wolf tales; his own "wolfish" mischief as a child.

According to Charles K Cowdery, in his book *Blues Legends* (Gibbs-Smith, Salt Lake City, 1995), Burnett appropriated the nickname of an older bluesman, John T Smith, who had adopted the name The Howling Wolf after his 1930 record of that song became popular. By the time Burnett came along, Smith had faded into obscurity, so no one objected when Big Foot rechristened himself Howlin' Wolf.

Cowdery writes that Sam Hopkins' nickname, Lightnin', came from an early recording partnership with a piano player named Wilson "Thunder" Smith. Their manager thought that "Thunder And Lightning" would look good on the marquee. The name also fit Hopkins' rapid-fire playing style. Muddy Waters, meanwhile, was born McKinley Morganfield, named after the president and his grandmother Ola, with whom he lived almost from birth, and it was she who nicknamed him Muddy. "Waters" came from his playmates on the Stovall plantation, near Clarksdale, Mississippi, where he grew up. And Memphis Minnie was originally christened Lizzie Douglas, but was always known as Kid to her family. A white record-company executive gave her the tag Memphis Minnie.

The subject of nicknames comes up in the dressing room of Jazz Alley, a Seattle club, where Taj is performing solo. He sits tilted against the back wall, waiting for his second set to begin. There's just enough room for a folding table – which is littered with instruments, plastic cups, and plates of half-eaten food – and three chairs. Shouts and bangs come through the open door from the kitchen, just outside the door. Seven people are packed into the room. It's loud, with everyone talking at crosscurrents. Taj's booming, raspy voice skips like a stone across the surface of the chatter about record sales and writing film scores and books, as he explains how he chose the name Taj Mahal.

"My thoughts about the name Taj Mahal started as early as the late 1940s and early 1950s. As a boy, I spent a lot of time looking at the *World Book* encyclopedias, because I was very interested in the world. I went to those books for information. I didn't allow the fact that I, as part of a people, did or did not exist depending on whether we are in the history books or not. A lot of people say, 'There's nothing about me in the history books, so I guess I'm nobody.' Well, I don't think so. Excuse me. If you really look at the point, you realize that history is the story of the person, or culture, that wrote it from their point of view, so it's not your story. It's up to you to get your story together.

"When I was a boy, there was a music program on television called Stage Eight. Stage Eight had a harmonium and organ player, an East Indian guy, Korla Pandit – very popular. He would stare at the camera with this incredible gaze and play this unbelievable music, so that memory lodged in my mind. As I grew older, I was impressed by Gandhi and Jawaharlal Nehru. I was a young child when Gandhi was doing his stuff to liberate India from British colonial rule. I was very impressed that Gandhi raised not a hand, not a weapon, not anything towards people, and yet completely created something very peaceful.

"I looked up to a lot of different people – Albert Schweitzer, Albert Einstein, Paul Robeson, Julius Nyerere, Kwame Nkrumah, Jomo Kenyatta. They made no compromise with the negative forces in the world. That's always been of interest to me. Like Anwar Sadat. Unbelievable. It's people like that, whatever it is that their brainwaves send across the world. Yeah, they took Sadat out, but he's still heard, because he was a very high thinker.

"Even at a young age, I sought out different people whose image and energy came across the planet as a positive human, people who lived for all the reasons of being a good person, as opposed to making money as the object of life. That's how I make my decisions. I don't step on everybody to get ahead.

"Coming to my name, over a period of time, it was a dream space. I say dream because it was a series of spaces in life that went out in what I realize now were out-of-the-body experiences. As I became more involved in music, I thought about naming myself. What kind of name would I have if I was a musician or an actor? Nobody ever shoots for the moon or for the stars, or past the stars, so I decided I'd have a really interesting name. I wanted a different kind of name that had more meaning than 'I'm just another guy out here trying to take your money.' I'm sure that, to a certain degree, living up to the idea of the name has helped me develop a different set of values.

"A seed of my new name was planted by my parents. They told me that I could do anything I wanted in this life, as opposed to saying, 'You're black and it's going to be hard for you. You ain't going to be able to make it.' I never thought that way about myself, ever. *Ever*. Not even for one minute. I thought that, when people were trying to stop me, impede my movement forward, that they were kinda stupid.

"So I never had a hard time struggling to be who I was or to do what I wanted. Still, I know the blues. You don't have to live a hard, tragic life to know the blues. The pain and sorrow that we recognize in the blues, as well as the joy and happiness, it's an enigma. You ain't playing the blues until you're *playing* them. How do you intellectually know a music that has that kind of feel? You can sit there and play every single note in an arrangement but no blues to be found; but you can find a guy with absolutely no school education who can sit down and beat the blues out so you just don't miss it.

"My thing is that the music came before all the lessons and notes and philosophy about it. Music is an extension of what my people did as an ancient people, what most people did as an ancient people. So the music is not necessarily the blues but music. You can try, from your brain and thought process, to write a blues song, but the authentic blues songs write themselves. You don't play the blues; the music plays you. After all the talk is said and done, the whole point is, does the music happen? See, the music...the music... Ultimately, we don't play it; we are being played. Some waterfalls are deep, some waterfalls are wide, some waterfalls are long, some make a lot of noise, and some don't make much noise, but it's still water over a falls. The blues is like that. Water is coming down.

"People would ask me, 'Why play this old-form music that does not have a future? Why not play jazz or contemporary?' Because the music is a connection to a people's culture and history. It's legitimate music. That's why I play it. There are times when I could have easily gone off into some kind of trash version of the blues and not stayed to the plan of how it's supposed to be played. I think my ancestors are very happy with the way I went with it. I want my ancestors to be proud of me.

"You know, the Africans didn't come off the slave ships singing the Delta blues. The Mandingoes and Ibo and Coromantees and all the other distinct tribal groups didn't even share a common culture or language, but they did share a *griot* style of passing on their history. In West Africa, the *griots* were members of a special caste who, through song and stories, passed on the news, past and present, into the collective memory of their tribes. The *griots* didn't perform solo but involved the entire community, revival style, with singing, clapping, dancing, and call-and-answer shouting. They had the responsibility, as carriers of the culture. That's also my responsibility. How far back to go to hear the older form? That's what I want to know.

"The easiest weight to carry with you is knowledge. There is a tendency – especially in our fast-paced society – to focus on what's happening now at the expense of what came before. In truth, there is not much of a gap between the what happened and the what is, in the big scheme of things, especially when considering music. My song 'African Blues' is based on a 13th-century Mali classic, and it sounds completely fresh today.

"We have the myth that this country is a big melting pot, that everyone throws away the information from their tribal history, or cultural, and jumps into this big pot. You're supposed to negate, ignore, deny all that which sets you apart from all the others. It's supposed to be that whatever you bring to the table should be easy for everybody else to digest. What kind of crap is that? I'm supposed to negate my African and Caribbean cultural roots just so I can be more readily accepted into the dominant European-culture-based society? I don't think so. That kind of thinking leads to cultural domination, assimilation. 'Let's all be brothers' has always carried the subtext in this country of, 'All you other peoples, be like white folks. Then we'll all get along.' There needs to be a shift of perception, an honoring and respect for the other cultural sources of strength, if we're all really going to be brothers and sisters.

"Here in the United States, you had a group of people injected as slaves into a system and into a language that was foreign to them. They were oppressed, physically and spiritually and emotionally. You can certainly use the blues as a platform to talk about past and present political and social injustices – the blues have been used that way; that role is and always will be there – but for me, there is a bigger picture. My picture is talking about what is happening larger than in the past 200 to 300 years in the United States. Some folks have a short-run vision that says, 'Ya, that reminds me of being down South, where we can't eat nowhere, can't stop nowhere, can't use the toilet nowhere.' I'm saying that's the short history. This music is timeless. The headlines 200 years ago are the headlines today. The blues brings the news.

"I thought for a long time about several different names, but Taj Mahal was the one that stuck. It was an interesting name, and I thought that the building was a classic. I first started performing under Taj Mahal in 1961, while I was going to the University of Massachusetts.

"In 1995, I did a CD named after the lady buried in the Taj Mahal, the

Empress Mumtaz Mahal, which means 'chosen one of the palace,' or 'jewel of the palace.' [*Mumtaz Mahal, Water Lily Acoustics*, Santa Barbara.] I recorded in a monastery's chapel in Santa Barbara with two Indian classical musicians, Narasimhan Ravikiran and Vishwa Mohan Bhatt."

Often called "the illuminated tomb," the Taj Mahal is the mausoleum of the Empress Arjumand Banu Begam (Mumtaz Mahal), the beloved wife of Shah Jahan, "lord of all the world," the Moghul emperor of India. They were betrothed when he was 15 and she was 14, and were married when he was 20 and she was 19. The union was originally conceived as a political alliance to ensure the stability of the government and the continuity of the Moghul dynasty. (His father was the ruler and her father was the prime minister.) What started as a politically expedient marriage blossomed into a sincere love-match. She died at the age of 44, in 1631, following the birth of their 14th child.

Upon his wife's death, the broken-hearted Shah Jahan ordered her tomb to be built on the bank of the Jumna River, outside the Indian city of Agra. The tomb and its setting were to be a model of the Islamic Paradise on the day of Resurrection: an exquisite garden watered by the four rivers of heaven, where the faithful would be entertained throughout eternity in circumstances of unparalleled beauty and order, surrounded by pavilions of superb craftsmanship. It took eleven years and 20,000 craftsman and laborers to create the Taj Mahal.

Most of the complex was built of brick and finished in the local red sandstone, but the mausoleum itself was faced entirely with white marble inlaid with semi-precious stones – bloodstone, jasper, cornelian, jade, agate, and many others – while the most sacred parts were originally decorated with emeralds, rubies, and diamonds. The Shah Jahan took at least two other wives, as was required of him, but his first wife was always his favorite. He died 36 years after her, with his eyes fixed on a small mirror mounted above his bed so that he could gaze at the Taj Mahal.

7 Now For Serious

In 1961, at the age of 19, Taj embarked on a two-year course in animal husbandry at the University of Massachusetts, Amherst. He didn't want to go to college, but his parents explained that, as the "oldest of all the kids, you ought to set some example," recalls Mr Williams. "If you don't go to college, the other kids coming behind you will say, 'He didn't go to college. Why should I go?' He went because we asked him to set an example."

Taj agreed, as long as he could study what he wanted: agriculture. No lawyer. No doctor. No business major. "I didn't see the reason for going to college. If I was going to be a farmer and a musician, as far as my mind was concerned, that would suffer from trying to learn about it from books. I didn't want to be taught away from my natural inclinations about farming or music, and academia does that.

"At the university, I joined the Folklore Society and a band called The Electras. There was strong competition and rivalry among the bands on campus to play at dances in the student union, a very desirable and lucrative gig. A university dean came up with the idea of a Battle Of The Bands, and to have the students vote for the top band. The Electras, we wanted to be the top band."

Taj's brother Richard – who at that time had a singing group, The Monticlovas – adds the details: "So he calls me up and says, 'Hey, you guys. You gotta come here. We're going to do this gig called the Battle Of The Bands.' We sang the doowops – myself, Albert Carter, Jimmy Foy, Alex O'Neil, Alto Daniels, and David McAlpine, who played the guitar, our only instrument. So we jump in Jimmy's car and drive to U-Mass. The Electras and The Monticlovas get together, and we nailed it. Tore the place up. Taj hands me the mic, jumps up, spins around, jumps off the stage, and goes twisting off into the audience. Taj is flamboyant – he loves to dance. Energy just flew off him. The audience just freaked out. Electras won the Battle Of The Bands. They were big time up there."

Taj begins the story about his Boston days after the final set at Jazz Alley. We're back in the dressing room. The autograph seekers and well wishers have finally cleared out. Taj wipes the sweat off his glistening bald head and orders a late dinner, which arrives straight from the Jazz Alley's kitchen. He pushes aside glasses, tapes, and a water pitcher to make room on the table for the food. He looks at the plate of chicken and pauses, as if torn between eating and talking. He decides to talk about making the move into music, about Jessie Lee Kincaid, his first musical partner, and their move into the big music business. He settles back with a cup of black coffee and tells the story of how he started as a professional musician.

"The Electras was my first shot at playing for money. It was a way to put myself through school. The drummer, Don Littlefield, was a business major; the bass player, Jack Moran, was in pre-med, and became a pediatrician; the guitar player, Marcel Crudele, was a forestry and landscape architecture major; one sax player, Ray Souza, was a phys-ed/English major; and the other sax player, Chuck Reed, was phys-ed. The piano player was a literary major, the alto player was in pre-med, and I was in agriculture.

"We played regularly on weekends at frat parties at all the Ivy League colleges, from Portland, Maine, to Philadelphia. Our drummer, Don Littlefield, did all our bookings in places like frat parties – Yale, Brown, Dartmouth, Smith, the Rhodes Island Design Institute. We were making an average of $50,000 a year, putting ourselves through college. By then, I had learned to play the mandolin, banjo, guitar, piano, harmonica, and autoharp. We played primary tunes that I brought to the band, mostly rhythm and blues – 'Shout' by The Isley Brothers, 'What'd I Say,' 'Irresistible You,' 'I Need Your Lovin' Every Day,' 'Do You Love Me' by The Contours, 'Let's Twist Again Like We Did Last Summer,' 'The Twist.' I had heard that music in my community years before it was marketed to the general public. I knew about Smokey Robinson And The Miracles before they were promoted as full-blown stars. Before that, Smokey Robinson was a huge star in the black community."

Marcel Crudele, The Electras' guitar player – now a landscape architect in Tupelo, Mississippi, with the National Park Service – recalls when Taj joined the band: "I was a founding member of The Electras. There was a group of us budding musicians in 1960 – three guitars, bass, drummer, singer – who started the group just for the fun of it. We had a successful year and broke up that summer to go our separate [ways] until the fall semester. Taj wasn't with us at that time. When we came back, our lead singer had flunked out. We limped along, doing mostly instrumentals. One night, we were playing at the student union and Taj bounced in – tall, slender. Before long, he started dancing. He had so much rhythm, it was unbelievable. He just attracted everybody. When Taj took the floor, everything just stopped. We handed him the microphone and he jumped onstage and sang a little bit. Then he put the mic down and jumped off the stage and started dancing. We had never been on such a high before; we had never experienced anything like that. We knew that Taj had something special. We all felt that Taj was destined to be in music.

"We became The Electras, Featuring Taj Mahal. We started branching out to other colleges and got the band in demand. As the demand increased, we started charging a little more. We were making pretty good money on the weekends.

"We had a driving beat and played what was popular at the time – a lot of Ray Charles – and Taj brought in a whole new repertoire. Taj took over, as far as setting the pace. He had a background mainly in rock and bluesy stuff. We had some nights that we sounded great. When we'd quit, we were all exhausted, but we knew – 'Hey, bud, we did great.' Then there were other nights when it was not so great. But we never *ever* had a bad night. We had good nights and we had great nights. What always amazed me about Taj was that he could perform all night long, work up an unbelievable sweat, and at the end, when everyone wanted to go to sleep, Taj would go off into the back room and keep making music after the job was over.

"The women just flocked around Taj. We were playing one night and Taj had the crowd in ecstasy, and this young, good-looking blonde said, 'I want to marry Taj.' They'd just flip out. He'd just capture them. I guess that is what music does to people, and Taj does have a force about him. Taj didn't have any trouble attracting women.

"He had a big heart, and was always concerned about people. I never heard him cuss or get vulgar. His parents did a good job – he's a gentleman. I'm proud to call him a close friend. He didn't throw money around, either.

"I was a year older than anybody in the group. I graduated in 1962; they graduated in 1963, and the band broke up. I was having such a good time I didn't want to leave the band, so I stuck around for another year. I had my degree in landscape architecture and found a job in Springfield,

Massachusetts, right up the street from where Taj's parents lived, at the Oak Grove Cemetery, as a manager/superintendent. One time, the band was in Springfield and Taj invited us to dinner with his folks. His mother cooked up a great big batch of fried chicken for us.

"I still play the guitar, but just for my own enjoyment. In those days, I started out playing a Les Paul gold Sunburst electric guitar. Now, when I think about getting rid of that guitar, it breaks my heart. It's a collector's item.

"Taj called me for my 60th birthday. That really meant a lot to me."

Taj continues with the story: "All the time, I was thinking, 'Why, in the early 1950s, was there real music on radio, and why was less and less of that real-sounding music being played in the 1960s?' I think people need to hear real music. I didn't know what, but something definitely shut off the real music. My idea was, if music is good, why would people opt with something that is less satisfying? I felt the music coming out of the radio was a lesser satisfaction.

"I was unaware of the whole commercial aspect of music. The record companies – who took the lion's share of the money – were trying to control music. I didn't have too much idea of what and why; I just knew that some things were going really crazy, and I didn't get it. It became clear to me that there was all this programming coming in on how to be or to work or to do music. I said, 'If that's the case, I'm going to program myself for what I want out of this.'

"When I got to college, I found this whole bunch of kids with guitars and banjos. I bumped into people pretty serious about learning older songs. I was very, very, *very* interested in the music, and trying not to play it in a glib or thin perspective. I wanted to play it from a deep perspective, where the music was coming from. I said to myself, 'You're not so far off from this whole thing, after all. You're not the only one who sees that a person can get overboard, in terms of being too intellectual about anything and everything in your whole life.'

"Then along came the folk movement, which led itself into popular music and popular television. The New Christie Minstrels and [The] Tarriers were on. I thought, 'This is interesting. These people are eventually going to get around to some really good music that it'll be fun to hear.' Couple that with the whole beat-generation/jazz thing – I was impressed that young white kids were into poetry and jazz and stretching out into different kinds of politics that surfaced around the beats and jazz in New York City, particularly Greenwich Village.

"With the folk movement came this big, huge discovery of older musicians, in lots of different traditions. I looked upon that as an absolutely major opportunity, because, if I had listened only to the media, those people were saying, 'No, there are no more real musicians. We have basically recorded all that music and information. It does not exist anymore, in terms of in the way it used to be.' But now, the opportunity was to have a new generation of people stimulated and inspired by finding these old guys and these old songs. To see people like Reverend Gary Davis, who now had a level of celebrity that didn't depend on the hype or the record industry – that was very interesting to me.

"I saw myself within the framework of being in that same sort of scene. It was something I wanted to be a part of. I didn't know a lot of the music the white musicians were playing, because it came from the more Celtic and Irish and French backgrounds – it wasn't something I really knew; but there were all kinds of people trying to play the blues and rags and marches on the guitar. People asked me if I knew certain older musicians, assuming that these black musicians were well known in the black community, but they weren't, only because of the way they were recorded and how they were recorded and where they ended up in the whole recording scene. Most of the black singers were recorded by white record companies for white audiences. And besides, economics – money, or the lack of – played a big part in the black community, as to whether a musician got heard. Most black folk didn't have the money for expensive – or, for that matter, even cheap – hi-fi equipment. If it wasn't free and on the radio, it didn't compute.

"I completed a two-year associated course and earned a BA in animal husbandry. I decided to leave the university after half of the first semester of the four-year degree course. I had learned everything I wanted from educational agriculture. I didn't want to become a technician, like a dairy technologist or an agronomist. The decision to leave school came over a period of time. I tend to make such decisions at a slow pace, rather than *achunk!* – I was there but now I'm over here. It was clear that I was moving more toward music, so I cruised out of school and started playing music in Boston.

"The folk era was hitting its stride. Buffy Sainte-Marie – also a student at the university – was performing at local coffeehouses; Bob Dylan, Jackie

Washington, Hamilton Camp, Bob Gibson, Joan Baez were starting to be heard. I'd go up to Greenwich Village to hear what was happening and play at open mics and hootenannies. I gravitated to where the older forms of indigenous music were happening, like where Lightnin' Hopkins performed. That man could play anything, most of it original, on standard blues motifs.

"I heard Furry Lewis, Gus Cannon, Memphis Willie B, Big Joe Williams (who sang an intensely personal, raw country blues), Roosevelt Sykes. Sykes was a transitional figure, connecting rural and urban blues traditions. I came onto Elizabeth Cotton, who was playing the old sound. I met Maria Muldaur at the first gig I played in New York City. I met Phil Ochs, John Sebastian, Barry Cornfeld, Jack Elliott. I met Dylan, who was discovered singing in a Greenwich Village coffeehouse called Gerdes Folk City. I liked Dylan's songs, the poetry, but I didn't get with the way he did his vocals. I got a solo act going and built up a following in the Boston clubs.

"What I wanted was, like, the way Mississippi John Hurt played, or the Reverend Gary Davis, or Elizabeth Cotton and Etta Baker. As soon as I heard that stumbling sort of rumble-tumble-rumble-tumble sound, I went, like, 'Oh, that's it.' That's what I call playing the guitar, as opposed to strumming the guitar. You see, Richie Havens is the king of strum. He strums the guitar. He does not pick the guitar. When I went to New York, at 19, I saw Havens and how he was playing. It would have been very easy – had I been an unprincipled kid – to go after his style, but the law of musicians was that you never copped anybody's style. You might learn from it, but you never copped it. I can remember looking up and hearing him play and saying, 'Oh, okay, you got that covered. Well, I'm going to get picking together, because that's another direction this music comes from.' So that's where I went, towards the picking sound, because I heard it; I felt it. Once I heard a little of it, like when I heard Jessie Fuller, then I always heard it. I've heard other guys finger-pick, but what happens it that they get a bland sound of doing it. It needs to be more lopey, like animals running. It has to have that feeling. That's what I was after."

One weekend, Taj's brother Richard went to visit Taj in Boston. "I was supposed to meet him in downtown Boston, and I'm walking around, waiting, wondering if I have the right place, when I see this guy walk up to me with a cowboy hat, bandanna, boots, and dark glasses. I didn't recognize him until he said, 'Hey, brother, how ya doin'?' He looked sort

Taj aged 19 at the University of Massachusetts, Amherst

Hughan Williams, Taj's stepfather, aged 24, new to the States from Jamaica

Taj's mother with (l-r) Samuel, Taj and baby Richard

L-r: Charles Bigbee, Taj, Edward Fredericks, Malcolm Jenkins and Skipper Cook in front of the family house in Springfield

Taj aged 11

The house at 163 Marion Street, always referred to as "163"

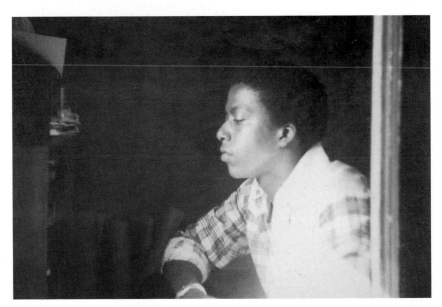

Ozzie Williams in his mid 20s

The marriage of Taj
and Anna de León on
Zuma Beach,
California

Taj and Anna after
the ceremony

The newlyweds in
front of their home
in Santa Monica

Taj Mahal and The Rising Sons

Hughan Williams Jr, Taj's stepbrother, in Springfield in his early 30s

Aya aged ten

Richard Fredericks' high-school
graduation photo

Samuel Fredericks' high-school
graduation photo

Robert Williams in his late 20s in San
Francisco

Taj while he was studying at college

Taj playing with Sleepy John Estes (center) and Yank Rachel (left) at the Ash Grove, 1965-66

The Taj Mahal Band in New York, 1967-8. Jessie "Ed" Davis is in the front window making the "V" sign. Taj is in the background wearing a white hat

The Taj Mahal Band at the 1968 Newport Jazz Festival

Taj playing backstage in Copenhagen, 1969-70

of western and casual and hip at the same time, way before hip was hip. As kids, we all thought Taj was sorta weird and different. Growing up, he tried to dress different, get into his individual style. He always went to get 'Sunday clean,' as we called it, where you'd wear a real nice single-breasted suit and tie and shined shoes. He really liked doing that, dressing differently. He and I would experiment in creating styles."

That's how Sallie Comins remembers Taj from those early Boston days, when she gave him his own night at her folk club, the Turk's Head. "He was a beautiful, big guy. He looked kinda country, because he wore jeans and a shirt and high-top country boots and an old cap like people down South did in those days – a golfer-type cap. He had nice woolly hair then, which he shaved off later. He was fun to hang out with, nice and friendly with people. He had a very magnetic personality. People were drawn to him very easily. That was in 1964.

"I was the wife of a doctor and mother of four young children when I took ownership of the Turk's Head coffeeshop in 1963. I had heard Taj play at Club 47 in Cambridge, where many leading lights of folk music played, and thought he was absolutely fascinating, totally engrossing. I asked him if he'd like to play at my coffeehouse across the river, in Boston."

The Turk's Head – named after one of the oldest coffeehouses in London, founded by Samuel Johnson and the actor David Garrick – was in the Back Bay section of Boston, on Charles Street, a narrow cobblestone street near the bottom of Beacon Hill, a couple of blocks from Boston Harbor. It was originally the basement kitchen of a 1700s row house, and the entrance was several steps below street level. The place was small, with room for 30 people sitting at small black-top tables. A large, ornate espresso machine with a marble base, copper tubing, and a regal brass eagle on top dominated the coffee bar. The machine had come from a coffee bar in Rome that had once been owned by Benito Mussolini. At the end of the low-ceilinged room, a Spanish blanket nailed across the door to a closet marked the stage. The blanket was covered with embroidered little multi-colored birds. "Taj sat in front of the blanket on a high stool and played blues and folk on his big guitar. His fans pulled their chairs around him and listened, so there wasn't any turnover," recalls Sallie. "We didn't do as well, financially, as when other people performed. It didn't matter, because I thought he was so great. I was one of his fans.

"He sang with his eyes closed, the way he still sings today, because he was listening to the music. Every now and then, he would give a little smile, like when he hit a chord he thought was really good. He just went into his world, but other people related to it. He'd get the people all working with him, get them involved, put them to work. He made you want to move. He was very dynamic.

"My favorite song of his was 'High Flying Bird.' It's about being down in the coalmines and feeling trapped and looking up at that high-flying bird. 'Lordie, look at me here, rooted like a tree here, and the only way to fly is to die.' He sang it in such a poignant and soaring way.

"Taj was singing mostly folk from his mother's roots then. Odetta was an influence on him in the early days. Odetta was trained as an opera singer, a highly intelligent, well-read, educated person. She sang the songs of the people, could belt out 'John Henry' in a powerful bass voice that could also soar. One night, Taj cut his set short because he was having trouble breathing. He said to my husband, 'Hey, Doc, can you give me something for my asthma?' Arn wrote him a prescription and he went to a drug store down the street at the break in the set. After his last set, Arn suspected something more than asthma was wrong. 'Is something brothering you?' he asked Taj.

"'You'd better believe it. I'm supposed to report for the army tomorrow,' Taj replied.

"'But they don't take people with asthma.'

"'Well, I told them, but they didn't believe me. And I have this bad knee, from falling off a tractor.'

"The next day," Sallie says, "Taj came out to our house, where Arn had an office downstairs. Arn wrote him a letter to help get him out of the army. He took the army's physical but failed, because of his poor lungs.

"When my husband died, after the children were grown and gone, I sold our big old sea-captain's house on Cape Cod. I drove around the country in a van to find a place to live that felt right. I tried Aspen, where my daughters lived, but it was too rich for my taste. Finally, I settled in Sedona, Arizona, attracted by the spiritual energy of the place and the number of people involved with metaphysics. I tapped into my ability to channel spirits, and have built a career doing reading and drawing portraits of the spirits I channel. Now I go by the name Sakina Blue Star, a name given to me by the daughter of Wallace Black Elk, the respected Ogallala Sioux elder and medicine man. I have a direct heritage to Native

American blood, and have studied very much about my people's traditional spirituality."

In the Jazz Alley's dressing room, Taj remembers his dinner and starts to eat. Then he remembers Jessie Lee Kincaid and how they went to California to start a serious career. "While in Boston, I joined up with Jessie, whose real name was Stephen Nicholas Gerlach. Boy, could he pick! He learned from his Uncle Fred and from the Reverend Gary Davis, whom he was a good friend with. So Jessie Lee and I teamed up and started doing some business for ourselves. Jessie was an interesting guy. He really knew his stuff, and I liked his sound and style. He was a good player, but he didn't sing very well. He sings great now. He was a player who could feel the inside of the music. He always came from where the music was, as opposed to where the notes were. It was a good deal to work with him.

"Jessie and I lived on Franklin Street in Cambridge, a neighborhood of triple-storey houses near Harvard, sort of a radial white neighborhood. [A] lot of students and families. Pigpen, who later played with The Grateful Dead, lived up the street. I'd see him all the time on his porch, playing the banjo. Al Wilson, of Canned Heat, was one of my neighbors just down the street. Mimi and Richard Farina lived around the corner on Putnam. There were a lot of musicians within a two-block-square area.

"A lot of people didn't particularly like that Jessie and I played together, a black guy and a white guy. They thought it wasn't a complementary situation. I'm pretty hardheaded, so I didn't listen. It worked for us. The whole civil rights movement was going then – Martin Luther King had given his 'I have a dream' speech, the Civil Rights Act had become law – but still, harmony did not reign between the races. This race thing, it's almost impossible to figure out, so I didn't and don't really pay much attention to it. I'm not going to waste my time worrying about what people are going to do. There's nothing I can do about that. It's like, today it's rainy. Nothing is going to change that rain. It's going to fall on everyone.

"The way the world is today is because a whole bunch of people went out and decided that they wanted to make the world over in their image. They said, 'This bunch of unwashed heathens over here, according to how we think, can never be more than three-fifths of a human being. So, therefore, us being of a higher and more intelligent nature, we can inflict whatever the hell we want on them with no consequences.'

"Now, look at it in these terms. Suppose these self-righteous people were on a path that everybody goes through in stages of their history. All people on the planet have been slaves to others at some point in their history, regardless of color. The Greeks and the Romans had white slaves and black slaves – they were equal-opportunity slavemasters. All people have been in a position of superiority to another group of people, white or black. Look at Bosnia and Rwanda, two modern-day examples.

"Jessie and I, we had a lot of things to talk about, music we could play. I started asking Jessie where he learned a lot of his music. He talked about this guy, Ry, who lived out in California, who was a good player and knew a lot about the music. He talked about the Ash Grove and the different kinds of places to play around Los Angeles. It sounded a lot more positive there than the East Coast attitude about folk music, which was a bit jaded and doubtful. The West Coast energy was more, 'Yeah, let's go with it.'

"Jessie Lee and I were just scraping by, doing the gigs and giving guitar and harmonica lessons to people. I had my feet in both the folk and contemporary music worlds. I was playing contemporary rhythm and blues music for a living while enjoying blues and folk for myself, but it was becoming clear that the Cambridge scene was coming to an end. By 1965, I was ready to go to California. I saw that the East Coast music scene was too locked in. Boston wasn't close enough to New York to attract people. Everyone I knew who went to New York and got inside the music business, that changed what their music sounded like. They patterned themselves after what the music business wanted.

"I thought, 'Well, maybe those musicians are not ready to understand what real music sounds like.' I was saying, 'What should my music sound like?' rather than, 'How can I shape my music to make a living?' My first thing was, 'Look, if I can't come up with something that is worthwhile, playing for a bunch of people, then I'll find a way to support really good music.'"

Jessie Lee Kincaid now lives in Mill Valley, California, where he recalls the early days with Taj: "I got with Taj, in part, because of Reverend Gary Davis. I had met Reverend Davis when he came to LA to play the Ash Grove in 1964, at the Folk Festival. Then I was living in Los Angeles, going to college, playing guitar – not professional, but just for myself. I got interested in other folk guitar players. One of those players was the Reverend Davis.

"I went to the Ash Grove to say hello to him. During our chat, I realized that he had noplace to stay, so I invited him to stay with me. He stayed with me for two weeks in my apartment. We sat around playing guitar a lot. Since he was blind, he didn't have a sense of night and day, so we'd be up all night, sometimes. He started teaching me his guitar style and songs.

"I learned Reverend Gary Davis' finger-picking on top of my Uncle Fred's style. When the Reverend left, he invited me to stay with him whenever I was on the East Coast. One April day in 1964, when I was 20, I got in my car in LA and drove to New York. I was awed by New York, found it intimidating. I called Reverend Gary. He said come on out to his house on Long Island, Jamaica. He gave me a room. I stayed about three weeks and drove him around – because he was blind – with his wife. He was a real minister and a real kindly man, with a soft Southern drawl.

"While I stayed with him, we'd sit around playing guitar with other people. He was like a mini-college for finger-picking guitar. He was an influential guy, because he had a unique style. In New York, everybody who was around checked him out. They were pretty much awed by him. It was like the presence of a guru.

"One day, I drove Reverend Gary to a folk festival in Amherst, where we were to perform. I met some people at the folk festival who lived in Cambridge and I decided to move there. I didn't have a place to stay, but met this guy named Philip Roger Johnson, and he said, 'Come on over.' Taj was living upstairs in the same three-storey house, with a woman named Maud. We had bedrooms across from each other.

"In those days, I looked like a fifth Beatle, without the suit and tie. I dressed in blue jeans and T-shirts and Beatle boots. I started getting little gigs in the coffeehouses in Cambridge. I had seen Taj playing in the Cambridge clubs, like Club 47. In Club 47, a lot of the other performers were doing imitative Bob Dylan stuff. Taj had a distinct style of his own, so he was a real strong presence. He was kind of a sexy guy, playing hard-driven blues. He wore sleeveless T-shirts, and the girls would go, 'Woo-ooo-ooo.'

"One night, in the house where we were living, we sat down together and played. It really clicked. We started playing this blues thing he had going, and I came up with something. He said, 'Look, I'm going to Philadelphia tomorrow to play a gig at the Second Fret for two weeks. You want to come with me and play?' So the next day we went to Philadelphia and did the gig. That led to another gig. Taj had an agent, Manny Greenhill, who started booking me with Taj. The only thing odd about Taj and I playing together was [that we were] a white guy and a black guy. Basically, we were doing Taj's thing. He drew the crowds.

"We played around the East Coast for about six months, in various cities and clubs. We didn't have a decadent, debauched time – no drugged-out orgies. The two of us would traipse around to these low-rent places, where we'd stay, do our gigs, hang out, and that was about it. It wasn't a wild scene or anything. It was pretty conservative, really. We'd get a hotel, play, practice, do the gig, eat, come back to the hotel, play, practice. Taj likes to talk.

"We got a gig in Detroit. Taj and I stayed in the coffeehouse where we played. I had an uncle in Detroit, an optometrist with lots of clients in the music business, like The Supremes, The Temptations – a lot of Motown clientele. There was the possibility of moving in on that, but we avoided trading on my uncle's contacts. We were not into Motown pop music. We were blues boys, playing acoustical. Our whole focus was not those popular-music type of people. We'd been more happy to spend all day with Booker White, or Elmore James, or Brownie McGhee and Sonny Terry, than with The Supremes. We looked on the Motown popular music as manufactured music. It was not the writer/poet kind of music – the extension of the culture – we felt that folk musicians were about.

"It was January, freezing, really cold. I said to Taj, 'Listen, why don't we do something different? We should go to Europe.' But since I was from LA, I thought, 'Why don't we go to LA? It's warm in LA. There are clubs. We should try it out.' Taj said, 'Yeah.'

"I knew of the folk clubs – the Ash Grove, the Troubadour, the New Balladeer. I also knew Ryland Peter Cooder. Ry took lessons as a young kid from my Uncle Fred. Ry was a really good guitar player, pretty much a little legend in LA. I connected with him through my uncle and started taking lessons with him. Ry gave me about five lessons, then wouldn't teach me anymore. He said that I was learning all his stuff. He was real protective about it. He had a definite style at an early age, and was definitely into the old blues.

"I contacted a car dealer, and he gave us a brand-new 1965 silver Cadillac to deliver in LA. When we got there, we stayed at my dad's house. He lived in a very small house he rented in the Silver Lake district of LA. He had remarried and had a baby son. We showed up one night unannounced. There was a little shack in back of the house with one small bed and a futon. We had sleeping bags. We stayed there a few weeks before moving over to my mom's.

"My mother lived on the other side of town, in West Los Angeles, near the Ash Grove. We stayed there in a little room in her apartment. We went right out to the Ash Grove, the Troubadour, the New Balladeer, and started playing gigs. Everywhere we went, people loved it, right up front. We were immediately booked in the clubs.

"What got their attention was our boots. We had matching boots made in Montreal. High, brown-leather sheepskin jobs that came up to almost our knees. In addition, we had developed our act. We were pretty hard driving, singing harmonies. We had a good little show. We were different than what was being heard in LA at the time. Our act was blues-based, first of all. It was Taj – he was very strong, as a performer. A lot of the blues boys were white boys emulating the blues sound. They didn't sound like the sound. Taj sounded like the real thing. He *was* the real thing. We were being successful in the clubs, but neither one of us had a place to live on our own."

8 The Ash Grove

We're at the apartment provided by the Jazz Alley, with an almost-view of an arm of Seattle's Puget Sound. Taj is resting for the next night's performance. He settles back into the too-cushy sofa and fools with a big cigar, finally getting it lit. He's subdued, perhaps just tired. "The Ash Grove," he says after a little prodding. "Yeah, well, that's where it all started really happening." He blows out a big cloud of smoke and tells the story.

"When I got to LA, I gave myself five years to make it as a musician. If I didn't, then I'd find a way to support people who were playing really good music. And the best place to start was at the Ash Grove. The Ash Grove was the focus of folk music in LA. Before it burned down, under somewhat mysterious circumstances, the Ash Grove was a pretty unassuming-looking building, with just the name on a sign out front.

"Now, I want you to picture this place, because it was important to me. I spent an awful lot of time there. You came into a foyer plastered with announcements about who was playing and what events were going on about town. To the right was a little guitar shop, a branch of the main McCabe's guitar store. To the left was a gallery, where local artists showed. A little to the left of the gallery was a small room, where music was taught on Sundays. Straight ahead was the front room, with a stage, and behind that the office, kitchen, and lavatories.

"I hung out there so much that I eventually moved in. At night, I'd pull out the big couch in the room where the guitar lessons were taught, set out my sleeping bag, and go to sleep. I'd set the couch at an angle to a corner so that, if someone came in during the day for music lessons, I could still sleep, as long as I didn't snore loudly.

"The Ash Grove was a gathering place for people knowledgeable about folk and ethnic music. The aficionados. It was also a family-oriented-type place, in the sense that the regulars there, the people who hung out, felt like a family. The cook would get pissed off and throw a pot of spaghetti on the wall and go walk around the block smoking a cigar until he calmed down. The whole place had that lived-in feel.

"Sandy Getz was the manager, a very bright-eyed, very smart accountant/business-type person who was actually a softie. She made the decisions and always worked from the point of view that business was business. Lots of people thought she was very terrible, hard hearted, but I thought, 'She's just doing her job. What's the matter with you all?' Somebody had to do the business there and give a little reality check. Otherwise, there would be overspending and things getting sloppy. If it wasn't for the fact that there were certain people who financially supported Ed Pearl, the owner, the Ash Grove would have gone bust a long time before.

"The musical and political tone was set by Ed. It was very progressive, positive toward all people. There was lots of grassroots politics and grassroots music going on at the Ash Grove [and], at the center of it, real music from all over the place.

"The McCabe guitar shop was the place where we hung out when we weren't listening to the music or performing. People gathered for conversations, drifted in and out from the performance scene to the conversation scene. You saw the performance, came out, talked about it, and that reminded you of a bunch of other things you wanted to talk about. On any night, there'd be conversations about Tolstoy, Jung, Martin Luther King – all kinds of people talking politics, art, philosophy. Cesar Chavez and the farm workers had their meetings in one of the rooms during the time they were organizing into a union. The Teatro Campasino – run by Edward James Olmos, before he became a well-known actor – put on plays.

"The Vietnam War was always a hot topic. The lines were well drawn, in those days. If you didn't like the war, there were people who accused you of being a Communist: 'Your own country is out there fighting and you're saying no against it, you red bastard!' I'd say, 'Come on, guys, would you wake up? You just can't genuflect over to the side. You have to think about, What the hell are we doing over there, thousands of miles away, killing thousands of young people? For what? Is there oil there? No. Is there gold there? No. What is the point?' 'Well, [to] stop the threat of the spread of Communism.'

"What does that mean, now, in 1999? We wasted all those lives and energy. The real deal was that the war was profitable. The bottom line was that it was an economical situation. To me, it was clear that it was a stupid war. All those people were getting killed, and for what? What can anyone say that it was really all about? I was with a lot of young Americans who protested against the war. I didn't think the war was a correct war. I knew that I wasn't going to be part of it. I wasn't going over there to shoot and kill. We had a situation in this country that was out of balance, and we needed to tend to that. Why would I be going somewhere to kill somebody on the basis that I was just being told to do that? I couldn't work with that.

"During that time, I marched in support of the farm workers, who were trying to organize. That was when Cesar Chavez was organizing them and leading the boycott against the California grape growers. I've always been interested in helping people help people. Even now, I have a little co-op that makes my shirts, the ones I wear onstage and that I sell. Not the T-shirts you can buy at the shows and concerts, but real shirts. I'm thinking about a little store, or putting up a section on my website [at www.taj-mo-roots.com] for Mahal designs. I started designing shirts as a teenager – no front buttons, just a head hole with a button on the shoulders to give room for it to slip on, and full sleeves. Drop it over your head and that dog is *on*.

"Anyway, I have a sewing circle of women – about six – who hand-sew my shirts. They make 25-50 shirts a week. They are single moms with little kids to care for, or women caring for an elderly parent, or widows who don't want to be stuck in black grief. They work at home, often together, chatting, feeding the children, sewing. It's more than giving those women some income without pulling them out of the home. It's not about retailing but about doing something to help preserve the handcrafting of something of quality. It's about pride in work. Some people only take from the table rather than bringing to the table. This is another way I can bring something to the table.

"But mainly, in the early '60s, I was working on my music, and the Ash Grove was great for that. I could always hear the old-time music from either the Appalachian-European tradition or the Afro-American tradition, plus Balkan music, Slavic music – music from all angles. I saw everybody from Mississippi John Hurt to Bill Monroe and everything inbetween, if it had a connection to the authentic music. Canned Heat, Kaleidoscope, The Firesign Theater all performed there during this time. An Israeli dance troupe would open up for Lightnin' Hopkins. Bill Monroe, Gila Gill, and Lightnin' Hopkins on the same bill, and people would handle that. The place was packed, packed out every night. Great gospel groups – like Betsy

Griffin And The Gospel Pearls – played there. The Chambers Brothers would be in for a week or two. During the Christmas week, they sang spirituals and carols all week. One night, there were 42 Chambers onstage, all singing. They were a very spiritually based family, part of a big church down in South-Central LA. All those Chambers, they could lift you right up to look God in the eye.

"The first time I saw Johnny 'Guitar' Watson was at the Ash Grove, and he played the piano. He played the hell out of a piano. Big Mama Thornton was a regular there. When I was ten years old, I heard her recording of 'You Ain't Nothing But A Hound Dog.' Later, Elvis Presley brought it out. She was an interesting woman. Willie Mae could play – she could play real good. She was gruff and rough and funny, a really interesting character. A strong presence. She was real serious, but a wonderful entertainer. You'd know what time it was when she came on.

"I saw Merle Travis, one the great pickers of all time, at the Ash Grove. Where did Merle learn to pick from? An old black man. Now Merle takes what he knows and contributes that to country music. When I was learning to pick, he'd come in many times and see what I was doing. Howlin' Wolf and Lightnin', they checked me out. They didn't say, 'Look, do it this way or that way,' and I didn't say, 'Now, Mr Lightnin', is this the way to play it?' It wasn't done that way. They would watch, not saying anything. That's how they told me I was doing all right.

"When I started listening to Lightnin', I said, 'Okay, in order to listen to this music, or be a part of this music, I can't come into it with a frame that Lightnin', or whoever, [thinks] I'm supposed to fit into. I've got to go with the way the music goes.' That's a lot more refreshing, and makes the music more personal.

"Other musicians often said that 'You can't play with Lightnin', because Lightnin' change when Lightnin' do.' Well, all right, so don't rush it. I used my ears. I never counted by the bars. Let him lead, and as long as you get in the right relationship with it, you can play with him. You got trouble when you start deciding that you know what guys like Lightnin' are going to do before they get there.

"When Bill Monroe played the Ash Grove, I sat on the bench nearly on the edge of the stage to watch him. I first heard Monroe back when I was eleven years old. Now I got to see him up close and how he played. I understood where he was coming from, and how he played the music, and where it came from. The country tunes were based on old English, Scottish, and Irish songs and reels that got an American feel as the music moved into the back hills of Kentucky, Tennessee, the Carolinas. It got a distinctive American sound to it, part of which was Afro-American-created. I was always looking to where music benefited from African sounds, or vice versa.

"The Ash Grove gave me the opportunity to meet people like Howlin' Wolf, Muddy Waters, Junior Wells, Buddy Guy, Louis and Dave Meyers, Sleepy John Estes, Yank Rachel, and Hammy Nixon, a great harmonica player. To meet them in person, rather than knowing them only as a sound happening through an electronic reproduction device, that gave me a deeper connection to their music. I'd ask them what's happening with their lives, and got to know about things going on in their music life that a record, as good as it is, only hints at.

"At the Ash Grove, I was in the position to be learning from people I considered my real peers. It was important whether or not I passed their inspection, not the inspection of the popular-music industry. The learning was in a lot of other directions rather than the actual music itself. Going to see Albert King for the first time – whew! That was a tremendous experience, to watch and hear how he played music.

"Being around people like Albert and Howlin' Wolf and Lightnin' made me eager to keep the authentic music alive. The music industry often doesn't pay proper attention to authentic music like the old blues, because that music doesn't deliver a big profit. The industry didn't see the quirky places where interest in such music turns up, like in lawyers' heads. As law students in Chicago, they'd go down to the South Side, where all the black blues clubs were, and listen to Muddy Waters and Lightnin' Hopkins and Big Joe Williams and BB King. That was the blues education those budding lawyers were getting. Now, as grown lawyers, they don't particularly care for the popular version of the blues. They like Muddy Waters and Junior Wells, the players who were directly connected to the straight music. So I thought that the music had a life unto itself.

"I had been listening to the old-time blues players since I was a kid. By the time I got to meet these people, I had already settled myself about their influences on me. This was just the opportunity to support them. I was supporting a musical explosion that was not being picked up by the music industry at large. Folk and blues records didn't sell much, in those days. 25,000, tops. If you got 25,000, people thought it was akin to platinum.

"I felt that, if I didn't put my time in supporting the music and the players out there – going to see them, getting to know them, finding out the human experiences of these people – then what would I have to offer when it came my time to play? Did I have the real juice to do it?

"At the Ash Grove, I was seeing the raw, natural energy of survivalists. They had survived in the music business over all these years and had created something that was extremely high, a highly creative art form, without all the trappings of the business. And then how does the business inter-work with that? Well, these musicians got ripped off. They weren't paid publishing rights, got cheated on royalties. That's why, when I recorded 'She Caught The Katy And Left Me A Mule To Ride,' half of the publishing and writing goes to Yank Rachel, who worked on it with me.

"A lot of old hardcore blues players and their audience got dumped by the wayside, because the music companies found the so-called modern-day music easier to sell. Most of the industry's decision-makers didn't know what blues was, let alone rock 'n' roll, but rock 'n' roll was modern-day music, and they saw money in rock 'n' roll. They didn't see money in blues. By blues, I take a wide swath: all-encompassing happy, sad, horns, sideways jump, single guitar, big band.

"The solo singer was seen as marginal, especially a black solo singer. As a solo singer, you could only make it big if you were white doing the blues, or the rock 'n' roll version of the blues, like Elvis Presley. Rock 'n' roll was a type of modern blues. The industry basically said that, if you're black, playing your own music, you had no opportunity to make it. This was not said out front, but the conversations over the years expressed this.

"Music is a very flat-out business, and by extension we live in a flat-out society. If the record companies didn't have interest, they wouldn't put money into a record, but they were putting money into recording the blues. Now why, if it had no significance, why were young black musicians totally discouraged, not only from their own culture but from the business end of it? Yet young white musicians were encouraged to record this music, encouraged to do this, encouraged to learn how. I'm really saddened that musicians like Alvin Youngblood Hart, Cory Harris, Billy Branch, Ben Harper, Joanna Connor, Barbara Blue, Eric Bibb, Curt Fletcher – young blues players – are not being heard large scale.

"At the Ash Grove, the musicians were revered. The audience knew who they were listening to. For me, it was coming to a natural place. If there was anything I was learning from those times, it was to see individual musicians get up by themselves and be completely entertaining, deliver the story, deliver the music. That was re-affirming for me.

"Linda Ronstadt hung out there a lot, too, along with her band, The Stone Poneys, with Kenny Edwards and Bobbie Kimble. Al Ross – who ran McCabe's – let us treat it like our own private museum of amazing old instruments. We were always picking up groovy pearl-inlay guitars off the shelf and playing them. Nobody ever stole anything or broke anything. The instruments were just there and, like, you picked up whatever you fancied, and wondered at it, and marveled at it, and played it, and wished it was yours. But we could never own it, because we didn't have any money.

"Linda was really nice. She's a feet-on-the-ground lady. I remember back then she was interested in legalizing prostitution, not because she thought it was such a great way to make a living but because a lot of the working ladies were supporting a family. She thought it was stupid to throw those mothers in jail and put the kids in foster care.

"Sometimes she'd be hitchhiking from her place up Topanga Canyon down to the old post office at Topanga Center and I'd give her a ride in an old school bus painted black I had then. It didn't have any windows in it. I bought a bunch of cheap wind chimes and hung them in the empty windows all over the inside so the wind rushing through the bus made me sound like a traveling music box. Linda would hear me coming and stick her thumb out. Seemed like she always wore those off-shoulder Mexican blouses and never wore shoes. She said that she had extra bones in her feet, and that shoes hurt.

"The Ash Grove was torched and burned down to the ground in retaliation to statements Ed made in support of what was thought – by some unknown people – of radical and innovative political ideas. I don't know the details, just the rumors. He opened it again, and it was burnt down again. It was torched a third time, and that put it out of business. That was after I had got my own career started and was traveling out away from the Ash Grove, so I never really knew what it was all about."

On a lovely San Francisco spring day, Linda Ronstadt sits in her living room after a morning's voice lesson and talks about Taj. "Taj was the guy that everybody wanted to be. We all wanted to be Taj. We couldn't help it. When he touched your life, you felt that he really knew you. It was very cool. He was the highlight of the scene, the shining zenith. It was unbelievable how people would congregate around him. He was made out of warmth, in a certain kind of way. He was just overwhelming, overflowing, and larger than life in his personality and in his music. It seemed to penetrate everything he did.

"He was extremely bright. He was very well prepared for things that turned out not to be music. He was very well prepared for music, too. I have always loved the way that he has run around and found that thing that really, truly inspires him [and] then completely steeps himself in whatever that is. He was the be all to end all of what we all wanted to emulate, in terms of natural, authentic-sounding music. I'm a great believer that you don't have to be original; you simply have to be authentic. You get a lot farther with authenticity. Taj embodied that.

"I remember playing a show in Tanglewood, or a similar place near Boston – a big, classical, outdoor place. It was one of those afternoons where there were a lot of stars on the same bill, a big walk-on show, one band after another. Everybody would come out and play their biggest, loudest thing to really get the crowd rocking and get their attention. I thought, 'Oh my god.' I had come from basically acoustic music, and was always sure I wasn't loud enough. I thought, 'Oh my god, we have to get our biggest, loudest thing for the first song to get the crowd's attention.'

"When Taj's turn came onstage, he took out a kalimba – a thumb-piano – and started to play. He didn't sing or have music with words. The crowd – which was grilling hot-dogs, scoring drugs, and doing all the things that people do at summer outdoor concerts – started to quiet down. Pretty soon, everybody's attention was riveted on Taj. He eventually started to sing, but it was just one of those grunting syllable things that he does. He had the entire crowd.

"All the other acts had huge amplifiers, drums, roadies, big songs, lots of words, screaming and hollering, skin-tight clothes, boobs hanging out, crotches hanging out. He wore a big caftan and played a finger-piano. It was *so* good. There was a case of being authentic and original. Taj has a big case of both, when it comes to his collision with pop music.

"I admire him so much, because he really carries a style, and never compromises it. I just love what he's done with his music. He's been a real pure spirit in that way. I remember him telling me one time that he had kept one instrument at home for his own personal, private soul. I am very much that way, too. I have certain private music that I do. I thought it was so wonderful that Taj kept a whole instrument for himself.

"Yes, I was, and am, very interested in the legalization of prostitution. In the early '70s, I got involved with Margaret St James, a madam and working girl, and her organization COYOTE (Cast Off Your Old, Tired Ethics). One of the things she wrote was that prostitutes will often keep a part of their own self for the person they love. It might be kissing, or a place on their elbow. The rest of it they sell. I think musicians sell this big part of our music, but there is a part we keep for our own. As musicians, we give away part of our soul and heart, but it's there to share and enjoy. In a way, it is a public service, but I think of it as a service to myself.

"I've always found it to be a privilege and joy to be in Taj's presence. When you run into Taj, it's like a day when you got an extra helping of cake."

9 Rising Sons Rising

Late-afternoon shadows fill the apartment as Taj talks. A couple of times, he mentions that it's time to stop, that he needs to rest and prepare his spirit for the evening's show, but each time, after a long pause, he takes another pull on the cigar, holds the smoke, and lets it seep past his lips. The smoke smells like a contradiction: musty autumn leaves and spring loam mixed with rich, moist brownie dough. He takes another deep draught on the cigar and, in a soft voice that he never uses onstage, starts to tell the story of his rude awakening.

"One night, Jessie Lee Kincaid and I were playing the Ash Grove and Ry Cooder came to hear us. Ry comes up and asks if he could join in on the next set. Sure. Ry was, and is, a great instrumentalist. He was 17 at the time, and already had the reputation as a prodigy. He knew a lot about blues, ragtime, country music, R&B, and blues. He had a good feel for indigenous music. He could render the music in a very believable manner, whereas a lot of guys played a lot of notes that didn't have a lot of believability. But with him, he was always up around 100-plus in believability. The kid was out there. He had a good understanding of music-business politics, too. His parents were folklorists, and he grew up in the LA music business.

"Things went really well, so I visited him at his place on Rambla Vista Road in Malibu. We sat out with our guitars and played and talked a bit. He was a real quiet guy. Ry had an upcoming gig at the Teenage Fair at the Hollywood Palladium. He was in charge of the Martin guitar booth, giving demonstrations, showing off the guitars. He invited Jessie and me to come out and play with him and a buddy of his, Gary Marker, who played bass.

"Now, the Teenage Fair was designed to show off products to teenagers – you know, hype them up to buy stuff. There were lots of bands there for entertainment. All the other bands were guys wearing matching suits and playing 'Gloria' and covering tunes of the day. We wore our ordinary street clothes and played some crazy Delta music. We were like a funky electric jug band. It drew a lot of kids. That made us think that maybe we got something going.

"We got hired at the Ash Grove as a band – Ry, Jessie, Gary, and myself. Ed 'Cass' Cassidy came on as the drummer. The basic idea was to take old-time music and bring it up to date, give it some modern arrangements, a modern sound. We were trying to take a more basic roots approach to popular music. We needed a name for the band, and Jessie came up with The Rising Sons. The play between *suns* and *sons* was to make it different, something for people to remember.

"As material and backgrounds, we had this big pile of blues and country and country blues, with folk in the center. All of us had a direct folk link and cultural links to these kinds of music. So we were putting something together. There were regular rehearsals. Cass – who is the world's oldest rock 'n' roll drummer – started playing with Randy California and Spirit, so we got Chris Hillman's cousin, Kevin Kelly, to take his place.

"Ry didn't have any confidence about singing at all. I'd tell him, 'Hey, man, relax. If you don't want to sing the front parts then sing harmony. Just don't make it a big issue.' He did a lot of arranging. That's how the band was built.

"We were excited to play the music we wanted. At this time, The Byrds were happening, Kenny Rogers was playing with The New Christie Minstrels, The Association was going together, Joe And Eddie was happening. The Turtles, The Lovin' Spoonful, Tracy Nelson, Janis Joplin, The Pair Extraordinaire, Arthur Lee and Love, The Dillards, Hoyt Axton were all there. The Stones were kicking in with the blues. Paul Butterfield was playing in that direction. Mike Bloomfield was coming. Jimi Hendrix popped up in the middle of the whole thing. This stuff was blowing up all over the place. The bulk of the musicians came from a background of listening to the blues and the Appalachian music. They were starting to mix it up with musicians who came out of rhythm and blues or the gospel bag, so the music was starting to grow. It was like a hybrid that was going towards something.

"It was a good time, musically. Music was happening around at the time, like a multi-layered cake: Joel Scott Hill, Three Dog Night, The Gentle Soul, Mama Lion, Eleventh Floor Elevator, Peanut Butter

Conspiracy, Mandrill, Sweet Water, Linda Albertano, Dick Dale And [His] Deltones. I personally liked Dick Dale's music. This mélange of music was full of pop and R&B stuff, and underneath is all the folk and blues. Also the San Fernando Valley Mexican rock and R&B bands, like The Three Midniters, Cannibal And The Headhunters, Tierra, and The Outlaw Blues Band.

"On the outside of this music was the Southern California surf sound, The Beach Boys. I had no idea what the hell that was about. Sounded like lousy blues to me. It was like nobody in that scene thought about, or looked into, the historical cultures where surfing came from. The Australian Aborigines, the Pacific Polynesians islanders, the Melanesian islanders and Africans have all been into surfing. Surfing had more cultural roots than just Southern California weirdness. The whole picture of the music wasn't there because nobody made the broader cultural link to it; the music was only linked to a bunch of kids who had lots of time and nothing else better to do than create some kind of sport. That's how it came across to me. I didn't get out of it that there was a broader cultural sight to that music, and there certainly was. The same way really good music from the Pacific islands is masked behind misinformation, surfing music was masked behind misinformation – or no information – of the youth culture emerging in Southern California.

"I once sat in on a Beach Boys recording session. A friend from back East, Robin Hemingway, was working with The Beach Boys and got me in. I was absolutely amazed about the way they recorded. Every word, every breath, every pause was done over and over. I frowned on that way of making music. It seems as though you are using the machine to create the picture of reality when you yourself couldn't come up with a reality to put on a four-minute record. I thought that you should start at the beginning and go to the end, [although] I've modified my thoughts on that after I've recorded 34 albums.

"The Rising Sons just wanted to play music. At that time it wasn't a very simple thing, because in LA film took precedent. Music was kinda considered a dirty little cousin, someone you really didn't want to get involved with. We came through at a time when music was trying to get its rightful place and respect. This was pre-John Travolta's *Saturday Night Fever*. That record put the music industry and the film industry in a much more positive, win-win situation with each other.

"The Rising Sons quickly got to be a hot sensation. *Rolling Stone* magazine called us a combination of 'ardent folk-blues scholarship, brawny Delta grind and Beatles-esque pop vigor.' Each of us was still doing solos and playing with this person and that person, but as a band we started working it, putting together a promotion packet, with photos. The record companies started coming around. They realized that the Mitch Miller sound was dead. The Beatles were hot. The companies were all in line to get the next product, running around, signing everyone. Warners, Columbia, Elektra, Capitol were all bidding for The Rising Sons. We did demos for each of them and signed with Columbia, which proved to be a mistake.

"We started playing some great gigs, like being the opening act for The Temptations, Martha And The Vandellas, and Otis Redding. Our first big show was with The Temptations at the Trip, on Sunset Strip. It was the most amazing scene in the world. LA at that time was highly segregated. You had the black area in South Central, the white and Mexican in the Valley, and East LA – that was solidly Mexican. Everyone listened to the same radio stations, but they didn't know that the other folks liked the same kind of music, too. Whatever their suspicion and weirdness about each other came together standing in the long line outside the club. Sunset Strip was, like, all the hippies were happy hanging out there, [having] hippie parties all over the place. People coming in from the Valley were afraid of these hippies, of being attacked. Sunset Strip was then semi-segregated. Blacks there were either working as waiters or cooks or maids or whatever.

"The people in the different sections of LA liked the same performers. That's what brought the diverse crowds together. My hat is always off to Elmer Valentine and Mario, those guys who are now running the Whiskey A Go Go and the Rainbow and the Roxy. They were the first guys to really come out of Chicago and say, 'Let's bring some real music to LA.' They started bringing in Marvin Gaye and Martha Reeves And The Vandellas, who had the hit 'Heat Wave'; The Miracles; The Temptations; Mary Wells, who hit the pop charts with 'You Beat Me To The Punch.'

"When The Rising Sons opened for The Temptations, the audience did not know what to do with us, a band with a black lead singer, who was me, and four white musicians, playing this kind of music that was not on the radio. They came only to see The Temptations. They were not there to see anything else at all. No way, no how.

"Basically, most white people went to see white bands. Here was The

Temptations, five obviously black men with an orchestra led by a black bandleader. That was okay, because the record companies put them in the mainstream. The people knew The Temptations from their records, which the record industry promoted as the sound of 'Young America,' which was Motown's slogan. The people came to hear the hits. Here was a city audience being fed what came off the radio. It's all marketing. It has nothing to do with you having a personal choice. If people were told that hit music was hip, they were supposed to like it, and then there were people jumping up to get with it.

"The Temptations had a slick, urban sound. They were hip, sophisticated, and had the power and the means to make people respect them. That was something young black kids wanted for themselves. White kids dug The Temptations' music because it came in a form they weren't intimidated by. It was gospel-based, and blues-based, but not delivered by some old black guy mumbling down in the cotton field. They weren't being preached at by a black gospel choir but entertained by real professionals who made the music danceable.

"Our band – a white band, with a black lead singer – was totally off to the side. We were into country blues, which for some black people represented some sort of retro they didn't want to be in. Here they were forced to listen to this embarrassing music in front of all these other people. They didn't want to be reminded that their people came from the country and sharecropping and the like. It embarrassed them at a time when they were trying to shake the dust off their feet and drive shiny Cadillacs.

"There was a racial consciousness in the black community that didn't want to be reminded of the old form. They rejected it. They didn't want to hear Sleepy John Estes or Muddy Waters or BB King or Lightnin' Hopkins, not back then. And here I was, saying, 'Hey, this country blues music is wonderful. It's about where you came from and who you are.' Well, they didn't want to be that anymore. The audience wasn't there to sing the praise of the country, which carried the baggage of a painful past. After we played our set, only one person clapped. People couldn't deal with it.

"The week we spent working with The Temptations was probably the hardest week we as a band had ever spent. The Temptations were great to us as individuals, open and warm and friendly. They related great to us backstage, always nice to us, not like the people out front. But they were a completely different trip than we were. They wore matching suits and make-up; we wore our street clothes. I had on the same jeans that I went fishing in, only they were clean.

"Every night after our set we'd hurry to get upstage, because we loved to watch The Temptations and their band. That was a serious learning situation, to watch the musicians play and their interaction, to see Norman Roberts, The Temptations' drummer, play. I never saw any guy finesse and play like that. And Cornelius Grant on guitar and Bill Upchurch on bass. Musicians play with musicians, regardless of color. Chuck Berry, Buddy Holly, Ruth Brown, LaVern Baker, Jimmy Reed, The Big Bopper, Ritchie Valens – all these people played together. They knew one another, worked on each other's records. It was almost like a subterranean existence inside the music business.

"Then, there was the face that the music business wanted. They wanted you to look like Bobby Vee. Bobby Vee had to be perpetually 17 years old. The music business' creations – creatures – couldn't have any bad records. All the record companies had to do was suggest that you drank or smoked dope or did anything that was out of the ordinary and your career was down the tubes. That's what the music business did. They created this kind of thing, and people – the public – learned their music out of that. Anything else that was different from that, the music business didn't know what to do, except put out a negative toward it.

"Our next great gig was opening for Otis Redding at the Whiskey A Go Go for a week. Boy, I cannot tell you how good that was! Otis and his band were really nice people, overly friendly to us, coming out to us. It was all a real deal, no hype stuff. His performances were absolutely the best of anything I'd seen live. It really resonated in me. Otis was from Macon, Georgia. He and his music had roots in country, and he didn't mind letting you all know. He never pretended that he didn't have major country roots, and his audience was very accepting of that. Otis' music celebrated his roots and where the music came from. His and our music were very compatible. He liked our music, really listened to it, and that was re-affirming.

"Although The Rising Sons was getting a following, our biggest problems were with Columbia, whom we signed with. We had a warning there would be trouble when we did the demo. We were in the studio recording a bottleneck-guitar piece based on 'Travelin' Riverside.' We're calling it 'Down In The Bottom,' because the first line is, 'Meet me down in the bottom/Bring my travelin' shoes.' We got the tune going, got the vocals to go through, and then Ry starts to play a bottleneck solo.

"Midway into the song, a buzzer from the production booth comes in. *Annnt! Annnt!* 'What's that weird, eerie, sliding, distorting guitar?' Alan Stanton asked over the intercom. (He was the head of A&R.) We looked at each other, couldn't believe it. Ry held up the bottleneck and said, 'It's supposed to sound like that.'

"Those guys didn't know what a bottleneck guitar was. That was our warning. They had no feel for the blues or for our sound. When you're learning to play with a group of people, the music is an elusive thing. It's escaping you, each of you, at different times. You really concentrate within yourself and on what you're hearing from the other guys and make it all work, the separate pieces, as a whole. Here we had hit a groove, jerked this music off the ground, and Alan throws this grating buzzer into it.

"We finally got all these tunes organized so we knew what we wanted to do with them. Then we had to fight the producer to get our vision over. He was the keeper of the corporate vision, so was trying to get that corporate sound, the sound that says *bottom line*. It was really nuts.

"For our first album, Columbia gave us one of the staff producers, Terry Melcher, the son of Doris Day and Marty Melcher. In those days, you couldn't ask for a specific person as your producer – the record company assigned you a producer. Melcher was a 23-year-old Californian, silver-spoon, movie-society, entertainment-industry kid. Our question was, did he know what he was doing? He had produced people like Bruce Johnston, Al Jardin, The Beach Boys, Paul Revere And The Raiders. That was the orientation of his music.

"Melcher called us to a meeting up at his house in Benedict Canyon, so we drove up there, pressed the squawk box at the big gate, and got permission to enter. We drove up this long driveway to this big house at the top of the hill. Melcher and Billy James – another A&R guy at Columbia – were waiting for us in the living room, with a tall A-frame ceiling. The juice of the meeting was that, if we didn't give Melcher and James, personally, 100 percent of our publishing and make them our managers, we didn't have a hope of success at Columbia. They said, 'You have to do this our way. If you don't, you're history, baby.'

"Now, in The Rising Sons, Jessie and I were the primary writers. The others would help on the arrangements and some writing, so the copyright would go to all of us as a band. We didn't own the song, but we owned the way we arranged it. We'd copyright that arrangement. In our band, more often than not, we were not willing to compromise our vision to fit into what the music business would get behind. I saw the band as an agreement to collaborate and to present human synergy in front of an audience. The singer was not any more important than the drummer or the bass or the guitar. This was a democratic way of playing, of sharing – a universal, human way to connect with one another. It lets musicians bring something of their own style and culture to the music. I've always formed bands on those principles.

"The implication was that, if Melcher and James didn't control us, Columbia would dump us. We turned them down on the spot. I looked at Melcher and said, 'You know, that's extortion. What the hell you mean, that you're going to take 100 percent of my publishing?' You've got to watch out in this life. 'It won't be me,' I looked him right in the eye, 'but if you continue this kind of stuff somebody is going to come and get you. You're going to run against someone who is not going to be as generous and peaceful as we are about how you do business.'

"Looking back on that now, I would have said, 'If you want 100 percent, give us $2.5 million plus stock options and then we can do business.' Now I can laugh about that incident, but back then I carried a lot of personal anger because I didn't come from the business; I didn't understand how to do the music business. Right now, I'm re-assessing what I've been doing over the years. I've been delivering live music on an event-by-event basis, but the real deal is that I've been helping people get a leg up in the music business, so now I'm thinking more about the production and independent record company end of things. This does not mean, and does not sound, the knell of me saying, 'I'm not going to play or tour anymore.' No. I've just outfitted my own studio, and will produce records on my own label, Kan-Du Records.

"I want to make young performers realize that the music business is not all glamour. One percent is about talent and 99 percent is about business. Kashif – a veteran producer, artist, someone who's been on the inside of the record industry for a long time – and Gary Greenberg wrote a book, *Everything You'd Better Know About The Record Industry* [Brooklyn Boy

Books]. This book completely turned my world around, whereas I'd been wasting a lot of my energy being annoyed at the record industry. In my record company, anyone working with me will be knowledgeable in the music business. I won't deal with people – including artists – who are not knowledgeable, so we can all work on the same page.

"To the best of my knowledge, Melcher was going to produce Charles Manson, who had a group. I don't know if Manson actually played music. A lot of people in the studios didn't play music worth a fart in a haystack. It might have been a case of somebody who knew somebody who didn't know anything about music and thought Manson might have talent, so they'd get into the studio or get a promise of getting studio time. It might have been a situation like that.

"This is what I learned about the studio situation: there were a lot of people who made records but didn't play on their own records. We wanted to play on our own records, but the producer wanted to bring in studio musicians. What the hell is that? I don't need that. That sounded like I would be getting credit for something I didn't create.

"I had bumped into Manson several times on the north side of Sunset, between the Hamburger Hamlet and San Vincente Street, by Whiskey A Go Go. It was clear that he was looking for trouble, that he was a majorly dangerous human being. When I walk on the street, I can pick up on someone like that. I'm actually looking to see what's going on around me. It's just the way my vision is, that it picks up the visual and the feelings or vibes behind the visuals. I also happen to see eagles a lot, even in cities. I don't know what that is. I guess that I'm not afraid to be out there.

"I decided to try to loosen Melcher up, and took him to a Bo Diddley show. After the show, Melcher told me that, to be successful, I should sing like a white 17 year old imitating Ray Charles. We didn't work with Melcher anymore. The band languished at Columbia for a while, then we finally decided to get out of the record contract. A lot of bad blood was created. There got to be this attitude problem. As The Rising Sons, we thought the record company didn't know what it was doing with our music. It seemed nobody there knew anything about the blues, or cared. They didn't know what was happening, in terms of our style of music, how to market us. We figured that we were covering everything that was out there. The band's sound was in two camps: the real funky American blues camp and the influence of Jessie Lee, who was Dylan-inspired. Columbia's marketing department was confused by it.

"Melcher's threat that we would be buried at Columbia and dumped came true. The record he produced for us wasn't released until 1992, as *The Rising Sons, Featuring Taj Mahal And Ry Cooder*. In all fairness, it turned out pretty good, for what it was, but Melcher and James didn't get what they wanted. We hadn't had a hit, so Columbia didn't pick up our option. They wanted hits, not albums."

The Rising Sons were called by *Rolling Stone* magazine "...the missing link between Beatlemania and the late-'60s electric-blues explosion, an exciting, highly commercial proposition that missed stardom by just a hairsbreadth," according to reviewer David Fricke. "At their best, the Rising Sons were precocious blues adventurers who took the music out of the beatnik coffeehouses and into the discotheques, where people could really dance to it. The Sons' version of 'Take A Giant Step' is the best example of their derring-do, a lithe roadhouse overhaul of The Monkees' song combining Taj Mahal's energetic howl and Cooder's bottleneck maneuvers with bursts of cheesy '60s fuzz guitar and a weird neo-Byrdsy *a cappella* vocal break. They definitely don't make 'em like that anymore."

Jessie Lee Kincaid confirms Taj's take on The Rising Sons and the encounter with Terry Melcher: "Initially, the vibe between the band and Melcher was pretty good. We thought, 'Whoa, Columbia, we're really cooking,' but we weren't. He had an attitude. We had a clash right up front. We didn't feel that he knew a damn thing about what we were doing, blues-wise. In retrospect, it was a mistake to go with Columbia. They didn't really know what we were doing. They didn't tap into the blues thing. They were trying to make us into a pop entity, and that never happened. It wasn't Terry Melcher's fault. He wasn't the right guy to develop the sound of the band. He was inexperienced in the blues.

"The Rising Sons was half blues and half pop music, that I was writing – Dylan, Beatles. We thought we had it all covered for the market. Problem was, once we did sign with Columbia, and started recording, we couldn't find anything that was commercially viable. The split in the music – blues/pop – was something that the company couldn't really get together. We never got the hit single.

"There got to be an attitude problem. As Rising Sons, we thought the record company didn't know what it was doing. Nobody there knew anything about the blues. Columbia looked at us and said, 'How are we going to make something out of these guys?'

"At this point, it had been a year and half or so [of] slugging through the LA music scene. It was a lot of work. We hadn't got a hit. People were getting a little discontented with the whole situation. It was, like, the final straw to have Melcher and James strong-arm us – threatening us, basically, to either control us or dump us. We didn't like the vibe. We said no. They said we were making a big mistake. That was that.

"The consequence was that Columbia dropped our contract. We hadn't had a hit, so when option time came they let us go. I think something else could have been happening behind the scene: Ry was getting tired of the band; Taj realized that he could function without all these guys in this ensemble – he had his own thing that he could do. He had enough attention – as did Ry – from the music scene to step on out and become a solo act. Columbia dropped the band and signed Taj. [Ry Cooder declined to be interviewed for this book, through his agent.]

"I went back to LA City College and studied classical guitar with Vincente Gomez. I was still writing songs, and did get signed – to Capitol Records. I did a couple of singles, but they weren't a hit. I didn't have much of a solo career. Then I got a scholarship to the California Institute of the Arts, where I auditioned as a classical guitarist. Now I live in Mill Valley, teaching guitar, composing, playing, and I have a production company."

10 *The Taj Mahal Band*

It's nearly time to leave the apartment for Taj's evening performance, but he lingers over the cigar, wanting to wrap up the story. The Rising Sons dispersed. Ry Cooder played in the studios. Gary Marker was off. Ed Cassidy joined the band Spirit. Kevin Kelly went with The Byrds and Sweethearts Of The Rodeo, and spent time with Clarence White and Gram Parsons.

Taj tells how he formed his first band: "All of us in The Rising Sons still played with each other, helped out on records. That is when I first met Dr John. He was playing guitar at a Watts 103rd Rhythm Band session. I played some harmonica on it. This session work, people were doing favors – 'Hey, man, I got $75 for a harmonica, so come out and play' – or it was a union deal. We were helping each other out. I played with Steve Mann, a real genius but not always mentally there.

"We had been signed individually, rather than as a band. Since I had a contract, I started calling Clive Davis – who was then president of Columbia – and telling him that I had some ideas I wanted to talk about. Davis sent David Rubinson out to talk to me. Rubinson was doing classical music. Davis kept calling and talking to me and sending David out to find out what's going on. By now, I'm somewhat established; I'm playing with a lot of people, so I looked like a commodity to the record suits.

"This was in 1967, a free-floating time. I was out of The Rising Sons. At the time, I was teaching guitar, growing a garden, working at the Ash Grove. I won a banjo contest at the Topanga Canyon Fiddlers Convention. Canned Heat used to come over, and we jammed in the garage. We tried to put something together, but didn't quite get the vibe we wanted.

"I was playing solo gigs wherever, doing some session work, looking for other musicians whose sound I liked. I wanted to put together another band, but I wanted to do it with the right people. I spent a lot of time listening to bands like The Outlaw Blues Band, a Latin blues band. Those guys were great. The bass player, Joe Bass, looked exactly like Cesar Rosas from Los Lobos – same Ray Bans, the whole look. They brought to the blues another enthusiasm, the same way Carlos Santana did with The Santana Blues Band before it became Santana. I was always excited to see other cultures interpret rock and rhythm and blues and the type of energy they brought to it.

"When I research musicians, I listen for a unique language they create based upon the original language of the music. I also look for common information on music we like. I'd find musicians like that and we'd go hang out, get high, listen to some records, or bring some songs, play, and jam. Plus, I want musicians who are dependable and on time, guys I can count on. If we're to meet at two o'clock, they'd be there. A lot of musicians were not accountable. I look for musicians who are interested in playing music first and being famous second. Some musicians went where they could make the best money and the music was second. Okay, fine, go do it. But I want guys who are with the music first, whatever their race, creed, background. I am an equal-opportunity employer.

"There are a lot of blues-hacker guitar players. They don't really listen to the information of the music, the soul of it, the tone of it, the pathos of it; they just put a bland dressing on it. Since the people might never have heard the real stuff, they believe they're hearing the truth.

"One day, I heard Jessie 'Ed' Davis play at the Corral up in Topanga Canyon. He lived out in Sherman Oaks with Gary Gilmore. Jessie and Gary came out of Oklahoma. A block from their place was the Plantation, a big old house where other musicians from Oklahoma lived – Bill Boatman, Chuck Blackwell, and Leon Russell, who was kind of the grand nabob of all those guys from Oklahoma. I was still working to get a recording agreement with Columbia and wanted to put a band together. As soon as I heard Jessie, I knew he was a major possibility. He was a sensitive player with really good tone touch. Jessie and I wrote several songs together and did some albums."

Jessie Edwin Davis is a minor legend as a guitar player. Taj deeply appreciated him as a musician, as did Mick Jagger, John Lennon, Rod Stewart, and many others. His mother was a full-blood Kiowa and his father half Comanche, one-quarter Seminole and one-quarter Scottish. He was born in Norman, Oklahoma, but grew up in Oklahoma City.

Taj's nickname for Jessie was the Agent, as in Indian Agent, and Jessie called Taj the Captain, according to Jessie's widow, Kelly Davis. "Jessie wrote a song for Taj, 'The Captain,' that appeared on Jessie's second album, *Ululu*," she recalls from her home in California. "Jessie was a natural musician. He had music in his being. He was artistic first and foremost in everything he did. He was a good painter, as was his father, Jessie 'Ed' Davis II, who has been widely collected. Jessie was a great cook. His sensibilities were very poetic. He was an English major, but he wasn't too big on lyric-writing. He died at 4.40pm, June 22, 1988 from a combination of alcohol, heroin, and Librium."

Taj continues: "I sat in with Jessie and Chuck Blackwell, a drummer – both of whom became part of my Taj Mahal Band – and those guys a couple times. We started doing some gigs together, using my material and stuff they had. People really liked it. I had knowledge of a lot of songs that the other players had never heard before, old information that hadn't been translated into modern times. A lot of those old-time authentic people were country players, and their music didn't get transferred into the more contemporary styles of music, whereas 'Dust My Broom' – originally known as 'Dust My Room,' according to Homesick James – went from Robert Johnson to Elmore James to Chicago, because Elmo went there a lot, where he played with Homesick James. In fact, Elmo died at the age of 45 after taking a shower at Homesick's house in Chicago. Other players in the Chicago blues clubs picked up the song, and it became a Chicago standard, but most people have never heard of it.

"I thought this band of a Native American, a black American, and European Americans could have a solid impact. We were what the country was formed of. Over time, the band settled into Jessie Davis, Gary Gilmore, Chuck Blackwell, and myself. We brought in James Thomas because I wanted someone who understood my bass lines. Sandy Konikoff was originally on drums, Ry Cooder on guitar and mandolin, Jessie Davis on guitar, and me on harmonica and guitar. Bill Boatman played guitar and a couple of other things. We basically took tunes I knew, worked them out, and recorded them with Columbia.

"Sometimes we called ourselves The Blue Flames, or The Great Plains Boogie Band, but most of the time the band was referred to as Taj Mahal. I often called it The Davis Band. Gilmore, Blackwell, Jessie, and myself were a powerful mix. Gilmore looked like Kit Carson, with a beard, handlebar mustache, and long hair. Blackwell had long hair and a mustache. I had a big 'fro up under a cowboy hat, and Davis was a straight Indian. We were slamming it. You couldn't have hit it harder.

"Jessie's parents were first-generation assimilated Indians – you know, living in a house and everything in Western organization. I really adored Jessie's father, Big Ed, and I love his mother, Vivian. Vivian is like putting your arms around the sun – she's always that warm. She is so wonderful, and loves the music. Even with her arthritis, she'd come out to a show with all her jewelry and the music would be going and the horns playing and the band hooting and hollering, and she'd be right there with us. She is really beautiful still today.

"Jessie Ed, the second-generation, educated Native American, was working to figure this whole Indian/Western culture thing out. At first, he was a little cautious with me. He was endowed with a certain amount of self-preservation, and so was I. I was, like, no nonsense, didn't take no shit from anyone, no how, no way. The situation intimidated him a bit, in the beginning. What I didn't realize was the level of indoctrination that Native Americans went through to be wary about being out front with who they were. They had learned that it was dangerous, in the white society, to be an Indian. But it worked out, because we all had the feeling together that we were crusading for good music, good-time music, and real music. Jessie had his own taste and touch on his music."

Chuck Blackwell, another member of the original Taj Mahal Band, says, "Jessie Ed was one of my best experiences. I just love the guitar, but I got so I hated the screaming guitar. It didn't make sense to me. But Jessie Ed made sense. He had some kind of deal in there that no one else had, a melodic, haunting deal that he did and still played in the three-chord blues progression. The whole Taj Mahal Band was some of the most real music I've played. We had a good time, more than I can say. The experience of being on the road with the band in the '60s was great."

Chuck swivels away from the piano in his home in Tulsa, where he had been working out some old tunes and learning a new one. He's a trim man, clean-shaven, with a short haircut, now "that I've got to deal with doctors, lawyers and Indian chiefs," he explains in his pure Oklahoma drawl. "I've stopped playing professionally, but music is my relief. I've had my own business for the past 18 years, Blackwell Beveled Glass, in Broken Arrow, just outside Tulsa. During the day, I design and build beveled glass entryway systems for homes and do some stained-glass church windows.

It's just making stuff up. That's what I do. I draw from all the experiences I've had, like with Taj. Taj enters my mind so often. I love to send Taj a tune every now and then.

"I was Taj's drummer for about three years. Musically, I'm self-taught. As a boy, I had me a bass-drum pedal but I didn't have me a bass drum. I hooked up a cardboard box and I'd wait at this big ol' console radio for honky-tonk to come on. That's how I learned to play. Later, I linked up with Leon Russell – a local boy, too. We'd play the nightclubs, Leon on piano, then went out to California, where I met Taj up in Topanga Canyon. I stopped touring when I was 30 years old. I saw that the road was killing me. I didn't want to pay the toll the road was taking. Too many good people had fallen by the wayside. I feel fortunate to be still standing."

Gary Gilmore, the bass guitarist in The Taj Mahal Band for two years, also recalls those days fondly: "I got started with Taj in such an amazing way. One day, I drove Jessie Ed to the airport to catch a plane for a gig with Taj. When we got to airport, Taj was sitting on the curb kind of depressed, bummed out because the bass player they had been using for the sessions on Taj's first solo album, *Taj Mahal*, wouldn't go. I don't know if he wouldn't fly or didn't want to go out of town or what. Jessie asked me if I wanted to go play the gig. I said, 'Yeah.'

"Taj was such an easy performer to back up, such a good singer. I thought he was a great singer, because he could do that raspy sound of the old blues and could also get a tender sound on the ballads. To be the back-up band for him wasn't like work; it was an inspiration. The music flowed real easy. When recording in the studio, if we couldn't get a song down in three takes, we'd scrap that song and go to something else. We all liked to keep things fresh. They didn't have to be perfect. We wanted the feel and energy behind the songs. We created our own sound. We felt that we were an all-American band, but when people would see us together they were in shock. There wasn't that kind of mix around. When we showed up, people noticed.

"Growing up around Tulsa, I grew up with R&B with a little bit of country and country blues thrown in. The guys I grew up with listened to Jimmy Reed and Chuck Berry, maybe Jerry Lee Lewis – those were the records we learned how to play from. The music Taj wanted to play was right down my alley. It was different from a lot of the other bands in the '60s. We played just the music, and didn't get into any of the show stuff.

One time we opened for Alice Cooper, and they had a guillotine onstage and all sorts of stuff. That was one reason I quit the band. It seemed like the music business was so crazy to want stuff like that. If all you were doing was playing real music, your chances for big success weren't too good.

"When I left the band, I went back to Tulsa and played professionally for another ten years. I've still got my guitar and amp, and play now and then for a benefit or recording gig here, but in the last couple years I've just about quit playing altogether. I have a 120-acre farm north of Tahlequah, which was the capital of the Cherokee nation before Oklahoma became a state. I've been out here about 23 years and have some cattle. That's really a sideline for me now. I drive a truck to pay the bills. I work four days a week and am home three days."

After the album *Taj Mahal* came out, things started happening for the band. "We got gigs in LA, were traveling across the country, playing in Texas, Ohio, Seattle, Portland, Salt Lake City," says Taj. "One time we opened for The Jefferson Airplane. Nobody there had heard us play. After they heard us play, everybody said, 'Geez, these guys are really good.' One of our regular gigs was the Whiskey A Go Go. Bill Cosby would come out and play cow bell with us while smoking a big cigar."

During this time, Taj moved from Santa Monica to Topanga Canyon, a location made infamous by the movies stars, musicians, and hippies who lived in the large, secluded houses, cabins, and small communities tucked away in the wooded sides of the canyon. Bernie Leadon, of The Eagles; John Densmore, drummer for The Doors; Mick Fleetwood, of Fleetwood Mac; and Lowell George, of Little Feat, were a few of musicians who lived in the canyon. Topanga Canyon was the closest thing to living in the country and still being within sight of Los Angeles. Taj went up there to get out of the city smog and bustle. He hung out at the Center, at the junction of Old Topanga Road and Topanga Canyon Boulevard. The club where he met Jessie Davis, Topanga Corral, was at the top of the canyon, straight up the "boulevard," which was a fancy name for a two-lane road.

At that time, the Center was a large, long Quonset hut that housed a grocery store, a post office, and several shops. It was the hub of the loose Topanga community, the meeting place. Taj would sit on a grassy knoll next to the Center and play his guitar. Naturally, he drew a crowd. He and his fishing buddy, Ron Nahoda, who later became Taj's road manager, drew a crowd every time they gave away their catch of the day to whomever wanted free fish. A free meal was always welcomed by the cash-poor hippies.

One day when Taj was at the Center, a friend of his asked him to come and look at her goat, which had been badly mauled by a coyote. She couldn't afford a veterinarian, but she knew that Taj had a degree in animal husbandry. Could he help her goat? Unfortunately, the goat was beyond help, but while examining it he met Marie Janisse, to whom he later gave the affectionate name "Sweet Mama." The only black woman living in the canyon, she was attractive – slim, with long legs and an open heart. Taj took to calling her "Highpockets." She loved to talk, enjoyed a high-spirited time, and had a generous, nurturing nature. She and Taj quickly became very dear friends. Several weeks later, he said that he wanted to get out of the city but didn't have a place to stay in the canyon. Marie invited him to stay at her house.

"I didn't consider myself a couple with Taj when he was living in my house. How could I? I had to call all these other women up and down [the] canyon to find him because he wasn't in my bed. We had a very close relationship, a friendship that can be had between a man and a woman and them not being lovers, you understand what I'm talking about? We loved each other dearly. I totally treasured our friendship. Mainly the reason I love him so much, and he loves me so much, is because we had that different kind of relationship."

"Sweet Mama" is now Marie Janisse Wilkins, married mother of a 28-year-old daughter, Desiree. While telling her story about Taj, she sits in her bedroom quilting a wall hanging with large, solid squares of purple and smaller squares of green and red, her favorite colors. She's wearing a beautiful, white, embroidered dress and a pair of abalone earrings that Taj had sent to her from the Caribbean. "I was working the front door at the Topanga Corral at the time, checking IDs and collecting money. My reputation was that you could get across an international border easier than you could get into the door of the Corral if you didn't have a proper ID. I knew Leon Russell, Jessie Davis – all those guys. Leon always had his pants too short and wore white socks.

"I knew Jessie Davis very well. Before we – me and my husband and daughter – moved out of Topanga, we helped him out a bit. It was kind of a drag. He called us up one day out of the clear blue sky. This was in 1986 or '87 – we hadn't seen or heard of him for years. He asked if he could stop by. Yeah, sure, come on by. He told us that he had this problem: he was a total junkie. He said, 'I need to clean up. I got to get away from this crowd.' We had a big treehouse in our yard for our daughter. He asked if he could stay there and clean up from drugs, so we let him stay there.

"He never came out of the treehouse. One day he left without saying anything to us. The treehouse was such a mess, so bad, that we should have burned it down, but we cleaned it up. About six months later, he called again. Said that he needed a place again. We read him the riot act but let him stay at the treehouse again. Same thing happened. He left, and less than a year later [June 22, 1988] we heard that he was dead.

"But back in the early Topanga days, Jessie was playing in The Taj Mahal Band. Every Monday night, Taj and his band played at the Corral for free. Mondays were always a slow night, and Taj would bring in the crowd. One time they played a benefit for me. Water lines were being put in along the canyon, and the property owners had to pay so much per foot for the frontage of their property. I didn't have any money. All the money made on the front door of the benefit was given to me to pay for the water line. The club owner asked what the band would charge him to play that night. Taj said they'd play free if I made them dinner of fried chicken, black-eyed peas, mustard greens, and corn bread."

Marie pauses with her quilting and looks around her bedroom. A picture of her daughter and her boyfriend hangs over the bed, along with a picture of Marie's best friend, Julie, and her husband, Vinny, and their daughter, Oliva Marie DiBenedetto, Marie's goddaughter. On the wall behind her is a picture of her and Magic Johnson from the days when Marie was a caterer to the movie business. On the opposite wall is a picture of a deceased favorite aunt, a statue of the Blessed Virgin Mary, and a picture of Christ. Marie's gaze finally rests on a small bell on a cord hanging on the wall. "That's the bell Taj wore around his neck when he lived at my house the first time. I wasn't married then, in the late '60s. He lived there on and off for about a year, because lots of the time he was on the road. I'd take care of him, tell him, 'You've got to wash those armpits. You got to wear deodorant.' I'd wash his clothes all the time. He went through different phases of the clothes he wore. For a while, he was wearing these pants made by a company [called] A Smile. They'd give him pants to wear. The pants would fit his body perfectly for the way he was built. He wore blue denim shirts and bell-bottom jeans. Then he got into wearing African-print shirts and a little crocheted tam on his head. Then he got into wearing an African bush jacket, a brown jacket with the flap pockets. I'd wash them and use spray starch so they looked real crisp and good all the time.

"There'd be times when I'd be at the house and the band would have a gig and a plane to catch. Nobody knew where Taj was. I'd put in calls to all the ladies in the canyon, because I knew that he'd be at one of their houses. Then I'd take his guitars, clean clothes, and a bag of trail mix to the airport and be sitting there waiting for him with Miss National, his guitar. I'd get a tap on my shoulder: 'Hey, Marie. Hey, Marie.' I'd be so mad at him. I would! I'd say, 'Man, you gotta stop. You're out doing your thing and I've got to put the word out to every woman in Topanga and ask them to pass it onto the next one to see if one of them will kick you out of bed.' The ladies had a 'Taj network.'

"All the women never got mad at Taj. Everybody was mellow, loved each other. He wasn't making any promises to anybody. He wasn't swearing on a stack of Bibles. None of that stuff. He didn't do anybody no wrong. He's not a nasty individual. Everybody loved Taj and loved the band, no matter what group of guys he had with him. They'd give them anything, even their house to stay in whenever one of his bands came into town. 'Hey, the house is yours.' People used to fight over whose house the band would stay at.

"At my house in Topanga, we had the best time. I'd make grilled cheese sandwiches, all kinds of food, and Taj would sit there and play music and we'd sing, stomp our feet. It was always happy at the house, always beautiful, all the times he was there. He had a big black bus then, the kind that carried farm workers. The bus had no window glass, so he put all these wind chimes in. Whenever he drove up and down the canyon, you'd hear it coming for miles. He parked it around the corner from the house. I had to go through a lot of shit with the woman whose property it was on – she didn't want it parked there. We decided to pay extra dollars per month to let the bus be parked there. Finally, Taj sold it. We also had a blue mailbox that we put trailer vines on."

Later, in the early '70s, Taj again stayed at Marie's, but things ended badly. A woman he was seeing – Inshirah, who later became his second and is presently his estranged wife – moved into the house. Taj was working on the film *Sounder II* at the time, and was often away. Marie and Inshirah did not become friends. "I feel that I got stomped on pretty bad when he got with Inshirah. I thought that Taj and my friendship was unsinkable. Then she came into his life and she started getting rid of everybody in his life who meant anything to him." Even now, 27 years later, Marie has difficulty uttering Inshirah's name. When she does spit it out, bitterness drips from it like venom from a serpent's fang.

"One night, I got a phone call from his brother Samuel. He tells me, 'Watch out for that woman. She's gotten rid of me. But we said, "Wait until she gets to Sweet Mama's house, and that will be the end of her."' Well, it wasn't. She did me in, terribly. She was living in my home and treating me like I was a servant. She said to Taj, 'You don't want to have anything to do with this woman. This is a black woman who has no respect for you. She treats you like a second-class citizen. All of her friends are white. You don't need to be hanging out with these dirty hippies in Topanga. You're a black man.' She got on this whole black trip.

"By then, Taj had a couple of young children, twins, who lived with their mother in San Francisco. My daughter was the same age. Taj paid $30 a month for diaper service for my daughter. One day, the call came that the twins might spend some time with Taj. Inshirah said, 'Oh, let them come. I'll take care of them.' Taj was going to send her back to Berkeley and she wanted to stay with him. Taking care of the children was her ploy to stay. She never took care of the kids at all. I was the one who washed his clothes, who ironed his clothes. *I* fed his kids. *I* took care of them. Inshirah did nothing. *Nothing*. She was nasty to the kids.

"Taj turned on me. I don't know what she said, but whatever it was, it did the trick. I've always wanted to know from him what it was, because I think it was a lot of lies that need to be cleared up. I heard that Inshirah told him that I didn't like black men. What the *heck* you talking about?

"When he left, it was such an ugly scene, lots of anger and terrible things said. I didn't know where he went. Up to San Francisco, I think. We had no contact for 25 years. If he would have just called and said, 'Hey, Mama, what's going on?' That's all I needed.

"For the longest time – when this distance was between us, when we had no contact – it was like a hole in my heart. Like this huge, gaping hole in my heart. No matter what came along in my life, nothing could fill that hole in my heart. I talked to my daughter, Desiree, about it all the time. As she grew older, I would still talk to her about it. She said to me, 'You know,

Mom, if I'm ever in an area where he is appearing, I'm just going to walk in and give him a piece of my mind and let him know how much he's hurt you.' She was old enough to know him and know what he was about. She didn't like the fact that I was hurting all the time because I had lost this very dear person.

"Then, in 1995, when he played the Hog Farm, I gave my number to a friend to give to him. About four months later, I got a call, and there he was, singing the song he wrote for me, 'Sweet Mama Janisse,' over the phone. Then he started talking, and I thought that I was going to die. It was like this hole in my heart just healed up.

"Some time later, he played at the Eureka Inn, near where I live. I walked in. He was sitting on a couch and had all these people around him. He looked up, and it was like Moses parting the water. He went through all the people to me and we hugged, cried, and laughed. It was so great. That same night, he called me up onstage, introduced me to the audience, and he apologized to me. He said that he made a mistake, that he owes me an apology, and that he'd never let anything like that ever happen again.

"Everybody loved Taj, because he brought so much joy into people's lives – his smile, his warmth, his music. He would come into a house and sit there and start playing whatever instrument was around and sing. He made you feel good. He never did anything bad to anyone. If he did, it would have been done maybe accidentally. He never went out to hurt anybody. Everywhere he went, he brought that joyful smile and wonderful loving feeling and beautiful music. Everyone loved him. This guy could write his ticket in Topanga. He didn't do anything wrong to anybody. He didn't go out to hurt people. He never intentionally set out to do anything wrong to anybody. You understand?

"I never hated him. I always loved. I felt in my heart that it would come around again, and it did. I believe in miracles. That was my miracle. If circumstances hadn't come down the way they came down, Taj and I probably would have been together. I think that might have happened, at some point. But he'd come and go, come and go, on the road. My life just kept going. You can tell from the letters that he wrote to me that there is that thing, that underlying thing. No matter where he went, he always kept in touch with me.

"Now I live in Arcata, in Northern California, and run my business, Bless My Soul, a line of spicy sauces good on everything. I call them 'Sweet Mama

Janisse's,' like 'Sweet Mama Janisse's Soul Q Sauce,' which is a barbecue sauce. Taj gave me $2,000 for the expenses to get Soul Q Sauce and Smokin' Hot Soy Gin Sauce out. He gave me the name Sweet Mama. I didn't think about that for a long time. It wasn't until I came out with my products that my daughter said I should use it. At first, I was very upset, because of what had come down, but if you love a person, you love them. That name was very endearing. He gave me that name long before Inshirah."

11 Marriage With Anna

One reason why Taj spent so much time in Topanga Canyon was that his marriage with Anna de León was in trouble.

"Yeah, Anna. She's my best friend." We're in Los Angeles with Taj as he drives away from the Hollywood Hills in a borrowed 17-year-old BMW with uncomfortably sprung front seats. He's due to perform this evening at a gala record launch for the House Of Blues, on West Hollywood Boulevard. Right now we're headed to a falafel place – the Hungry Pocket, in Santa Monica – for dinner. Taj knows the place from when he lived in the neighborhood with Anna.

"I wanted to come back to the old neighborhood before telling about Anna. That was a confusing time."

As we edge our way through LA traffic, Taj says, "There's the short road of doing whatever it takes to make a living. On that road, so many people have to turn down what their real feelings are because they got a job to cover their needs. That's not necessarily a bad thing, but it's a sacrifice. I refuse to put myself in that position. I take the long road – that is, to look into myself to see what I need to do, what I need to feel, to stay connected. I always wanted to be independent of someone telling me what the hell I should be doing. The more you can keep your independence, the more authentic is your art. You just lean into it and you're goin'."

After one of the long pauses that often punctuate Taj's conversation when he's giving serious thought, he continues, "The first thing is not being afraid to say the truth." Long pause. "With me, the big thing is whether or not my ancestors are proud of what I'm doin'. There's information in your DNA that will allow you to hear and feel things that have been planned for by ancestors a long, long, long time ago. I heard sounds inside my head, but it wasn't until I heard musicians from West Africa and the Caribbean and from the South that I actually heard the music that was those sounds."

We drive to 2019 21st Street in Santa Monica and stop in front of a modest bungalow. Taj leans over the wheel to look at the house and tells the story of Anna de León.

"Anna was gorgeous – tall, shapely, with a fine-toned dancer's body, hair down to her waist. Her mom was Puerto Rican and her dad an Estonian out of Chicago. She had style, and it wasn't the all-American style. She was a flashy dresser but tight, *tight*. She was a Hollywood girl.

"At the time, I was working with Yank Rachel and Sleepy John Estes, recording the old songs. Yank was a really warm, funny, big teddy-bear kind of a guy, a really warmhearted, warm person with a big sense of humor, and told lots of stories. He was a mandolin player who developed the technique of catching the blues atmosphere on that instrument, but he also played the electric guitar and composed songs. Like Sleepy John, Yank became known before World War Two, when he wrote 'Hobo Blues,' covered by John Lee Hooker, and 'Army Man Blues,' that Big Joe Williams sang.

"John was blind, small-boned, frail-looking, and had a reedy voice. He got called 'Sleepy' John because he'd take naps all the time. Like a lot of blind people, he didn't have the same orientation to day and night as sighted people, so you had the sense that he was awake a lot. John passed on in 1977. He sure is missed.

"Those two old guys had been famous, then forgotten, then famous again, especially Sleepy John. They played together back in the 1920s, Yank on mandolin and Sleepy John on guitar. He had a real simple style, a purity that was rediscovered by the folk/blues fans in the 1960s. He cried the blues as much as sang them. His vocal style influenced Sonny Boy Williamson and his cousin, Homesick James, both of who had an impact on the Chicago blues. I regularly play one of Sleepy John's songs, 'Diving Duck Blues.' Listen to that song and you know he had a real poetic touch. He was 62 when I knew him, an important connection to the pre-World War Two blues. His song 'Someday, Baby' – also known as 'Worried Life Blues' – became a blues standard back in the '40s. Both those guys are important in the development of the blues, and that's why I listened to them.

"Anyways, Anna's best friend, Alicia James, at the time was the secretary in the University of California Los Angles [UCLA] music department. She thought Anna and I would be a perfect match and invited us to Thanksgiving dinner with her family. At first, things were a bit tense at the dinner table. Anna lived by herself, and was a pretty cool lady, but a bit on the shy side about being set up with someone, so she was really upset about the situation. She thought it smacked too much of matchmaking.

"I said, 'Hey, I thought it was cool. I see that this is stressing you out so, hey, you don't have to be part of anything you don't want to do.' That helped to calm the situation. We started talking back and forth and found out we liked a lot of the same things, especially about music.

"Her dad loved the blues, gospel and country western. He was a retired army career officer who died when she was twelve – oddly, two weeks after my father died. He played the piano and gave Anna a harmonica when she was five years old. That became her instrument of choice and, as I found out, she could play just about anything on the harmonica. And she sang. Her mother was Catholic, so she and Anna would sing Gregorian chants around the house, sometimes in Latin.

"At the time, Anna was at UCLA, majoring in fine arts, although she started out in physics. She was a painter, and she sang in jazz clubs, and she danced. She was a major, avid jazz person, but knew her rhythm and blues, BB King, the old Ray Charles stuff, and Louis Jordan. During that dinner, we figured out that we had enough energy for one another, really liked each other. She had a little apartment on 21st Street in Santa Monica, so little that the bedroom was her studio. We moved in there, then to a house on Eleventh Street, then, about a year later, to this house on 21st Street.

"This was a good neighborhood to live in – lots of ethnic groups hangin' out, everybody friendly. I once painted the mailbox. I always thought that, if I slowed down a little bit, I'd paint. I always liked drafting in school.

"My song 'Going up to the country, paint my mailbox blue' started with that city mailbox, although the song isn't about it. The story behind that song is pretty simple. I had actually left Santa Monica and moved up to Topanga Canyon ten, twelve years before. I was catching up writing tunes about my own life, sort of autobiographical, about leaving LA. The idea started with a phrase I heard once: 'I'm going to move to the outskirts of town.' I don't know who that was by. Maybe Louis Jordan, or somebody like that. 'Mailbox Blues' is dealing with getting out of the city life and having a country life. The color of the mailbox, blue, has to do with the color of the sky, not a mood. The sky was blue up in the canyon, above the smog.

"When we lived here on 21st Street, I got a rototiller and plowed up the front yard and put in a ton of vegetables. If I see a piece of land around me, and I have an opportunity to put a garden on it, the garden goes in. Just like that. I always feel good when I have a garden down. I sort of have roots. I always have a garden wherever I live, if possible.

"The importance of gardening is that it connects you with what people did throughout their history and culture. At one time, all peoples and tribes where nomadic, following herds of animals or going to where the food was. Then they became agrarian, and settled down and started domesticating many of the animals that they once chased down the road. A garden is a stabilizing, visual, physical, philosophical statement relating to that human history.

"A more practical reason for our garden was that we were poor. The garden gave us food. We could live on about $20 or $25 a week. The Rising Sons wasn't making big money. Gigs were hard to come by, despite our growing reputation, and money went into equipment and the business. Basically, Anna and I had very little money. We seldom went to see the old-time blues guys who played at the Knights Of Columbus Hall, a half-block from the house; we sat out on the front porch and listened. For a while, I had a paper route. After a gig, I'd throw paper from 2am until 6am. There was a time I washed dishes at the Ash Grove and Anna was the cashier. One summer, she worked on a tutorial program to bring in money.

"Anna did a of lot canning and always had a crock of homemade wine or mead brewing. She pickled watermelon rind, made wine out of peaches, beets, celery, you name it. At that time, she did most of the cooking – greens, fried chicken, and fish. She did this because it was the food that the older blues guys – who stayed with us at times – could understand.

"When we moved over to Eleventh Street, Joseph Spence stayed with us for a while. He was from Nassau, Bahamas, and played unusual gospel/military-style music. Ry Cooder was a great fan of his. There were times when Joseph didn't eat for days, when he stayed with other people, because they didn't prepare anything he understood. They were well meaning but offered him only raw vegetables. He didn't understand that rabbit food. He lived for days on nothing but milk and cake. Anna thought that was terrible, that people would have such cultural insensitivity to those old guys, so she cooked what they knew, even if it wasn't the most healthy for your heart.

"I baked the bread. I had always been a good cook, since I was a kid. All the men in our family can cook. It's no big thing. Anna introduced me to a lot of food that I didn't know from back East, like guacamole and eating Japanese. It was absolutely frustrating, learning how to use chopsticks.

"We scuffled along. I grew our food and fished. We'd go next door to Myrt and Clay's – old friends of Anna's from when she first lived in that apartment on 21st Street – and eat fish and fried corn bread. We could do that for days.

"I fished nearly every day, down off the pier, to bring home food. For me, fishing was about more than catching food. Fishing has been a meditative place for me. It puts me in a place of my own where, if nothing happens, that's okay, or if music happens, that's okay, too. A song might happen in my head when it appears that I'm just staring into space, blanked out, like nothing is happening. When I get out on the sea, away from the crosscurrent of land noises, I hear music, lots of music, all around me.

"Sometimes Anna would come down to the pier and stay until maybe eleven at night. I'd fish until one or two in the morning, then go home with the catch. She'd get up and fry up the fish and we'd have a candlelit dinner. If I had a night gig, I'd fish from four in the afternoon until around eight. Anna would come to get me, or I might forget I was supposed to play that night. She'd always insist that I change clothes and not wear the fishy-smelling ones to the gig.

"Sometimes the neighbors pitched in money so I could go out on a boat to fish. The neighborhood was a mix of whites, blacks, Asians, and Latinos – working-class neighborhood, very friendly, with everyone looking out for his neighbor. I'd fish all day, come home about suppertime, and distribute the catch around the neighborhood.

"I had a very domestic, settled life with Anna. I loved it. I was with someone I really appreciated. It was really strong energy for me. Up until then, my life had been unsettled. For a lot of people, it was the time of drugs, sex, and rock 'n' roll. Women had the liberation of birth control pills. But I've always been kind of traditional, in my core, about family. I came out of those types of values. It wasn't until I got with Anna that I got with someone willing to say, 'Okay, let's go. Let's do this.'

"We didn't have a rock 'n' roll household or lifestyle. Our house was never a crash pad. Only the older, traditional blues players ever stayed with us, like Mance Lipscomb, Sleepy John Estes and Yank Rachel, when they played in town. Mance was a farmer, a singer, an exceptional guitar player. That man could *pick*. He had a real light, soft touch, and I learned from that. He wasn't known as a musician until he was around 64 years old, and even then he still farmed. Mostly, he played in his town, Navasota, Texas, until a couple of ethnomusicologists discovered him. He was a real human being, with lots of warmth. There was nothing fake about him. He'd rather be a farmer than famous. He died a year before Sleepy John.

"When John or Yank stayed, we'd sit around the living room playing, or out on the front porch playing for the neighborhood kids. John and Yank visited with music – the way people have conversations with words – [and] other guys from the band, and we'd jam. There was constant music around the house. Anna and I sang a lot together.

"We had a real lived-in house. The dining room was my model airplane room, where I'd build the planes. I'd been making model planes since I was a kid. The table was always littered with bits of balsa wood and wings and glue and tiny motors. Building model airplanes and flying them calmed me down, allowed me to get into my own space. It was like meditation, like fishing, playing the guitar, having a garden. It settled me, got me in my own trip.

"Anna had a room for painting. She was getting her master's degree in painting at the time, and had a research assistant's job in the master's program at UCLA. She did really big paintings with lots of colors. She had never used blue much in her paintings until she lived with me, maybe because I wore lots of blue at that time. She was always working in all sorts of mediums. Even made tables out of tiles. Her output was intense.

"Our house wasn't so different than the type of household Anna grew up in. In her family's house, the whole living room would be devoted to big art projects, and a pet monkey had the run of it. Anna and I raised German shepherds instead of monkeys. Oftentimes, we'd have ten puppies underfoot, which we eventually gave away or sold.

"She introduced me to a lot of things about art from the point of view of a painter. I had no references. 'Okay, there's a painting on the wall. What does that mean?' Talking with Anna, I started to understand where the artists were at the time, what was going on, politically, around them. She educated me to the different kinds of art.

"We were part of an artistic community. A lot of the people we knew painted, danced, wrote poetry. I got tuned into Charles Bukowski through Anna. She met him through a poet friend and got to know him pretty good. They became long-time good friends. He liked her paintings and asked her to do a cover for one of his books. She also did the covers for two of my albums, *The Natch'l Blues* and the double album *The Real Thing*.

"They wrote letters and visited, and I'd often go with her. I thought Charles was straight up. There was nothing superficial about him. Anna and I found him very insightful, very deep, very perceptive, very easygoing. He wasn't judgmental. He was a gentle person. Then he was working at the post office, drinking beer, and writing his poetry. Anna maintained that people paid a lot more attention to his drinking than was really the issue. Drinking was his way of deflecting people.

"Anna and I supported each other in our art forms. It was a lot of fun. I had a settled life, and I really enjoyed it. I wasn't traveling all the time; I worked at the Ash Grove, went out dancing here and there, got to people's shows – I had a pretty organized life. The relationship was a very win-win, counter-inspiring situation. That worked real good.

"Anna got really sick and was in the hospital for a few weeks. That's when we decided to get married. I formally asked her mom for Anna's hand in marriage. We planned the wedding from Anna's hospital room."

Anna is now an attorney specializing in Constitutional law regarding civil rights and First Amendment issues on the state and federal levels. She takes up the story: "I was in the hospital, really sick, with an abscess on my lung. I don't know exactly why Taj decided that was the time to get married, but he did. Maybe seeing me so vulnerable. He went to my mom and formally asked for my hand in marriage. I wanted him to look serious for my mami, so he got a burgundy-colored band jacket for $3.50 at the Goodwill. He wore it over his blue jeans and a blue work shirt.

"Taj is very formal in the West Indian rural sense. All the men in his family are. It's a turn-of-the-century formality based on what is proper and respectful. It's a respect that country people who grow their own food learn. You don't treat the important things in life trivially.

"He didn't get down on his knee to me. We just agreed. We made all the plans from my hospital room. As soon as I got out of the hospital, we met with a preacher at his rectory and made those arrangements. I made myself a short, comfortable dress. It was green, to go with nature. I wore a maidenhair fern crown in my hair and was barefoot. Taj wore boots, jeans, a shirt with a jacket, and a dark-brown cowboy hat.

"The ceremony was held on the rocks on the edge of the ocean, at Zuma Beach. I have a picture of Taj making a dramatic gesture, as if claiming the

Pacific. The day had that kind of energy – big, open, exuberant, anything and everything is possible. It was big fun. Alicia, who had introduced us, was the maid of honor, and brought her daughter as the flower girl, and her dog. Jessie Lee was our best man. His wife, Jennifer, was there with a small group of other friends, and three dogs. The preacher, dressed in a suit, read words of Khalil Gibran we had chosen. Just as Taj and I said, 'I do,' the tenth wave came in and splashed all of us. We laughed and shook off the water. Then Taj and I exchanged rings, gold-colored brass ones we had bought for 99¢ each at Cost Plus. They were really pretty.

"Yes, I thought the original set-up at that dinner a little odd, intense, but there was a charge between Taj and myself. I've never lacked male attention, but I'm a pretty shy person. I've never been much for superficial dating, was never comfortable with that. I have friends or I have intense relationships. That middle sort of bullshit area has never been one I've understood. I got married at 19 for a short time, because I didn't understand dating.

"When I met Taj, I was completely knocked out. It was 100 percent clear that he cared about all the things I cared about. His dreams were like mine. I remember at that Thanksgiving dinner standing on the front porch, discussing how we each wanted to have nine kids. We started living together right away – like, the next day.

"In lots of ways, our relationship was really, *really* traditional. Taj was very domestically oriented with me. We had a wonderful life. It was a dream come true. We spent nearly all our time together. I think that, in a way, the life Taj and I lived was the life of the old-time music. It was kind of an organic whole: music, fishing, growing vegetables, raising dogs, having a child. I painted pictures, I sewed most of his clothes. I loved every moment of it. He'd come home and work on his model airplanes or in the garden or do something with the dogs. I loved the life we were living. It was so terrific.

"Maybe it was because I didn't marry somebody who was famous. I wouldn't have cared, and he wasn't famous back then – that's not why I got together with him. I didn't even get together with him thinking that he was going to make music a career. I thought he was going to be a farmer. I got together with Taj in part because I could see that he was the male completion of me as a woman. He was, and is, gentle, passionate, and deeply good. I didn't make him nervous. He wasn't afraid of me or of letting me lead a full life. He never felt diminished by me or what I was doing in my life. He gave me plenty of room for my art, or whatever I was doing, and I was always doing something. He was always happy to do it with me, whether it was making sandals or walking the dogs.

"I like a great big rich life. The life Taj and I lived together was the great big rich life. Our connection was very, very deep, culturally and personally. He's half West Indian, and so am I. He's an artist, and so am I. He's very traditional, in many ways, and so am I. Music was a huge connection for us. I went to all his gigs and recording sessions. I don't think that a deep connection like between Taj and myself happens that often in life. We connected in a way that happens when people don't claw each other apart. I cannot imagine loving a person I'm fighting with all the time. We didn't do that. That says a lot about the love between us. I don't want to be a person who is raving and screaming. He doesn't either. We never had a harsh word for each other. I don't recall ever having an argument with him.

"I think that was one of the things that drew me to Taj. That, and that he doesn't have a speck of competition in him. He is not driven by competition. That's one of the things I love about him most. He never seeks advantage over anybody. I've never, *never* known him to do that. He makes sure that everyone gets their fair share, often in ways that no one even knows. As powerful as he is, he's not competitive. There is a sense of power with him, even when he sits still. It's more than his physical size. I think that sense of power comes from a kind of internal harmony, that he is not about bullshit. He is strong because he is not competing. I think that people who are competitive, in the way to beat others or put them down, those people feel at risk. Taj never felt internally at risk.

"The thing about that is that it's lonely. There's really no choice for him. Taj is who he is. That's one reason why I think people – audiences – connect so strongly with him. He isn't funky. His life is like an organic blend. If he played in the living room with just John and Yank, or on the front porch for the neighborhood kids, or at the Ash Grove for 100 people, or at a concert for 5,000 people, there was no difference. There was no artifice between Taj and the audience.

"He'll say what's on his mind, sing what's in his heart. He doesn't phony up. Left to his own devices, he'd go straight from fishing to a gig without changing clothes. There's music in him, and it's got to come out. He plays what comes out of him. I don't mean that he is childish or not in control of it; I mean that it is authentic.

"Our life wasn't separated into music and another life, but as he became better known, and spent more time on the road touring, his music life started pulling him away. We tried real hard to have a child, but it wasn't happening. We even consulted a doctor. Then, *boom!* I was pregnant, like a miracle. Our daughter, Aya, was born in 1967, but Taj and I separated in 1969. The next year, we got back together for a while, then separated again in 1972.

"I'm not sure there are words to describe what happened. The one thing I can say is that neither he nor I had ever heard of marriage counseling back then. I have to tell you, I'm not really sure what happened. I just don't know.

"While we were separated in 1972, I wasn't seeing anybody, and I don't think he was, either. I thought that he liked it that way, us living apart but still seeing each other. Nothing nudged us together. He was on the road a lot. I was still relating to his family a lot. It just became too painful for me, too painful to live by myself with Aya, have him live somewhere else. It was like a stasis. We weren't together and we weren't apart. I somehow thought that was what he wanted. We never talked about it. I never said, 'What are we doing? This is what I want.' He never said, 'What are we doing? This is what I want.' That had gone on for years.

"It was a time when people weren't very skilled in having those kinds of conversations. I wouldn't have known, at that time, to say, 'What do we want from each other? Where are you headed? Where am I headed?' I'm not sure why we never had that conversation. That's the part I'm mystified about. I don't know why, as strange as that may sound. Part of why, I think, is because his life changed so much. He was on the road all the time. He had a band. He was gone. Now he was well known. With Taj, he can talk all day, all week, all month about big issues, and it will be interesting, but he has difficulty talking about what's right in front of him today, about who is standing next to his shoulder as part of his life.

"I thought that love was supposed to be like a poem – it just sort of came. Words won't improve love. It was what it was, and you couldn't change it. I didn't think that you could understand a person better by talking about the love, or the problems with the love, so I never talked about my relationship with him.

"One day, I went to see him play at Glide Memorial Methodist Church in San Francisco. I was with his sister, brothers, their families, all of us as family. He and I had been separated for four years, were still seeing each other but were living apart. That day I just couldn't stand the pain one more minute. It was so painful for me to be there with his family that I couldn't stand it one more second. I never told Taj that. Seems odd now.

"I sought the divorce. I left. You know what did it for me? Aya was in the hospital for an urgent tonsillectomy. Her tonsils were so large that she wasn't getting enough air. She was about three at the time. Taj was rehearsing with Howard Johnson and the tuba band up in Calistoga, in Napa Valley, which is only a two- or three-hour drive from Berkeley. Aya's operation was planned, so this was not a sudden thing. He knew it was happening, but he didn't come to the hospital. I spent three days and nights at the hospital. My upstairs neighbors, who I didn't know very well, brought me Chinese food. I thought, 'They do this for me, and what has Taj done? Where is he?' Something in me snapped. His definition of family was clearly different from mine. I couldn't see any reason to go forward. I didn't see life as a pit-stop.

"I ended up marrying the guy who gave me a ride home from Glide Memorial that day. We had known each other for a long time. He was truly a nice person, but we had little in common. Taj married his second wife, Inshirah, when he heard that I was getting married, according to his brothers. We both remarried on the rebound.

"After the divorce, I was appointed to the Civic Arts Commission in Berkeley, where I was living. I was elected to the Berkeley school board for a four-year term and re-elected to a second term.

"In 1979, I became a foster mom to Martha. Martha's birth mother was mentally handicapped and her father was a drug addict. She had been a burn victim, and spent six months tied to a hospital bed while suffering through skin grafts. At the age of seven, she could only put together three-word sentences. She called Taj 'Daddy.'

"I wasn't allowed to adopt Martha, because the law at the time said foster parents couldn't adopt. The parental rights to her birth mother were never terminated. It was like biology meant ownership. I had a lot of trouble with that. I couldn't stand it. Basically, that's why I went to law school in 1979 – Boalt Hall, at UC Berkeley. I was a working single parent going to law school and serving on the school board. Nobody said that I wasn't smart. I did very well, and have been a practising attorney since I passed the bar.

"In 1991, I opened a restaurant, Anna's, in Oakland, so I'd have a place to sing. Taj and I sang there together once. It was cute. The restaurant closed because of a fire in the apartment over it. I've opened another restaurant in Berkeley, a kind of community cultural spot.

"Taj and I were, and are, best friends. Well, I don't know if I was always his best friend, [but] I did everything I could to be a good and dear friend. That didn't change just because we got divorced. The connection between us is very, very deep. Recently, he stopped by and we had a four-hour talk. This was not unusual. In truth, the loss of the life that joined love and family and music was very devastating for me."

Taj pulls away from the house in Santa Monica and drives back toward the House Of Blues. He is quiet most of the way. As we start the climb up the Hollywood Hills, he says, "Recently, Anna and I were talking about all this. We were saying that neither of us, when we look back on what it was that we split up on... We really didn't have any problems. Our problem was communication. She didn't talk, and I didn't like to talk about it. We worked pretty much off our feelings. When it felt good, it felt good, and that was it, we went with that, realizing now [that], if we had been able to communicate a little bit better, we probably more than likely would have stayed together. It was a painful time for both of us. The song 'Why Did You Have To Desert Me?' on the *Mo' Roots* album is about that pain. It's about what was going on with me in those last four or five years, my take on that time.

"At one point I knew my relationship with Anna was really deteriorating. My anger was starting to surface. I was working real hard not to go there. Seemed to me, from my point of view, she was really working hard to take me there – which, in retrospect, it was up to me not to go there. When I did, I realized that I couldn't stay. That energy got ahead of me. It bothered me then, and still bothers me. 'You can have anything from me, but you don't have to push me in that kind of direction. Why are you pushing me into this corner? To force some kind of reaction?' That was my headspace at the time. When a relationship gets into that, it can't go anywhere but down. There can be nothing but a war between energies. Still, I'm responsible for my actions. It's not like, 'You pushed me, therefore you're responsible.' No, I'm still responsible."

The gutbucket blues, crying heart, soul in confusion, and pain in his voice can't be missed when Taj sings 'Why Did You Have To Desert Me?'

The plaintive wail says all that he couldn't express to Anna: "Why did you have to desert me?/You didn't have to leave, run away/No, no, no, no, no/Why don't you confront me?...I can't understand, can't understand/No, no way, I can't understand." He breaks into Spanish, the language of Anna's mother, as if to send a private message. Later in the song, he complains about her friends: "They keep taking me for a fool/I'm supposed to deal with that."

Also in the song, though, is a plea for reconciliation: "Let us get it on for some time together/I know you'll be surprised at the difference." The last line of the song on the original cut is "De León, listen to my song," sung in Spanish.

"I'm not really a direct singer of a song inspired by the first person, the I, like in 'I myself,'" Taj explains, "and I'm not mercenary about being inspired by somebody to do something, like taking a private situation and mining it for public consumption. I'm more trying to open it up, not make it so narrow, focused – more on the greater situation that affects lots of people, rather than just my situation. It's probably made it hard for everybody to really figure out what the hell I was doing – again. 'Why Did You Have To Desert Me?' meant a lot to a whole lot of people. The New York Puerto Rican community just dug the hell out of that song. The Philadelphia R&B urban community got into it because a lot of cats were experiencing that situation in their lives, and there was no song for it. It was like blues for a new era, with a different kind of chord structure more organized behind jazz."

But self-references and glimpses of his life can be found in other songs that Taj has written. In 'Big Kneed Gal,' he sings of the Thanksgiving dinner at which he and Anna were introduced: "When that woman smiled at me, a whole new world begin/I really do love her/She's my lover, my baby, my pal." 'Queen Bee,' on the *Señor Blues* album, is for his second wife, Inshirah: "These songs were made for lovers...my soul, my soul/queen bee, queen." In 'Cakewalk Into Town,' he admits to having the "blues so bad one time it put my face in a permanent frown," and sings of his love for his daughter Aya and son Ahmen (by Inshirah) as a way out of those blues. The song 'Big Legged Mamas Are Back In Style Again' is, he admits, about his preference for a woman's body size, while the song 'When I Feel The Sea Beneath My Soul' is about his love for being on the sea.

His song that perhaps best expresses his fundamental stance in life is

'Nobody's Business But My Own,' in which he sings, "Don't care what you do/as long as you do what you say."

In 1997, Taj and Jon Cleary – former keyboard player for The Phantom Blues Band – wrote '21st Century Gypsy Singin' Lover Man,' which Taj sings on the *Señor Blues* album. It's a song about loneliness, the pain of being on the road, the longing to get back home to loved ones. It's about leaving without a word to avoid the sadness of the long goodbye, and about the undeniable lure of the freedom of being a wandering minstrel man. It's a song about the reality of a "21st-century gypsy singin' lover man," the life of a bluesman. And Taj knows from where he sings.

12 *The Rolling Stones Circus*

We pull into the parking lot of the House Of Blues. The white beams of three klieg lights spike the blue-black sky. Four television trucks transmit live interviews with performers filmed inside the club. The black-and-white cop car used in the original *Blues Brothers* film sits off to one side of the crowded parking lot. Taj played on the film's soundtrack, and became friends with the co-star, Dan Aykroyd, the MC for tonight's event.

From the outside, the club looks like the rural South mysteriously plonked down in striving California. The building's rusted and battered tin siding was taken off an old sugar mill that stood at the crossroads of Highways 61 and 49, outside Clarksdale, Mississippi. In 1936, Bluesmaster Robert Johnson immortalized the crossing in his song 'Crossroads,' a song made famous by Cream in the 1960s.

Highway 61 is also immortalized in blues history by a tragic accident. On the night of September 26, 1937, the car carrying Bessie Smith, the empress of blues, sideswiped a truck on one of the sudden curves that kink Highway 61 near Clarksdale. She died from her injuries the following morning.

We go up the back stairs to the Foundation room on the third floor, the private bar/dining room for members only, where the performers are putting on their stage make-up and glitter. Taj sits on a couch in the khakis that he'll wear onstage. Aykroyd stops to tell him that Mick Jagger is downstairs and wants to meet with him after the show. "Yeah, that'll be good," Taj replies.

As the first act goes onstage, Taj tells how he and Jagger first got together: "In 1968, the English invasion had come down pretty heavy in the American scene. For those of us who were playing the older music – like the blues, not disconnected from its culture – the attention given to the British bands was...well, irritating. I mean this in the sense that the American music scene really didn't move for us, but the industry made room for the English musicians to come over and play the older music that originally came from this country. The American kids were eating it up, like Led Zeppelin had invented the blues. That was a real strange trip for all of us.

"There was an openness to the music in England that was starting to flow back to this country. Jimi Hendrix had to go to England to get some attention in this country. You didn't hear about him in this country until the British music press started writing him up. He couldn't get arrested in this country, but in England he was supported for his creativity.

"The British musicians were listening to the older blues and the people who played it. Eric Clapton was the first one of the English musicians who really paid attention to The Taj Mahal Band. He told me that he heard one of our songs when clicking through the music channels on a plane from Singapore to somewhere. 'Whoa, who's this?' CBS was putting it out on the airwaves. Whenever he was flying on a regular basis, he kept coming back and listening to that.

"Word spread among the English musicians. When they came to play in LA – like Eric Burdon and The Animals, the Stones, Cream with Clapton – they stopped by the Ash Grove to listen to the hardcore blues. They came for the experience to catch Lightnin' Hopkins, or whoever was playing. They were really nice, very friendly. A bit on the rowdy side. Enthusiastic more than rowdy.

"When I first heard the Stones, I knew a lot of the original music from which their music came, so their stuff never sounded like 110 percent to me. But then, I wasn't a young white kid coming to this music for the first time and relating to it as Rolling Stones music. I knew the blues background behind it. I did enjoy the excitement that the Stones brought to the music. Jagger was working on becoming a really good performer. In the early days, he was pretty spastic, more like Axl Rose in Guns N' Roses than like Tina Turner or James Brown that he became later on.

"I was interested that these guys were covering old blues songs and were real positive towards blues people. The Stones wanted to meet Muddy Waters and talk to him. They were genuinely interested in the old blues guys as people and artists, whereas many of the young American rock 'n' rollers looked at the old black guys as someone they could steal from. The Stones – the British bands in general, at that time – never looked at it like that. They had an attitude of a friendly exchange between musicians, where they copy from each other, learn from each other. Other American musicians were into the vicious exchange, where they'd say, 'We know you're not going anywhere, so fuck you. We'll take this material from you. Who gives a shit about you?' There was never any of that coming from the British musicians. They always came from a respectful point of view. And I got that respect from them.

"The Taj Mahal Band was playing at the Whiskey one night. I was playing harmonica with my eyes closed. When I open my eyes and look down on the floor, I'll be damned – it's Mick Jagger, Marianne Faithfull, Keith Richards, and Brian Jones down there, dancing. I saw an opportunity. I said, 'I'm going to talk to Jagger about this music scene in England. I want to see where his head is at.' So, after the set, I went to the back of the club, where they were sitting. I said, 'Mick, let me put this to you. Seriously, the way things are going on here in the United States, Taj Mahal has a snowball's chance in hell of really making it. There must be something going on in England that is totally different than what is going on here. Jimi Hendrix is coming out. All this other stuff is happening. It seems that you guys have a really interesting music scene going on over there. Look, if there is any way that we can get with you guys, you can help us do anything, or we can assist you in doing anything – music, playing – don't be afraid to give us a shout out.' He took it in. I said what I had to say and went back up onstage to play. That was that.

"Three months later, through our management office, the Stones sent word that they wanted us to come over and be part of their *Rock 'n' Roll Circus* movie. 'Come on, don't worry about the dollars and cents. Just tell the people here that you're vacationing.' They sent tickets for the band, two road guys, two management.

"It was our first time to England, and very exciting. Everything was absolutely perfect. Only time we went into our own pocket for money was for personal needs. The way it was paid for was wonderful. Classic. Everybody was friends. Lots of lasting friendships came out of those circumstances. The film was shot in a London soundstage over two days in 1968. The Who, Eric Clapton, John Lennon and Yoko Ono, Peter Townshend were all there. Lennon, Clapton, Keith Richards put together a one-time band for the occasion, The Dirty Mac. Mitch Mitchell, drummer in Jimi Hendrix's Experience band, played the drums.

"Me and the band were in a weird situation. Basically, we weren't supposed to be in England without an exchange of English players and American players. We just showed up, so the Stones' organization had to be on the lookout that we didn't get arrested or run out of the country. They shot our bit the day before there was an audience so nobody would know we were playing in the film. On some of the shots, as the camera moves across the stage, you see that there are empty seats behind us, whereas on other people's performances there is an audience.

"In the film, you can see everyone is having fun. There was a wild energy to it that could get crazy and out of hand. Inbetween the music acts, there were acrobats and clowns and fire-breathers, but still, it was British and contained. We're talking British, not a bunch of wild kids in New Jersey. The film didn't come out for a long time, for lots of reasons. Then bootleg copies were passed around and the film was finally released.

"The actual original footage ended up in Ian Stewart's barn. Stewart was the sixth Stone. He was a wonderful guy, and a great boogie-woogie piano player. He did a lot of playing on 'Boogie-Woogie Explorer.' He didn't do the stage stuff, because he didn't have The Rolling Stones' look – you know, the foppish long hair, wiry body, kinda outlaw look. He had a big, square, Scottish jaw, and a wholesome look. He was one of the guys I locked into. I always looked for him when I got around the Stones, and he always came to see me whenever I played in London.

"After he died, his wife found the film footage and brought it to the attention of the Stones' office. Allen Klein, the Stones' manager – who was part of the whole operation from the beginning – put the money up with Mick to bring the film out. Klein's daughter and son got involved in finding all the footage. There were three great performances by us that didn't end up in the film. We did three songs and only one made it in.

"While we were doing the film, we'd hang out with Keith, Mick, and Marianne. The one I didn't talk to much was Charlie Watts. He doesn't seem to talk a whole lot, but he paid absolute attention to the way our band played, especially to our drummer, Chuck Blackwell. Mick and Keith were a tremendous amount of fun. They were very generous, extremely wonderful, warm people. We jammed together, exchanged songs. It was a time when we all thought that the music was going to save humanity. All of us were under 30, idealistic. It was real magical.

"Underneath all the music, Mick was a businessman, a graduate of the London School of Economics. After a show, when everyone goes off, Mick goes and sees what the receipts for the night are, then he goes to party. He's a sharp guy. He really knows his music. I liked, and like, the Stones because they stay with their own vision of the music. At first, they were happy to present real black American music, in terms of bringing the songs out. Basically, Mick and Keith wanted the kids to enjoy the music as much as they themselves did.

"The Rolling Stones definitely did more than their share of giving back. Over the years, they have always fostered a positive relationship with black music and supported the good musicians. Mick and Keith know who the players are. I am sorry Brian Jones isn't with us, because he was highly knowledgeable about music and black music. Keith and Mick were seriously into blues, knowledgeable about what the real music sounded like. American musicians, as a generality, tended to play the blues on the surface. If they played 52 percent of what the music was about, they thought they were a blues player. The English musicians were playing more into the 80-90 percentile range of knowing the music. When you get to John Mayall, you could hear it was John Mayall, but you could also hear it was a Muddy Waters song. The real form of the song came out.

"The blues came slower to England. Since it was slower, the musicians and the audiences took more time to find information. It's like me about fishing – when I'm not fishing, I'm reading about it. When they were not playing blues, they were reading about the blues, listening to records, going to each other's houses, and jamming. 'Come on over. We're going to listen to a bunch of old blues records and have a party.'

"The British didn't have all the painful background that went with the blues, such as the slavery history and injustice, so they could hear it more completely as a music without going, 'Oh, that reminds me of picking cotton in Mississippi,' 'Oh, that reminds me of those dangerous darkies down the street.' None of that kind of stuff. They just heard it as an art form, like Europeans usually do. That's why jazz has a bigger home in Europe than it does in America.

"The British blues came mainly out of the working class. Same in America. It's working-class music. The British players were the first generation of English who came of age after the Empire basically broke down, so they no longer had resources from their colonies. They weren't living the high life, as before. Blues was a lot closer to their existence. It was more like what their sentiments were about, so they could relate to it real good.

"We stayed in England for two weeks and then played gigs in Sweden and Germany, thanks to Jagger's people. This laid the groundwork for an international fan base, which in the coming years continued to grow. Later, when I was being frozen out of big concert dates by Bill Graham in the United States, I played a lot in Europe. Those fans supported me."

Before the soundcheck in Miami, on The Rolling Stones' 1998-99 No Security tour, Mick Jagger stops by to talk about why he invited Taj to be part of The Rolling Stones' *Rock 'n' Roll Circus*: "Back then, Taj was a new performer, relatively young but playing in a traditional manner, which we really hadn't heard in a long time. There weren't many young black blues players around that we knew about. We thought that if we were going to have a blues performer in the show, we'd have someone like Taj. He had good energy. We were listening a lot to the *Taj Mahal* album with 'Leaving Trunk' on it, so we knew the band, especially Ed Davis."

Mick's voice is free of the cold that hit him in the previous week in Detroit. After a four-day rest, his energy is back up to performance level. He has just finished a series of early-afternoon business meetings, and is now in the transition of folding the businessman back into the musician. The pre-show buzz is starting to build around him, but Mick doesn't take on any of its edge. "Though Taj has been through a lot of musical changes in his career – just look at all the different kind of albums he's put out – he's still very rooted in traditional blues music. He's a good player and interpreter of the music, and he's a really interesting historian of it. His grandparents came from the Caribbean, you know, and Taj reached back and looked at that musical background. He is interested in more than just one thing, and that informs all of his playing. Now he's considered a living link to the old blues traditions. That's exactly what he is.

"I saw Taj do his one-man thing in San Francisco recently, and he still has the same thing I liked in the first place. In St Louis, on this tour, he and I did a duet of 'Corrina,' which we put on the *No Security* record. That performance is also on the video of the tour. For that duet, Taj thought it would be better – and I totally agreed with him – to do 'Corrina' rather than straight-ahead old blues, which would be the expected thing. Better to do something more melodic."

In retrospect, it's not surprising that Mick would be attracted to Taj's music. They are only a year apart in age, and Mick became interested in the blues at about the same time that Taj tuned into the music. "I was a student of the blues from the time I was twelve years old. I loved rock 'n' roll, but I liked country blues and the Chicago blues particularly. Those were my thing. A lot of the American blues performers came to England and were quite visible. I didn't see all of them live; some I saw only on television. They did quite a lot of television. Leadbelly came. Muddy Waters came, but I never saw him. John Lee Hooker came a lot. Sonny Terry, Brownie McGhee. A lot of gospel performers came as a big show, so I got to see quite a few players on TV when I was really young, as well as hear them on records, which were relatively difficult to get. I really didn't think of them as legends, or old. It was just music, as far as I was concerned. I didn't know how old or young the performers were, or anything, really, until later on. That was the music I liked.

"The form of the blues, as you know, was a pretty traditional format for other types of music. English blues is a subgenus of the blues, if you want to be a musicologist about it. English blues has its own long history, back to the 1940s. It's like a colonial outpost, I suppose, but the other way around.

"As musicians, we were very admiring of the blues, we being The Rolling Stones. We didn't start up by trying recreate or change the blues; we just played it as it was. We tried to copy it as close as we could. We did Muddy Waters and Jimmy Reed. We just did them as far as we could, note for note, but we really couldn't play them note for note, [so] we did the best we could. We just copied. As for the emotional and economic background of the blues, that obviously didn't apply to us. We just liked the way the music sounded and the form of it. We didn't necessarily enter into any other part of it. It's a very easy music to understand, very direct.

"When we were 19 and 20, we really couldn't play the blues the way the Chicago blues were played, but over all this time I suppose we – The Rolling Stones – have collectively added to the language of the blues. We took a lot of the blues music into the rock 'n' roll style. Our treatment of the blues went through lots of subtle changes, but when we play the blues we play it in a very traditional way.

"What do I like to do when I'm not being a musician? I like hiking. I do that quite a lot. There are some really good hiking trails in France and Spain. I love reading. I've got lots of children, so I spend lots of time with them. I don't have any great political agenda."

It's time for the soundcheck. Mick excuses himself, says that he hopes that he's been useful, and walks out onto the stage.

13 Burn-Out

Onstage at the House Of Blues, The Clara Walker Gospel Group finishes a rousing set. Taj is on next, and goes to change into a fresh shirt. Dan Aykroyd appears onstage in midnight wraparound sunglasses and his Blues Brothers black hat and suit.

"And now, what you all have been waiting for. The man. The keeper of the flame. The man who knows so much about the blues he can't sing it all – Taj Mahal!"

Taj walks onstage, plugs his guitar into an amp, and launches directly into music. As he thumps into 'Mailbox Blues,' his shoulders jerk right, his toes swivel left, his big National steel-bodied guitar drops down, and his chin thrusts up. He rides the rhythm flat out and whips it into a lather, picking and pounding the strings. He plucks secretive notes, perfumed letters, bloodstained pleas from his guitar, and sings their news. He lets the ancestors come, doesn't doubt their voices, doesn't try to control whatever comes. He just opens up, with fierce concentration, and lets the mojo roll.

The crowd is on its feet from beginning to end. People stomp, shout, and whistle for more after two encores. Backstage, a couple of the women gospel singers bounce up and down, clapping their hands. "He's the *man!*" He's the *man!*" Taj wipes the sweat off his shaven head. "You're lookin' good, sisters," he says, and heads back up to the Foundation room for a post-show supper.

Later on, when the place quietens down, Taj tells of the time when he nearly quit the music business: "When I came back to the States in 1969, after the European tour and the *Rock 'n' Roll Circus*, Janis Joplin and I did shows together. I used to see her at the studio, or at gigs in San Francisco. I knew her pretty good. She was a down-to-earth person, not stuck up in star status, although the media surrounded her with that. She was a really simple, straightforward, direct person who wanted to be heard on the basis of her singing ability.

"She started working with The Holding Company, and basically said she was going to be with them. She finally started getting into a band that could meet her more than halfway with the music she was doing. I think that a lot of her frustration came from the musicians being good musicians but not really prepared to play the idiosyncratic music that she wanted.

"Janis wanted to sing more progressive chord structures that were developed out of a black gospel tradition, went into jazz, R&B, more like the old chitlin' circuit stuff. The musicians she was playing with knew folk and folky blues chords, but not the stuff she was going for. When Janis left The Kozmic Blues Band and got playing with a couple of R&B bands after that, I thought her music was much more cohesive. She was propelled by the music, whereas in the other circumstance she would get excited, the band would get excited, but the two would never really quite get together, so in the end it left her frustrated.

"I think she filled up the frustration with drugs and alcohol. For me, if she had really gotten off on the music all the time, then there wouldn't be a need for all that excess that happened. After a session when you do your music the way you want, you just want to cool out; but when you're left frustrated, with that same kind of energy as you experienced with the music onstage, then you're looking for something else to do to get you back down. It hurt me deep in the heart, *deep* in the heart, when that child went out.

"I remember one time I was flying to San Diego in '68 or '69. I was at the ticket counter in the airport, and I heard all this commotion in my right ear. I looked over, and there was Janis with this whole band of crazy-looking guys. I walked over and said, 'Hey, how you doing? What's going on, baby?' She was all cuted out, and introduced me to the band. She seemed to be so happy. I had never seen her so happy.

"The next year or so, I bumped into her in the studio and she was, like, really agitated. There were lots of shards of energy coming off of her. She had read a review that really chewed her up. I remember walking in and telling her not to worry about what those people say – it's only somebody's opinion. It's what they think based on what they know at the time. They've got a job. They're supposed to come up with something to put the beans on their table. She was really affected by negative reviews. Jimi was affected by that, too. I get upset, too, sometimes, by a bad review.

"We were both recording at Columbia about the same time. At that time, Columbia was trying to legitimately give me a shot out there, although not to the same degree as Mack Davis or Paul Revere And The Raiders. My next record project during this time – 1968 – was *Giant Step*. I had heard the song by The Monkees back when Melcher was producing The Rising Sons. When we recorded the song, we had technical problems with the engineers – they dumped all this work we had done. I thought the original version sounded better, and we had to do it again. I said, 'These lyrics are too good to be singing that fast, so I'm going to find another pace.'

"Turns out I was right. Ricki Lee Jones told me that she knew every word on *Giant Step* and *The Natch'l Blues*. She said that, when everybody else was talking about death and being negative toward women, my records always talked [about] reinforcing life, and were always positive toward women.

"'Big Legged Women' is such a song. It's artistic license I did on various themes of blues tunes. It makes a lot of overweight women – who are normally fighting against the skinny girls – feel good. The skinny women get all the play, yet here's a man who has sentiment towards women who are not threatened when they put on 30 pounds. That's very positive. Overweight women don't have a chance to get feedback about what is positive about them. The song says this is the more real situation of the human condition. That's taken as complimentary and flattering by overweight women. I like big-legged, big-hipped, big women. I understand that song.

"This was a time when I concentrated on developing my art. I could always hear ways to put songs in different arrangements and sequences and cadences and hear how they sound. 'Giant Step,' 'Give Your Woman What She Wants,' 'Good Morning Little Schoolgirl,' 'Further On Down The Road,' 'Big And Fat,' [and] 'Six Days Down The Road' are examples of that. I learned from both the culture and various jazz musicians, and Ray Charles, how to change the rhythm so as to accommodate the way I wanted to say the music. I worked on developing my art just by being open.

"There are several types of musicians. There is the kind the corporate record companies like – those are the ones who are completely malleable. The corporate people can put the song in the musician's mouth, put the musician they want in the studio, and the singer goes out and does everything they want him to do. That works for them. Then there are the natural musicians who listen to what they do, play how they play, play from what they learn. That's what I do.

"Then there are musicians who have both ends of it. They have some of the corporation and they throw in their ideas and personal thoughts. Then there are some musicians who don't care about personal thoughts. They just want to be working every night. 'You want us to sound like Michael Jackson tonight? All right. Or Bobby Womack? All right.' They'll do that to put beans in their bag to feed their family and themselves. Other musicians are not content with that. They want to have people recognize what they personally write and do. I have enough of an ego to go ahead and do what I'm doing.

"After 'Corrina, Corrina,' I recorded *Giant Step*, and it became a hit. 'Corrina, Corrina' has been through a lot, you'd better believe it. Blind Lemon Jefferson did the first 'Corrina Blues,' back in 1926. Bo Carter recorded his version in 1928, and it became a standard in the '30s. Everybody's had a hand at bending that song from western swing to pop. In the '60s, every folk singer and their cousin had it in their repertoire. Bob Dylan sang it. After our 'Corrina, Corrina' hit, it was a busy time for The Taj Mahal Band. We toured around the country – I went back to England to play with Santana and It's A Beautiful Day, then back here with the band and played folk festivals: the Newport Jazz Festival... [We] played all over. We'd now arrived at a place where we're playing with Steve Miller, Boz Scaggs, Tower Of Power. I got a base audience who were staying with me. People had money in their pocket and could buy records. There was a scene going on, and people were hanging out. Sex, drugs, and rock 'n' roll; free love; love-ins; flower power; hippies – all that was happening.

"In 1970, I was on my second tour of England. We had an intense time. Unbeknownst to us, our contract had created a lot of grief. The band was oversold by the promoters for the tour section from Los Angeles to New York and then oversold two or three times around London. The last guy was picking up the heavy money on the whole thing. The tour didn't go all that well, because the promoter put money into getting the musicians from here to there and not all that much money into promoting the gigs. The ticket sales weren't all that good, but we had to do it, because we were signed up.

"Because of the devious business that gets done, the promoter had to take a huge loss. That created a situation where some people on the England end were really pissed off. In Bournemouth, they sent some goons to destroy our bus. The road manager came out and found some guys trying to place explosives on the bus' axle. They were apprehended by the local constabulary.

"I thought, 'Here I am trying to work toward something really positive with my music, to contribute positively to these times, and I am coming into contact with the kind of energy that's trying to blow up my bus, and maybe me.' I needed to take a break. I had been focusing on trying to make it in the music business for five solid years. The years of traveling and running were catching up with me. I realized it was dangerous to stay in the industry just to go along. I needed to live out on the edge a little more by being willing to believe in myself and go into the music I wanted to do. I was really tired. I was over-abusing myself with cigarettes, herb, coke. I became a pretty intense macrobiotics vegetarian – mainly vegetables and rice – for health reasons, to clean up my system and get myself balanced.

"I never got involved with speed or uppers or downers in the sense of pills or any of that. I never did heroin. I didn't take acid, speed, Quaaludes, any of that. About three times, I got dosed with angel dust. Herb and hash and cocaine I did. I liked grass for one of the same reasons I like the older music: it slowed down the tempo. As a band, when we'd hit that slowed-down tempo, it seemed that the whole audience would get locked into a real nice tempo that allowed them to feel more time in the music, to feel positive about themselves. The same was true with me, both with the music and herb.

"I did deal with cocaine to a point, went to Ibiza to clean up, and had a bout with it after that in the '70s. Fortunately, family and friends said what they had to say about it, and I cleaned my life up from that situation. It was never that I was crawling around in the streets or out to score; the [abundance] of cocaine and herb and hash came from the fact that I was involved in the music business, and that it was available. Going out to score cocaine never happened. It was always offered. I just wouldn't buy it. I would buy herb on occasions. Then it was $20 a lid – reasonable. I got in, had to deal with it, got out. Glad to have been there and glad to have been out of there.

"I was really careful with coke, as I tend to have a pretty speedy personality anyway. But I had loosened up on myself, in terms of cocaine. I wasn't doing a lot, but enough. I didn't like the way I physically felt, like I was tightening up. I figured that I needed to calm down and take a little time off. One day, I told myself, 'This has got to stop. You've got to clean up your act.'

"I started to question this whole '60s thing, in terms of free love and drugs. From the end of the '60s, a lot of musicians – friends of mine – died because of drugs. When the '60s started, drugs were mostly herb and hallucinogenics and a natural grounding trip, but by the late '60s and early '70s a new, more dangerous element was coming in. The urban hardcore drugs were getting involved in this whole thing.

"For me, the whole drug thing came to a head when Jimi died, on September 18, 1970. I had gotten together with him almost exactly a year earlier, before I left for Europe. He was holed up in this apartment, despondent about all the shit that was going on. The record company gave him a big build-up and threw him out there. Then, once they saw that he was reacting to the big build-up, they started chopping him down. He was a very sensitive man – funny, but very sensitive. He was not that hard-edged.

"I was surprised that he wanted to play with me. His dad told me, a few years ago, that Jimi always talked really good about me, because I was one of the few young black guys who was playing something different out there at the same time he was playing something very different. He wanted to play with somebody he had respect for, who didn't seem to be so stained by the scene.

"I saw really strange stuff happen around him, strange enough for me to worry about him. I thought that a lot of the people around him were not out for his best interests. People started taking pot-shots at him. Because of what was going on in black politics at the time, a lot of brothers came and said to him, 'Yo, man, you're all over the place. You're high profile. How come you aren't making any political statements about what's going on, like supporting the Black Power movement?' He didn't have that gripe going; that was not where he was coming from. Hendrix's response to black injustice was to bring in some black musicians who hadn't been given a shot – like Buddy Miles, Billy Cox, Juma Sultan – to play with him. Nevertheless, he was being shot down in the papers, and he took it pretty hard.

"Anyway and anyhow, it worried me. If I was playing the stuff as wide open as he was playing, I would be shut down. He was way out, running cars off mountains, going through all sorts of equipment. Somehow he seemed not to know what was actually happening around him. Or maybe he did and the significance wasn't a big thing to him.

"It was too wild. I said, 'These people, the record companies, really aren't going for this. It only looks like it.' They tried to sabotage him in the reviews, put him down badly when he played with Buddy Miles and those guys. And then there was all the legal stuff – he was supposed to record only with the band Experience, so he had to sneak into sessions to get other things done.

"I thought, and think, that the record companies should show more responsibility to the people they were making money off of. Janis Joplin went out, Al Wilson of Canned Heat, Gram Parsons – these were people I really knew. It was starting to unnerve me that the record companies seemed to have an attitude of, 'Too bad they're dead, but that gets their name back in the news. Everybody knows they're dead and now people want to buy their records.' Even if the artists choose to put themselves in danger, the record companies should say, 'We want you around.' Then the person sliding down the slope might realize, 'Hey, I've got some people that I can depend on, and they depend on me to be there with my art.'

"That's why I wrote an eight-page letter to Clive Davis, then president of CBS records, in the September or October after Jimi died. [Davis is now the founding head of Arista Records.] In the letter, I said straight out, 'With the deaths of all these artists, doesn't the record company have any responsibility in this? Is this the signal for what's going to come, and we should be on the lookout for more tragedies? Look what's happening. We're losing some great people here who, down the road, are going to be of even more value. If you don't see their value now, you sure won't later, because they won't be here to finish the work that they started.'

"From my understanding, that letter was copied and sent around to important people in the record industry, but there's no copy of it in any of the archives. It was a personal letter to Clive, but looking back I should have written an open letter in the *Rolling Stone* so more people could have read it. But that wasn't my style.

"My mind was talking to what I thought the record companies were trying to do – that is, develop people for the long term. But the record executives may have been down the road further than I realized. They were, in fact, in the twilight between developing artists and just doing the distribution thing that the record companies have turned into now.

"An artist brought a record company revenue through sales of their effort and talents, and the record companies just took it for granted. They didn't have any sense of responsibility to the talent. They figured they could always get somebody else who had talent, was hungry, and was willing to go along. That's why I always played my stuff sorta close to the vest, which may or may not have accounted for how things have happened for me. Consequently, I may have been picked up on as a squeaky wheel and didn't get the resources put behind me.

"While in London, I had gotten a letter from my friend Nancy Mehagian, who used to book me in Phoenix. She was in Ibiza, running a restaurant, and invited me to come down. I had spent five years highly focused on my career, and had never taken time for myself. I had really pushed myself hard. I needed to center myself and let go. Boy, I could feel my body was aching from head to toe. I hadn't allowed myself to be conscious enough to go into my body and feel it. I was smoking three packs of Pall Malls a day, snorting cocaine, doing herb, just being crazy. I needed to hang out until I figured it was time to come back in the music business. Otherwise, I was going to be like a lot of other musicians, dead, and then I wouldn't get to do my work.

"After the England tour, I had a two-week break before I had to go do more work. During those two weeks, I decided, 'Fuck it, I'm not going back until I'm ready.' I went to Spain alone and stayed there for six months. After about two weeks of being there, I started to relax. I realized how tight I was holding myself. That's when I realized that I really felt like shit. I played with different musicians I ran into in Ibiza, Barcelona, Madrid, all around. It was, 'What comes along today, I'll do.'

"Ibiza was a hip, artist spot where creative people from all over Europe gathered. There were great places to go dancing. I met all kinds of people going in all types of creative directions. Clifford Irving, the writer, was there, Charles Mingus Jr – lots of people. There were people to talk to about painting. I was part of this group of people who danced, talked, got in and out of relationships with each other. I ran into Joni Mitchell and spent a couple of days talking with her. She was over there with Nico, from The Velvet Underground. They had been living in the caves on Crete with their lovers. Nico was a little strange but nice. She'd sit off the side and not say much.

"I also met Siena, one of the original Diggers. She was hardcore hippie but nice. We spent some time together, then moved off. I returned to the States and she went down to Morocco. Nearly a year later, I was told she gave birth to our twins, Ghamela and Taj Jr.

"That summer, I read *The Tempest*, Khalil Gibran's *The Prophet*, and re-read the autobiography of Malcolm X. I was glad to read that Malcolm finally came around to see that we're talking about the world. It wasn't just black Americans in this Muslim organization; it's an organization that includes people from all colors and all walks of life. That is what Malcolm discovered, which is what I knew. My Uncle Abdul told me years ago, when my father had some concern about perhaps joining the Black Muslims. Uncle Abdul – who was a Sunni Muslim – said, 'You don't have to join them to be a Muslim.'

"Many people thought that my going off to Spain was a tremendously bad move at the time. They thought that, whatever the cost, I should stay in place for the record companies to recognize me. I didn't think so. I thought the most important thing for me was to always play the music I wanted to play. I'm never playing something I don't want. If the record companies didn't like what was happening with my music, fine. Yet a lot of musicians were coming to me to learn what I was doing, to figure out what I was doing, to see how I did what I did. Then they'd go off and make big-money careers for themselves. Fine with me, but let me go off and be involved in my own development. I didn't want to listen to 'Fishin' Blues' 25 years later and think of myself as being an echo of that, as opposed to keep on creating. That song, 'Fishin' Blues,' was first recorded by Henry 'Ragtime Texas' Thomas in 1927. He was a hobo singer from Gladewater, Texas. Nobody remembers him now – at least, not in this country; but when I was in Argentina, they got his records down there.

"I didn't want to fall into the trap of complacency. I wanted to keep pushing the musical ideas I had about jazz, music from Africa and the Caribbean. The Caribbean was part of my background, but I hadn't spent time with Caribbean musicians. The same with African musicians, in terms of knowing their music. So I wondered what the hell was happening with Caribbean guys my age. I wrote 'West Indian Revelation' during my stay on Ibiza as part of that wondering.

"My parents belonged to the West Indian American Club in Springfield. They always played that music, so it was not foreign to me. It was not like I went to Jamaica once and came back and said, 'Oh, I've got to play reggae.' No, it was already happening with me, but it wasn't something I had taken time to clean off the table and say, 'Let's put this music up and see how it relates to this and that. I hear lots of stuff in it that I recognize and I don't recognize but I can feel.' So I wanted to explore the connections between different kinds of music. I had some ideas and wanted to know how they would sound in reality.

"That wonderful summer allowed me to relax. I had unglued myself from the guitar. I could listen to the music in my head and relax for the first time in years. I let the whole siesta, calm-down, tranquil thing happen to me, and I was really happy about it; but I loved the music, and I wasn't ready to let go, so I communicated with Howard Johnson in New York – the jazz and tuba player – about playing with him. I returned to New York on October 8, 1970."

When Taj left Ibiza, he went to Barcelona in August 1970. He wrote his dear friend Marie "Sweet Mama" Janisse a letter about his life in that moment. On the back of the envelope, he wrote the beginning lines of what would become his song 'Sweet Mama Janisse': "When a man gets worried, got to find some peace/he can find his welcome at the home of Sweet Mama Janisse/I ain't hurried, I ain't worried/My thoughts are happy and I'm smiling at my baby."

Dear Sweet Mama,

How the hell are you, anyway? I know you can't be nothing but in good shape. I'm fine in all respects, spiritually, physically, and mentally. I'm been eating so good I've lost weight! I really look trim and I've been exercising every day, running about 1,000 yards and walking in the sand and standing on my head, back bends, shoulder stands, Japanese push-ups, arches and so many more.

It's been good to be away for a while, and I've enjoyed it, but I feel the call of the canyon [Topanga Canyon] stirring in my heart and soul and I'm going to be heading home soon! I really miss a lot of people! You know! I've been on the road for such a long time it's about time I started enjoying some of the fruits of my efforts. The past few months have seen a great change in me, and believe me I welcome every bit that's happened. Mainly I'm just not uptight any more about anything. It's just a waste of time. That's not to say I can't get up and shake my ass and holla hallelujah and be an absolutely loud, rauckus [sic] nigger, but rest and thought have been my constant companions, along with fresh air, sunshine, good food, green trees, so much more.

I can also say that, if it hadn't been for your hospitality and affection and true friendship, I could never have lasted for as long as I did. Your home is forever implanted in my spirit, in thought and in song. There's not a day that goes by that I don't think of you, not just for one minute but for all day long inbetween my other thoughts. Anyway, I thought you'd like to know how I feel about you. Writing isn't enough, but this is the best I can do from here.

I'm playing for probably for the first time since May 4 at a little club in Calella, Spain, called El Caribe. I just been playing guitar, piano, harmonica, singing and foot stomping, and I've learned to play that brass flute of mine really well, and I'm playing that, too! New songs, loads of 'em, and my playing is the finest it's been in 20 years, and that's a mouthful for me to say. Whew!

So much for what I'm doing! Listen, Maria, I've neglected to keep my mailbox at the post office [in Topanga] and I think it's closed now! A friend of mind in Amsterdam wrote me a letter saying mail to me had been returned. I would really appreciate it if you could see about it for me. It can't be more than two or three dollars at the most. Box 804, Henry S Fredericks, aka Taj Mahal. If you can get it open, I'll appreciate it, Mama.

PS I saw Tony Puzo and his old lady on the Isle of Ibizi [*sic*]. Blow my mind, honey! I'll come home and bite you on the neck soon.

Love, Taj.

14 Coming Back On

Howard Johnson lies on his bed in the back of his loft in lower Manhattan's Chelsea district recalling his days with Taj. A round-faced man with a solid center, he's a highly respected veteran on the jazz scene. While recounting his times with Taj, he received a phone call. "Well, that was bad news," he says, hanging up. "I'll deal with it later." Without missing a beat, he continues the story.

"I got letters from Taj while he was in Ibiza, very poetic letters about the sea, the cantina he was hangin' in, the musicians he was playing with. He didn't say much about how he felt. You've got to pry info out of Taj. He kept talking about getting together with my band, Gravity, but I didn't take him seriously about wanting to play with tubas. When he came back from Spain, he stayed with me a couple of days in New York. He was the calmest I'd ever seen him, and that was good, because he can be a pretty angry guy. I don't think he's got much specific anger, but he's not pleased about a lot of what he sees and experiences around him.

"Charles Mingus, who everybody thought was a very angry guy, was very much like Taj. Anyone who is sensitive is not [going] to be happy about a lot of stuff they see around them. Taj is a very sensitive person. Black people go through things every day where people do and say things, and you just say, 'That racist idiot,' and forget about it; but anybody who says that slavery and its influence is all over, and everybody should be over it now, really doesn't understand what happens at all. That bondage is palpable, it's really there, even when you don't experience it every day in life. Mingus couldn't forget about it, and Taj doesn't really forget about it, either. It doesn't really roll off his back. It hurts and it pisses him off.

"Taj is hard to pin down. He's real solid and real mercurial at the same time. Other bandleaders I've worked for who are Taurus – Duke Ellington, Gil Evans, and Charles Mingus – have one thing in common with Taj, who is a Taurus: there's such a thing as gettin' in the doghouse with those guys, such a thing as them not wanting to hear your name, don't want to know you, wouldn't want to be with you.

"He's not a very constricted guy. He really knows who he is. He's also a guy who's working on it. He's just not satisfied with himself; he's always got to be something more. It's hard to really characterize him. He's got a really solid core, and can go off in a lot of directions, too. Maybe he can do that because he has that core to fall back on.

"He has so many talents, is so curious about different forms of music, that he appeals to a lot of people; but I think the real reason he has such a strong appeal is that he takes people to a very deep place. His kind of energy is more revolutionary, more dangerous to the establishment, than guys who get up and sing about burning the country down. I'd always laugh at those so-called revolutionaries who have a big recording contract. They ain't gonna burn nothing down except their limo bill.

"Taj is dangerous because the changes he makes in people are profound. The audience comes away feeling different, and a lot of times unconsciously so. They come away and take less shit. They come away gratified in a way they might not expect in a concert. They are moved more deeply than that. They find a kinder place within themselves, and strength, too. They are less tolerant to take a bunch of crap, and never know why they were able to stand up one day better than they were the day before. He's threatening exactly the right kind of stuff. Taj doesn't get any credit or blame. If we were in a world that didn't need that, he'd still be an important artist."

Joseph Daley, who performed with Taj as a member of the legendary tuba choir horn section, contributes this take on Taj: "I view Taj as an intellectual giant in his field. He should be bestowed an honorary doctorate for the vast knowledge he has assimilated over his career. His performances are a study in the African *griot* [and] West Indian and African-American systems of teaching, through storytelling and music. He embraces his audience as a village elder would when reciting historic information to the members of his community. His performances are history lessons on music proficiently performed on many intellectually stimulating instruments, with an embracing vocal delivery that just immediately draws you in for a closer listen.

"I say he's an intellectual giant in his field because of his multicultural perspective and assimilation of a wide variety of musical styles and forms, such as reggae, calypso, blues, jazz, and folk. He also plays instruments that fit those forms – the piano, guitar, banjo, and harmonica. He also has the languages for the music, including Spanish, French, Cajun, and many Caribbean and American dialects.

"As a storyteller and teacher, he has an historical perspective of the evolution of music that is learned and taught via the oral tradition. He has an understanding of his musical lineage via the study and assimilation of the styles of the earlier generations of African, Caribbean, and African-American musicians and reshapes it into something new.

"Everyone, young and old, loves a great storyteller. Taj can mesmerize an audience with wonderful stories of love, hate, betrayal, survival, family, and the full spectrum of life. The stories are both entertaining and educational. These storylines are also woven into his approach to instrumental music. When he is playing an instrumental selection, you can visualize a tale being woven for your enjoyment and enlightenment."

Shifting around to make himself more comfortable on his bed, Howard gives a quick history of how it was with the tuba choir and Taj: "In 1970, my friend and manager, Anne Tansey, insisted that Taj Mahal would love my band Gravity, which I formed in 1969. She brought him downtown to our rehearsal. I didn't know Taj personally then, and I was skeptical that *the* Taj Mahal was interested in tubas, even our fusion/jazz type of tuba playing. Even after Taj began to get excited about what he heard and declared that he wanted to use this tuba sound, I didn't quite take him seriously. I didn't know how focused and resolute he is until much later. Even when we structured the tuba section idea to include saxophone, flugelhorn, and trombone doubles – a perfectly workable concept – I never thought it would come to pass. Even when I got those wonderful letters Taj sent from Ibiza, I still somehow didn't believe he wanted to play with us. I was humoring the guy.

"About three months after he returned from Spain – a week before Christmas, to be exact – he called me from the West Coast and asked how much rehearsal time my band would need before an actual gig.

"'Are you kiddin'?' I said. 'With my guys, two weeks, tops.'

"'Well, good,' Taj said. 'We should start rehearsing about January 1, because we play Fillmore East January 15 and 16, open for Little Richard in Pittsburgh, and then we fly to the West Coast for another two weeks of concerts.'

"But my guys couldn't travel. One was conducting a show on Broadway, one had a jive-ass 'war on poverty' gig in Harlem left over from the Johnson administration, and some were teachers. They were booked! I was busted. Out loud, I bluffed, 'Gee, Taj, that's terrific. I'll call the guys right away.'

"I called Dave Bargeron. When Dave answered the phone, he said, 'Well, I guess you already heard the good news. I just joined Blood, Sweat And Tears.'

"'Oh, shit,' I blurted out.

"'What kind of reaction is that?' he said, and I had to explain.

"Then I called Bob Stewart, who had a teaching job. He said he couldn't get free. But before my depression could get any deeper, he called me back and said, 'Count me in. I'll find a way to do it.'

"Then I called Joe Daley, who had sat in one time with the band on a rehearsal. His wife said he was working at the Cheetah, down in the Flatiron district. I went down to the club that night. When I told him the offer, he said, 'I don't play the tuba anymore.'

"'What do you mean?'

"He said, 'I always thought I was a good tuba player, but after that rehearsal with you guys I realized that I can't play at all.'

"'You still have the instrument?'

"'Yeah, but it's for sale, and I got a buyer.' Also, he was in the last year of finishing up his college degree. He was the first one in his family to go to college, so it was important. The next day, he called back and said he'd dusted off his tuba and would work on college while touring with us.

"That same night, I called Earl McIntyre's mother. Earl wasn't in the band, but he had impressed us at rehearsals. Because he was just 17, I had to sweet-talk his mother into letting him join us on the road. I assured her that Earl would have a bunch of big brothers on the road. The band wasn't into drugs or anything, so I had no worries there. I told her that Earl had the talent and skills for this opportunity. She didn't want to hold back any opportunities for him, but if he didn't go to school she'd pull him off the road. He and Joe were bopping in and out of classes while touring for those six months.

"So, overnight, I got together the band. Taj probably still doesn't know how jive and full of it I was at that time.

"Taj rented a house and a place for the band to practice, a garage at

Pooh Corners in Bearsville, which is part of Woodstock. He hired a macrobiotic cook, which some of my band thought odd. Earl and Joe wanted pork chops.

"When we rehearsed, Taj appealed to the players' natural instincts more than anything else. He didn't want to give them any rules that would stand in the way of how they instinctively played. This works out with some guys and not with others. Some people needed to be told a little more than he would tell them, and then there's the guy that you tell what to do and he doesn't understand anyway.

"We never wrote anything down. I'd keep the line, the notes, the music marinating in my mind for several days. In rehearsal, I'd tell the guys, 'Now you play these notes, or this line, and you remember them because by tomorrow I won't remember them, so you remember your own. We're not taking any paper or music stands onstage.' I do that so the musicians feel how the music goes, rather than just reading the notes. And I don't like having music stands onstage, not even microphone stands.

"I wanted to set up a situation where the musicians would be more getting inside the music, as opposed to playing correctly. Taj did the same thing. He didn't want to have the musicians' native thing subverted by academic stuff.

"Our drummer wasn't bad, but there was a needed element that wasn't there. When we played opposite Little Richard, we really loved his drummer, Jimmy Otey, so Taj and I started plotting right away. In those days, the guys who worked with Richard were paid next to nothing. They had to keep their clothes really sharp and everything. They'd get fined for all sorts of crappy little stuff, and they had to pay their hotels out of this. Typically, after a gig, a bunch of them would share a cab to the airport and sleep in the airport before taking the plane to the next gig. But that night, when the drummer was packing up, I came across the stage and he said that he really loved our band, that's the type of band he'd like to play in. I said we'd already been thinking about it. He said, 'Really? I'd like you to have my number, but nobody can see you writing it down or it'll get me in trouble with Richard.' He joined us on the second leg of the tour.

"The band stayed together from January to June 1971. It just got to be too much to get around with, and Taj was getting in the hole, financially. He had to get himself back even. I don't know exactly how he actually felt about it. I think he was getting some money but getting along on less than he was used to, but digging on the music he was hearing.

"It was a nice run. My mother was very unhappy about the band breaking up. She said, 'Taj gets a good band then breaks it up. He makes more money in one night than it took to raise him, so why's he breaking up a good band?'"

Taj laughs at Howard's account. We're on our way to a Seattle radio station to do a promo spot for the Winston Blues Revival, a national tour Taj is heading to raise money for old-time blues performers. We're driven by Carey Williams, Taj's personal friend, tour manager, and sometimes producer for 20 years. Ahmen, Taj's 20-year-old son, sits in the back with his father and keeps commenting on the lack of visible signs of a subculture in the scrubbed-white downtown. "It's here, further out on the fringes of the city," Taj replies, then starts the story about his re-entry into the American music scene after returning from Spain.

"Mingus was one of my major heroes. He did what came to him without selling out. You think that selling out is the way to get there, like in success. You fit yourself into the corporate mold and you run the risk of having success meaning just going from hit to hit. Your popularity is based on that, not based on values that you're giving to the world or to humanity at large. There are singers and there are artists. Artists have a responsibility. Mingus was that.

"Yeah, you can get in the doghouse with me. There are some things I think people got to be on top of, musically and in life, so some things can really annoy me. Sometimes I'm unable to articulate what annoys me, because I get to the anger before I get to the thought. Instead of, 'You know what? If you feel this way about that, you should really say something to that person,' I was just, like, 'I can't go there. I can't talk at the moment.' I'd rather not be yelling and shouting at anybody. The bad thing was, I didn't learn a way to communicate what I felt was incorrect. To some extent, I wasn't willing to deal with people misinterpreting whatever the situation was. If they got it wrong, that's their problem. Now, as I get older, I'll say to someone, 'Hey, at the risk of losing my friendship with you, I'm going to be the one to tell you this. You can do with it whatever you want to do. You can misinterpret this – you can take it that I'm obviously not your friend – but I'm going to tell you what you're doing is bogus and why it's bogus.'

"I've been always in the position of, 'This is who I am, and this is what I see,' but I didn't take the responsibility in a friendship to be willing to lose it by telling the person that they were incorrect. They might get all up in your face and call you all sorts of names and talk all kinds of stuff about you, but then they're the ones who have to come back and apologize to you because you were correct. You valued their life and friendship and safety more than you valued to stay a friend of their's without telling them the truth.

"If you don't go for the truth, what are you going to get? A superficial relationship. What's the real outcome of that whole thing? At first, it feels like it's hard to confront a person, but then it becomes very easy. You're not wasting time with people you don't have to be around.

"And that getting over the bondage thing, the slave background – Howard's right, there's no getting over it. But there can be a complete direct healing in the situation, where people acknowledge that we came to the worst of who we are with one another and we're not that anymore, there's another way of being now. Getting over it is not on a monetary level, like buying your way into respect and dignity. Being a rich black man doesn't necessarily make your ancestors proud of you.

"Being in that tuba band was really a nice thing. When audiences first saw the band come onstage with all those horns and tubas, they couldn't figure out what it was going to sound like, but they were soon dancing and yelling. We were able to get people past themselves and into the moment. We made a heavy impression, both with our record and the live performances. The band gave me an opportunity to really test my mettle with a lot of other players. My idea was always to play with people who were ahead of me, so I was always learning, stretching to keep up. The guys in the tuba band had big chops. They played in all kinds of musical circumstances.

"We made an album called *The Real Thing* [1971], a double live at the Fillmore East, now available on cassette. Another album followed called *Happy Just To Be Like I Am* that same year, which was a studio album, [with] interesting tunes using tubas in the rhythm section. We started the new phase of the tuba being seen as a melodic instrument, so I at least got to go my way with that band. Now I don't have to say, 'Yeah, there was this tuba band and I really wished I'd done something'; now we have a living record of it. But it was just too hard to run that band on the road. Expensive. I worked with the tuba band until the economics became so I had to go back out onto the road solo to maintain the financial situation of making a living.

"When I was in Woodstock, with Howard and the band, I visited with my brother Samuel, who lived not far from there with his wife and two young daughters. He was working for IBM as a systems programmer, developing a time-sharing option system. We hadn't seen each other in some time, so it was good to reconnect. About seven months later, after the tour with the tuba band finished, I invited Samuel to be my manager. My finances were a bit stressed, as were a lot of other things. I thought Samuel could help me get it all straightened out.

"I called him, very humbly, and said, 'It would be really great if you would work with me.' He asked, 'What would I do?' I said, 'Well, you'll do something.' He was my manager from 1971 to 1976. He brought in my sister Connie, and all together we got things on the road again. Eventually, all my brothers and sisters worked for me during this period – all but Hughan Jr, who was deceased.

"When I came back to the United States, I realized that I really couldn't trust the corporate music-business people I was working with. I wanted to work with people I could personally trust, even if they weren't in the music business. I'm a private person, protective of myself, but I was willing to risk them getting on the inside and being in my space. That was better than me being surrounded by a bunch of people who really didn't have my best interests at heart.

"I felt that, from 1965 up to 1970, I was very open to what was going on in the music business, willing to be shaped by it, out there playing, putting forth what it was, trying to work with the record people and understand their point of view; but when I came back from Spain, I decided that I wasn't going to compromise with the record people ever again, for any reason. There was no reason to compromise. They take compromise as one step over the line into convincing you to do whatever they want, as opposed to, 'Here's our ideas. We want your input.' Or, 'We need your input so we can put something together that really works for you and for us.'

"I looked at my history in the music business and knew something had to change. From 1965 to 1970, I was solidly in the business, had a high profile. A lot of people knew what I was doing, but I still couldn't manage to break high ground in the music business. I just got tired of feeling like I was waiting my turn. I was idealistic about my chances to be considered as a major talent and contributor at that time. I knew that a lot of people were getting breaks that weren't coming to me. I thought that me and the band got the short end of the stick. We were a highly visible, well-playing bunch of musicians. Everyone was always sniffing at my records, or whatever I was doing, to see what was going on.

"We had played all the big shows – the Avalon, Fillmore – with all the big names. We were one of the few LA bands that the people in San Francisco accepted. The San Francisco fans were real persnickety about LA bands. They thought they were all plastic and weird. But we could play all the time in San Francisco. We just didn't get all the shots. We just couldn't get the big push that was behind Crosby, Stills And Nash, or Neil Young, or Neil Diamond. We didn't get that kind of investment. We didn't get the real high-up, inside-the-hierarchy kind of push. Management, promotion – that just didn't come our way.

"I wasn't happy, because it was still a real hard fight to get to the level I wanted. The record company still wasn't convinced that Taj Mahal was happening. I had hits like 'Corrina' and 'Giant Step,' 'You're Gonna Need Somebody On Your Bond,' 'Mailbox Blues,' 'Diving Duck [Blues],' 'Good Morning Little Schoolgirl,' and I still wasn't getting the backing. There was always someone bigger happening that the record executives could allude to. You got to realize that, if a record company has an inside policy – like some big corporations have their unofficial policy of keeping the upper management and boardroom male and white – they become adept in making it look like, 'Well, there's not very much we can do about why you ain't getting nowhere.' They'll pat you on the head and say, 'We'll look into the matter,' and that is that.

"I got tired of hearing the status-quo rhetoric from these guys. It was more important for me not to lose my connection with the music than to become disillusioned with the music because of what these guys were doing. The music didn't have anything to do with them. I was always playing gigs, but at times I'd say, 'Geez, why isn't this happening?' I'd think about quitting but say, 'No, this isn't time to quit. I got too much time in, too much effort in. If I quit, it's like saying that I agree with where they're at,' and I didn't agree with where they were at – that was impossible. My point was to really care for the music. I just liked the music, and I felt that I was connected to it. As an American citizen, as an African-American, this was part of my culture, and I had the right to express it. Why was there something wrong with what I was doing?

"My first three albums are good enough to stand up today, but the music industry looked at my music and said, 'He's a black. This is how we market black music, but he is totally different. We've got to come up with something different with him.'

"I saw that. I said, 'Okay, all this music I've put in context, it's ahead of the commercial. If you guys don't see anything, well then, you know what? There are other levels of music that are more rewarding, more fulfilling, so I'm going off and doing some of these other ideas I have, like more African music. I'm not ever going to compromise myself with what you guys got going. I'm just not going to compromise like that anymore.'"

15 Pushing The Boulder

The tuba band experience put Taj back on the American music scene, but not in the scene. He didn't have a record contract or a band. His stance was a bit like Sisyphus not compromising with the boulder: it was a hard, uphill struggle. The relaunching of Taj's career became a family effort. His brothers and sisters – Samuel, Connie, Carole, Robert, Richard, and Winston – all worked for Taj at one time or another from 1971 to 1976.

The family effort was a mixed bag. Taj got out of debt, bought the Tilden house in the hills above Berkeley, and started his career moving forward, but there were some serious family strains in the process, as well as personal strains on Taj. In the early '70s, he was divorced from Anna; learned the unexpected news that he was the father of twins; started the passionate and tumultuous relationship with Inshirah, who became his second wife; and suffered the death of their first two babies.

"There was a lot of growling going on," recalls Taj's brother Winston, who joined the family enterprise in 1974, when Taj had the seven-piece Intergalactic Soul Messengers band. Winston designed the cover for Taj's *Music Keeps Me Together* album, for which another brother, Hughan Jr, did the painting that appears on the cover. "Samuel took the brunt of the discontent, but Samuel was doing a lot of growling, too. They were young, trying to establish themselves in the business, where they wanted to get. It was supposed to be a support thing, but at times they got in each other's way. Taj would growl; Samuel would growl.

"Taj was fighting for his independence. That's what the growling was about. In a lot of ways, Sam felt things should be a certain way in order to get where they wanted to go. Taj felt that Sam's agenda was cramping his space and style, or that he didn't necessarily want to do it in that way. The growling with Columbia Records started before Sam came in. That came from Taj being abused by Columbia and his standing up for his rights. Part of his growling with record companies is that they wanted to put him into a niche. He said, '*I'm* my niche.'"

Taj agrees that it was a time "when I was growling like an eel. You stick your hand in my hole, you would come out with a stump. You get a jam up among the artist, the management, and the industry suits. Friction is a natural feeling, back and forth between those elements, but you have to grow past that. I didn't want to lose what I felt about the music or the value of the music I was playing. I saw a lot of guys who played the blues and then started playing in some other way because they could get rich."

Samuel also acknowledges that his stint as Taj's manager had its highs and lows: "As the manager, I was the person that got the flak when Taj didn't think things were going right. Antagonism happens when the creative person – who brings the capital in – has need for management. Both sides have the same goal, but a lot of friction happens between management and entertainers, or athletes, or whatever. The artist says, 'If I don't work, there's no money,' and you, as management, know damn well that, if you don't manage the money, the creative people don't have anything to stand on. As management, I had to be in control. I had to understand where this thing had to go in terms of management. I had to believe and trust in myself. I wanted to move his career to the top of his game."

As the manager, Samuel was the point man to get Taj secure, if not rich. His mission was to sell records, get air time on radio stations, sign to a major label. He and Taj had the same goals, but at times they were rowing in different directions to get across the river.

"When Taj came back from Spain, he more or less had to start over again," says Connie, Taj's oldest sister, who was working as a producer for ABC in San Francisco when Samuel asked her to join the Taj team. She had her fingers in the press and publicity pie, so her job was to increase the public's awareness of Taj. "Taj was ahead of his time. It was difficult for the traditional black radio stations to respond to him. Even today, it's still difficult for Taj to get play on black stations, quite frankly. Taj didn't come through the black hierarchy. He didn't come through the R&B circle. He didn't do the chitlin' circuit. He was opening acts like The Rolling Stones – that's where he was at – and there were very few, if any, African-American people in the Stones' *Rock 'n' Roll Circus*. So, when we said to R&B stations, 'Please play Taj Mahal,' they'd say, 'Who is he? What kind of music is this? Can I dance to it?'

"I think in his heart of hearts he wanted to be accepted by his own people. To not have them understand the kind of music he was playing was frustrating. Extremely frustrating. What makes him unique today is that he hung in there with what his heart and his creative genius and his soul were saying to him. If he had gone the way of everybody else, he wouldn't be the Taj Mahal of today.

"He's telling stories of the human spirit. That's why people of any color come to see him – they can relate to what he is talking about. He is just the receptor of the energy coming through. He has to be in touch with his own human spirit to be authentic. I think he is, but I also think sometimes the weight of the responsibility wears him down. It may not necessarily mean that his own life is as perfect as he'd like it to be, or as spiritual as he'd like it to be.

"Once he gets out onstage, he picks up the knowledge, that other energy, and he moves with it. It's almost like the experience of people in rural and, sometimes, Pentecostal black churches. A minister can be making a point, and you can see him being transformed from an easy, smooth-talking person to a person who is showing a bit more agitation in the spirit, then speaking in a completely different vocal range from where he started. Taj changes vocal styles right in the middle of a song. To some people, that's scary; to other people – the African-Americans – that's appropriate.

"Each song vibrates in him differently and brings up something different. If you sing the notes that he sings in certain songs, you can feel the notes inside you, in the solar plexus, inside the diaphragm. You can feel the vibration in the middle of your chest, resonating inside of you. He can't go up on that stage and sing those notes genuinely without having something being transformed. This is the appeal of Taj beyond just someone singing. On a scale from one to ten, as a vocalist, Taj is about a five, but with Taj you're not listening to the pure note – you're listening to the emotion behind the note. That's the key to black singing. That's the key to any singing.

"It's the immediacy, the playing who he is, that is the magnetism for an audience. He might have a set outlined in his mind and play the same songs set after set, but it looks like he never thought about it. It comes in such a spontaneous way that people start to sing along with him.

"His best arena has always been the intimate club setting, where he can talk to the people. Taj used to – and still does – go into real political conversations about the record companies when he was onstage. He used to really go into it. Sometimes I'd get a little nervous. I'd be saying, 'If you want people to support you, you don't necessarily want to say that they don't support you.' But he would. He'd say to the audience, 'Thank you, for you have supported me and my family by being here tonight, and sometimes the record industry doesn't do that.'

"Part of the difficulty was that, with the music industry in this country, you have to re-invent yourself. The way Taj re-invented himself was never, ever the straight-and-narrow way. I think that was the difficulty. A lot of people really expected black performers to look and sound and perform in a particular way. Taj didn't come through that. He didn't come from there. He came from the Buffy Sainte-Marie folksy blues way, with a mixture of rock. The music industry didn't know how to categorize him. It was always a little difficult to get the industry to be behind what he was doing."

For Samuel, in for the long haul, the experience was personally exhilarating and personally costly: "It wasn't like I went out to California to be a big manager, to get a stable of artists; it was to save my brother's life, to be very candid. I knew that, when Janis went, and when Jimi went, I saw Taj was in real trouble. I have premonition in the family. That's what I presented to my wife, Georgia, at the time when we moved. I said, 'Hey, I just feel that he is in trouble, and I'm going to do what I can do.' That was very much part of this.

"March 20, 1971, I flew out to California and spent three weeks with Taj and the Howard Johnson tuba band. I got hooked. I was really taken by the plight of musicians – problems they had with management, getting recognition – especially black musicians. Here I was, working with my brother, who was a musician doing real music, world music. I came back to Woodstock and packed up everything. In July 1971, I drove across the country in an 18-foot Ryder truck with all the household possessions. When I arrived in Berkeley, Anna de León loaned me her car and I found a place to live. I sent my wife and two young daughters – three and two years old – to Nashville, which was my wife's home. Later, they joined me in Berkeley. I did this all at my own expense.

"That started my California days. Bill Graham was Taj's manager at that time. Bill's office was located over on Market Street in San Francisco. On the ground floor was David Rubinson, who produced Taj. It was the same Rubinson from Columbia, during the Davis Band days. On the middle floor was the Millard booking agency, that booked Taj. All this was not as innocent as it looked, as I later found out.

"In the summer of 1971, Taj's road manager, Ron Nahoda, had to go on and do other things in his life. I ended up being Taj's stage/road manager. I found out that Taj was in tremendous debt, in the neighborhood of $50,000. Back then, you could buy a duplex in California for $28,000. He was behind in payments to Graham, union dues, old debts from the tuba band. He hadn't been paying child support to Anna for Aya. I made sure that she got a check every week. He didn't have a place of residency – he spent nights in Rubinson's office, or wherever. He didn't have a driver's license.

"Also, Taj had a disdain for his career and disdain for other musicians whose careers were getting the breaks. I was in an uphill battle with him. Music preoccupied his mind so that the mundane, practical stuff never got proper attention. When he got the house up by Tilden Park, I'd go up and fix plumbing problems or they never got the attention. Basically, what I tried to do was clean my brother up. Not that he was that bad. I tend to be a bit paternal. I'm the second eldest, Taj being the oldest, but I tend to want to fix things, if I can. I looked at his condition, financial and physical.

"Taj's spirit, under all that debt, was rather heavy. He didn't feel good, being in debt. That was around the time he and Anna had broken up for good. It was heavy for him all around. He rose to the occasion. He was wonderful. He was something to behold.

"When 1972 came around, Taj was having trouble with Columbia and Columbia was having trouble with Taj. They didn't know what to do with him, how to market him. Columbia had Aretha Franklin first, but they didn't know what to do with Aretha, either. Taj – a big, boisterous black man – was very forceful in how he felt about what the record companies weren't doing or should be doing for him. He wouldn't grab guys by the collar, but his voice would. You don't get a lot done that way when you ask someone to do something for you. There was always tension between him and the record company. I'd always hear him harping on about what wasn't being done, what guys were doing very well in terms of music, who had got a different break. He was very displeased.

"As Mr Fix-It brother, I tried to fix it. I fell into that bag. It wasn't a great place to be, but I felt that my job was to get closer to the record-company guys and build some kind of rapport. As you do it, you get more and more things for your artist. We worked out of Bill Graham's office. Bill was manager and I was road manager. We talked about Taj taking a solo act on the road. Taj had not gone out before as a primarily solo act. He had done solo shows, but this was a first time as a career move, so this was very new. We had to sell the promoters the concept that they were buying Taj Mahal, not a ten-piece tuba band or five-piece rock band.

"Graham was involved in a very positive way. He did the management responsibilities, co-ordinating with the agency that did the booking. We went on the road. Graham was real good at that time about Taj's debt to him. I don't think that he ate any debt, but he didn't call it in straight away. He was paid, but he gave time. He was in a good position – when the money came in, it came in through him.

"We toured all through the States and Canada. I can't say that I enjoyed the road, because I'm a homebody and loved my wife and children. The solo act lasted at least a year to a year and a half. By September 1974, Taj bought the house on Tilden, in the hills above Berkeley. His back yard was Tilden Park, where he spent a lot of time walking. He was completely free of debt. He'd got a driver's license. I wanted us to buy a rental property, a building of 30 units in the good section of Richmond, but he didn't want anything to do with it. 'I don't want to be a landlord,' he protested. I wish that I had bought it on the quiet, anyway. It would have been a good investment.

"So, within a few years of my arrival, he was free of debt and had his own house. I read the script to *Sounder* and said it was a must-do. He liked it. Bill Graham lobbied real hard for Taj. Originally, some big production group was going to do the soundtrack for $10,000. He got the soundtrack and went down in history for that, and he got a bit part for a third of that money. But a lot of good things were happening by 1974.

"I was working to gain him recognition amongst his own people. We'd tour nationwide and only a handful of black people came out. I was convinced that it was not necessarily because black people didn't like his music; it had more to do with the fact that he wasn't promoted to the black audience. The blacks I connected with said they never knew when Taj was coming to town. I tried to get Columbia to spend some time and appropriate dollars toward markets that were not Taj's usual market, but the record companies were quite comfortable with promoting Taj through discount chain stores.

"I was trying to build a bridge to his own people, where he comes from and where the music comes from. I wanted to include them in the whole process, to share in this experience. Taj talked about it a lot, so it was important. The flak we got from the record company, the booking agency, and the producers... They just lined up and said, 'Hey, we don't want to turn Taj into another rhythm and blues artist.' We said, 'We're not talking about that. We're talking about broadening his base.'

"Taj was out there playing the straight-up funky blues. Some part of the black community didn't want that music. They didn't want to be reminded of their country roots. One of the sad things is that most of our indigenous music – whether it be blues, reggae, folk or jazz – was really not supported wholeheartedly by the people that this music comes from. If we subtract white people out of the fan base of any of that music, we don't have an audience. That's kinda sad. That's a very real dynamic.

"I peeped it a different way. I peeped that there were black people who really did like his music, a lot, but didn't have access to him. I saw, as a road manager and as a manager, that he was being cut off from black people. That market wasn't being encouraged, and I was trying to encourage it. Now Taj is recognized for keeping the flame of straight blues, music of the people. He stayed with it. He showed his brothers and sisters that staying with things has a tremendous amount of merit.

"When *Mo' Roots* came out, in 1974, the dollars loosened up. I was a bit more seasoned, having been on the job for three years. We had a very competent road manager and road crew. We were getting to markets that we had not been to before. Taj was getting air play he had not gotten before. I had built a rapport with the Special Markets department of Columbia – every major label had a Special Markets division; that was the coin for the black market – so some real things were happening. Certain ducks were lined up.

"We played Philadelphia to a packed house. Half were black. We played at Howard University – black school – to a packed audience. We played Carnegie Hall to a full house, black and white. Some of what we were trying to do to get this music to all the people was starting to happen with *Mo' Roots*. That was a wonderful time: more money from the record companies, big crowds. We had control over the album rights, kept control, had a lot more say-so.

"I must say that Georgia, my ex-wife, was extremely important in these years. She made it easy for me to do the work with Taj. A spouse can make or break something like this. She never gave me any flak about what I had to do to put the foundation under Taj's career.

"But my wife and I split up. I felt I had outgrown her. We had four beautiful children together, and she did a tremendous job. I've come to realize that, if anyone outgrew the relationship, it wasn't me. You know, you get a little large and you think you need somebody with flowers on their dress, meditation, incense. I had left my wife for a beautiful transcendental meditation teacher. Truth be known, I changed women to move up. I thought that I had reached a place in life that I needed something better. But within two years, that relationship fell apart and I was throwing newspapers to make money. I learned a lot about higher truths and meditation, but I also realized what Georgia had given to me and our children: a living example of selflessness and kindness and generosity.

"Things between Taj and me became more difficult, started disintegrating. In 1976, he would go through serious mood swings. I thought it was just artist stuff. I don't think I really had a sense of what an artist – a musician – goes through, as far as the insecurities and whatever that makes them who they are. I don't know if there was any substance abuse at that particular time, but looking back now at the mood swings, he was cool one minute, then the next in a tirade about something.

"Managing a band is one of those things I felt that I had to do, and it's one of those things I [hope I] never have to do again. *Ever* again. I gave my life away. It was wonderful, a tremendous experience, but once I did it, 'Okay, got the T-shirt. No need to do it again.'

"Toward the end, I felt a tremendous sense that I was just plain wore out. The years took their toll. I no longer wanted to do it. I wanted a break. I wanted to get away for a couple of months and just cool out, which turned out to mean leaving it for good. Late in 1976, I left and went to a very menial existence. I felt as if I had been on drugs for five years, although I wasn't on drugs. I was almost like a zombie. I took in all that responsibility and pressure and I tried to raise up.

"I floated around for a few months to get my head together. I talked to some guy one day in a health-food store about a morning paper route. For two years I'd get up at four o'clock in the morning and throw papers. I had thrown papers as a boy, and I wasn't looking to do it again after college, not after working for IBM. My self-esteem was smaller than the width of my little pinkie.

"In 1977, I couldn't buy a job. I had been trying for over a year to get a job, but I'm sure that I gave off such a negative vibe I couldn't attract anything. Anna gave me a $500 money order, with instructions to pay her back in our next lifetime. That changed everything around for me. Within two weeks, I got a job as a substitute teacher in the Oakland schools for $85 a day. Shortly after that, I got the bookselling job. Anna giving me that money raised my self-esteem to where I could attract something good.

"Taj and I were on the outs. I had a lot of anger at Taj during that time. I put my life, my family, on the line for him. When I was going through it real heavy myself, I didn't feel like he offered or extended, even when I asked. He didn't respond in kind. There were some very, *very* rough years, in terms of my feelings about him. After managing Taj, I didn't make a lateral move; I took a dip. It was very frustrating. I was very, very angry. It was hurtful at the time.

"He was with Inshirah, whom he married in 1974. There was a lot of tension there. She didn't care for me. I always felt that the combination of the two was one of the reasons I was out. I chose to blame her. Taj was, after all, my brother. He would never see me out here doing this, eking out a living, and not help, especially after I moved out here on my own money. That's what I wanted to believe about my brother.

"In 1981, Taj started coming around, and made it known that he wanted me to come back and manage him. I said, 'Well, I don't know.' I kept working, selling books. I had spent five and a half years with Western Book Distributors, but it wasn't as fulfilling as I wanted it to be. It was probably the best job I had, working for somebody else, if I don't consider working for Taj as a job. That was working with my brother.

"Then, one time, he said something very meaningful to me: 'It ain't really about us; it's about the kids.' I really thought about that. That hit home. Then we were back to speaking, being cordial, being more comfortable with each other.

"We decided, on a handshake, that I'd go back in with him. He was living in close proximity, and we'd get together. Inshirah was pregnant. When she had the baby, Ahmen, we were all over there. Even though it was a difficult time between Taj and me, I was there in the spirit of bringing the child into the family. We wanted things to be right with the birth. He gave me some herbs from his garden that night. When the second child, Deva, was born, my whole family was there. We took photos of the baby and the happy family.

"Before I gave notice with Western Books, I called him to confirm that we had an agreement. Yes. So I gave notice. When I left that job, I was kicking down about $50,000. Shortly after that, I called over to his house and his wife mentioned that they were moving to Hawaii. Huh? We were talking about rebuilding a career, about bonding, about being close, and now he was moving to Hawaii without telling me.

"I came to the office one day and the phone was cut off. I ended up out again, for the second time. All I got was one pay day. So again I was out of a job, at 39 years old, the same age our father died. He was out of a job, trying to do some work. He had five children. I had four. I'm feeling, 'Does Taj understand what this is?' He was difficult to get a hold of.

"I had a hobby a couple years earlier of framing paintings and prints. I said, 'I can do this.' I made a couple of attempts to look for work, but I was pretty decent as a framer. Being out of work with the wife and four kids, that didn't bode well for the marriage. My heart really wasn't into looking for a job for someone else. I said, 'Well, hell, I'm going to do what's in my heart.' That was to collect African-American art, frame it, and make it available, make a business out of it. I just went after it. I didn't envision a gallery at that time.

"I started building the name Samuel's Gallery, worked full time out of my home for three and half years, then went down to Jack London Village in Oakland and opened the gallery."

16 Lawsuit – Mahal Versus Graham

We're driving away from a radio station after Taj did a promo spot for the Winston Blues Revival tour. Carey Williams is driving. Before he worked for Taj, Carey was the lead singer of a San-Francisco-based Latin band, with members of the original Santana band. He writes one-act plays, and he's working with his writing partner, Michael Nash, on a musical based on Satchel Paige's life. Bob Weir, of The Grateful Dead, is the producer and one of the music writers, along with Taj, and jazz sax player David Murray is another main writer. They've been working on the musical for four years, and don't know when it will be completed. Carey produced Taj's *Sacred Island* album (Private Music, 1997) and is Taj's personal friend. As he says, "I see more of Taj than do any of his wives and kids. I'm low-keyed, and so is Taj. We've hardly ever yelled at each other. Taj doesn't show his emotions that much, things like sorrow. He tries to be strong for everyone around him, like when his brother Hughan died, and his kids, but those deaths in the family took their toll."

The staff at the radio station had been effusive, eager, and respectful. The DJ wanted to know how Taj had met Mick Jagger, the unconscious implication being that Taj was anointed by the reflected glory of Jagger. The truth is that Jagger is a big fan of Taj's and looks at Taj as being a torchbearer of roots blues. Taj was gracious to the DJ, but in the car he says, "What was that all about? I was there to play and talk the blues, to let people know about the Winston Blues Revival tour, but I didn't see any pictures of blues players displayed on the walls, only rock and pop. No BB King, no Keb' Mo', not even Buddy Guy. Eric Clapton was the only bluesman they had up. I might as well have been at a sanitation engineers' convention. In that situation, it's hard not to get cheeky about music that melts the mind."

That brings him back to a favorite theme: his constantly waving the warning flag that corporate culture is bleaching the colors out of ethnic cultures. "When I came back from Spain, the people in the record companies, who controlled what type of music got national treatment, they wanted only one style of music. They still do. The record executives were saying, 'Here is what the music business is about.' I said, 'Bullshit. Music is about music. Business is about business. Your idea about the music business is not the world's idea of what music is about. You're forcing your idea on people.' I wasn't against marketing music; my point was that, if you could market bullshit, how come you couldn't market good music?

"This was before the record companies got this whole Special Markets thing, which means, ultimately, black music. From about 1969 on, there was a whole movement in the industry to consolidate black music under Warner Brothers, CBS, EMI, Polygram, and Sony. There was this umbrella, with maybe five or six people at the top, whereas before there used to be independent record companies putting out black music all over the place. John Lee Hooker, Muddy Waters, the others – all those years they were out carrying the music through the clubs, on the race records, the major labels weren't putting a big focus on what they were doing. You couldn't find them anywhere, unless you knew where to buy their records. There wasn't really a blues category. Only in the '70s and '80s did the record companies say, 'Okay, let's get this stuff organized.' Then they started re-releasing a lot of the old titles, because of the new CD technology. Then we started hearing a lot more of the old blues.

"It wasn't as simple as putting good music out. There was industry politics and organized crime that went down. The jukeboxes, the beer, the places where music was played... The teamsters and organized crime has always been involved with the music industry. Some bands were clearly connected to organized crime. Their stuff was out there all the time because they had somebody walking their stuff. That *had* to be done.

"The music business has always had some element of organized crime in it, just like the boxing business has it, and lots of others, too. You don't see people going to Las Vegas and getting upset about organized crime. There's not a lot to say about it. I worked in a lot of clubs where organized crime was behind it. I minded my business, came and did my show, got paid, didn't cause no trouble, didn't bring in no riff-raff, and didn't hassle the boss' daughter. Another name for the Mafia is a man looking out for his family, making sure they get fed, making sure they're safe.

"The music business finally hit the wall in the 1970s. The record companies had taken the music away from the composers and innovators, the players and singers, the singer/songwriters. They brought it completely over to the producer/arranger, in an attempt to control the financial end of the business and not to have to deal with the artists.

"Music is about the emotional investment you put into it. The music – especially the older blues – was elusive, like ether or quicksilver. You cannot hold it in your hand. The old blues was elusive, because a lot of the people I knew from the South would not talk to you about it. When I ran into people who did, they seemed like it was magic that had come to them. I was always interested in the way this magic was transferred from generation to generation. I think that is why I bothered a lot of people in the mainstream music industry – 'How did this guy get a hold of this information that wasn't available. What's his trip on it?'

"I wanted a more organic experience between myself and the music, and consequently a more organic experience between myself and the audience. That immediately puts me in conflict with the record industry, which wants a more sterile product approach to music. I'd rather do a lot of work at something I really want to do than work at something I don't like.

"In 1972, I wrote a soundtrack around the movie *Sounder*, and even played the part of Ike, opposite Cicely Tyson and Paul Winfield. We did *Sounder II* about a year later. Except for the one Lightnin' Hopkins tune, 'Jesus Won't You Come By Here,' I wrote all the stuff that was on there. Doing that movie was nice. I spent most of the time playing my music around people who had been in the rural setting that the music had been cast in. To go back and play in rural Louisiana, where things hadn't changed all that much, was very important for me. It was important to have a group of people listen to what I was doing and say what they had to say.

"They weren't shy about saying what they thought. They liked what I did. They heard where the music was, which caused me to relax and play it in a different kind of light. I was oftentimes playing music in a professional light, one which that audience wasn't into, as far as where the music was coming from; but with those people in rural Louisiana, the music came out of their experiences, and those notes meant an awful lot to them.

"While making the movie, the Klan came and tore down the set one time. It was interesting to see these LA people finally get the message that it was serious stuff, not just on TV at night. This was real life.

"After the movie, I recorded *Recycling The Blues And Other Related*

Stuff [1972]. That's all everyone was doing, recycling the blues. Nobody else was saying it. I did. Half the album was live at the Fillmore and the other half in the studio. That was an opportunity for me to bring The Pointer Sisters up front. I heard about them, finally got to meet and hang out with them. Bonnie, June, and Anita, originally. Ruth joined later, then Bonnie left the group in 1978. I thought they were really great, but I could see by the way they were raised, and how I knew the music industry ran, that the sound they naturally came to, that sound would be eventually changed by a record company. Before that happened, I wanted to record with them. Their sound definitely changed as they became popular. They were not about slick when they started.

"We did 'Sweet Home Chicago.' I told the sisters to sing like Basie's horn section. They understood that. They were very bright, they were just not given the opportunity. Well, let me put it this way: they were traditional in their awareness of how to wait until asked. They were not going to hit the dancefloor until the hand came to take them out there. Both their mother and father were Baptist ministers in Oakland. They grew up in a highly steeped religious household. They were very shy, proper girls who were just beginning to stretch their wings and step out there. The whole family was nice.

"I used to take them out to dinner. Oftentimes, I'd come by and hang out and talk with them. They were really interesting, funny people. They were some of the first people that I knew doing all the thrift shops for their clothing. They had kind of a wild look at that time.

"I took the sisters on tour. I took my upright bass and several guitars, banjo, mandolin with me. On the planes, I'd put the bass on the seat next to me, get its own seat. I remember one time we got in the plane from Seattle to Los Angeles. The plane got stuck on the runaway because of air traffic, so me and the sisters told the stewardess that we'd play some music. We were in the first-class cabin, putting on some music. Everybody in second class got mad and called us to come out, so we went back there and played.

"I taught the sisters some things about the music business. I told them that, any time they are in the studio and they come up with the vocal background and put all the stuff together, that is arranging. As group, they get arranging credit and a fee, along with their studio musician time as back-up singers. I brought them up to a lot of stuff in the business so they wouldn't get taken advantage of. If they didn't have a manager who knew what to ask for, they'd lose out. You'd think that other people you're dealing with will tell you what's your rights. No. They will not tell you. That's the music business. The bottom line of the business is, 'Hey, if you don't know, I don't have to tell you.'

"Morris Levy, the head of Roulette Records, had on his desk a plaque that said, 'Send me a talented, ignorant bastard.' That's what the music industry looks for to take advantage of. Morris had a booking agency called Queen. He got every R&B act that went down the road. With him, it was, 'If you want to play, we get a piece.' It wasn't what you did but who you knew.

"I was having some trouble with Columbia about that time. Working with the record companies, it's a goddamn deal, you know? No matter what. Look at the trouble and how long it took for Jimi Hendrix's family to get the rights to his stuff back after he was dead. It took years before his father got royalties and rights owed to the estate. The record companies think they can take advantage of you if you are black or a woman. Elizabeth Taylor said it clearly: 'You don't get paid what you deserve. You get paid what you negotiate.'

"Artists who sign with record companies think that the companies will treat them fair if they have talent, behave themselves, be good, and accept what they're told. Then the record companies will like them because they don't cause trouble. Then everything will work out, based on them being good. It has nothing to do with that. What it has to do with is who's making your business deal for you. At that time, Bill Graham was making my business deals. I had a run-in with Bill Graham. I had to take him to court.

"In 1973, [he] and I got into trouble with each other. Until then, people were getting away with being the booking agents and the management and taking a percent on each. Double-dipping. When I joined Graham, I was trying to come from the optimistic, positive place. I didn't have an attitude that this guy was going to do me wrong. I hoped this deal was on a straight and even keel. Well, that's extremely naïve. Music is a cutthroat business. If management or the record executives had to cut their own mom's throats, they would. That is what their business is about. It doesn't have anything to do with you, personally.

"When Samuel became my manager, that immediately created some steam between me and Graham Management. Like, why did I want some personal management beyond what they could offer me? I was very frank

Taj and Jessie "Ed" Davis of The Taj Mahal Band at the Newport Jazz Festival in 1968

Taj Jr, Ghamela and Aya

Taj while he was living in the Bay Area of San Francisco

A rare picture of Connie and Eddie together while they were working with Taj, still new in California

The cover of Taj's album *Music Keeps Me Together*, designed by Winston and painted by Hughan. Hughan had to paint several pictures, as the name of the album continued to change

Taj in the mid 1970s in the
Bay Area of San Francisco

The twins Taj Jr and Ghamela, taken when they were around four years old

Mildred Fredericks-Williams, after featuring as a guest soloist

Mildred and Hughan at a family birthday party

Inshirah

Taj in the mid 1970s fishing at the
Fairlawns in San Francisco Bay

Inshirah in college at the time that she met Taj

At home in Hawaii. L-r: Deva, Taj,
Ahmen and Inshirah

Inshirah with the twins Zoe (left) and
Sachi (right)

Nani, Deva and Taj in Hawaii

Taj and family performing in Hawaii. L-r: Deva, Taj, Ahmen and Inshirah

Deva, Taj and Nani celebrating a birthday

Taj and daughter Nani on the beach in Hawaii

Taj and Inshira, taken at their wedding

with them. I saw that it was very easy for me to be handled as a black artist within the framework of a larger, so-called popular – read 'white' – slick scene, whereby anything personal or cultural somehow doesn't come up on their roster of priorities. I'd watched a lot of black artists develop themselves, get a hit, and then disappear for the rest of their career.

"I watched a lot of artists become so separate from their source that whatever they were doing was not feeding into their own culture. In other words, nobody was taking anything back home. There wasn't anything being shared, very much like the situation with OJ Simpson. Until he really needed the black community, he wasn't paying a whole lot of attention to it or trying to put something back.

"The Graham people said we could have any agency we wanted, but recommended the Millard Agency, which was in the same building as Graham. Samuel and I asked the Graham organization flat out if Graham was connected to the Millard Agency. Graham's people said there was no connection. 'Oh, no no no. Millard is just in the same building.' Okay, fine.

"Samuel and I said, 'We'll think about it.' We talked about it for a long time. I said, 'Well, don't be so ready to see the negative,' so we decided to go with Millard. It turned out that Millard was part of the Graham organization. Instead of ten percent going to Millard and Graham getting a separate 15 percent, actually 25 percent was going to Graham.

"We had been with the Millard/Graham outfit one or two years when Samuel found out about the connection. The following Monday, I came in as usual to the office in the same building as Graham and Millard. I didn't have my key. I went and got a key from Graham's office. Graham walked down to the office with me. We stepped into an empty office. Samuel had cleaned it out over the weekend. Graham went ballistic. He couldn't believe it. That was a direct hit. I had no idea Samuel was going to do that. At that point, things went south between us and Graham and stayed that way through the whole deal of going to court.

"When it came down to the court case, Graham was represented by a black lawyer, Cecil Poole [now a federal judge], who was the brother of Elijah Muhammad, the founder of the Black Muslims. Muhammad's given name was Elijah Poole until he changed it to the Muslim name. We knew then that this was serious warfare, major warfare. I was determined that Graham was not going to win. He was not going to threaten me. Seeing Poole would have thrown a lot of guys off keel. Holy shit! The man got paid very well. He was a legitimate lawyer. Graham was his client. I decided, 'Bill, you really don't know what the game is.'

"We had three young boys out of Berkeley law school. These cats were voracious. There wasn't a river full of piranhas that was more ready than those guys. We had to constantly tell them to please sit down, that they couldn't climb across the table at Graham. Because of their aggressiveness, our youth, and the fact that we did have the right stuff going for us, we won.

"For years, Graham and I were not friendly. If somebody asks me what went down, I just tell the facts. Graham never directly threatened to ruin me in the music business, but I didn't need to be told that someone is out to ruin me when they are. I knew he was powerful enough to slow things down for me. It was pretty clear that he was definitely going to put some energy out there that would be difficult to deal with. There were no two ways about that.

"The dust-up with Graham didn't affect the amount of work I could get, but it affected my movement upward. Over the years, I had been making progress upward, but there seemed to be – especially in the '70s and the top of the '80s – a glass ceiling for me. I could see through it above, but I never got up there. I felt – real or imagined – the pressure of being clamped down. The basic deal was that I had been out there for years and years, listening to people in management who had bullshitted and lied to me in as many ways as possible.

"I stayed out of harmony with Graham for a long, long period of time. He was upset because he was double-dipping into my income and got caught. It wasn't until a couple of years before he left this planet that we reconnected. I figured that time had been long enough. My point was that he knew where I was coming from and that I didn't fuck him over."

Bill Graham died in 1990, at the age of 61, when the helicopter in which he was riding to leave an outdoor concert hit a high-power electricity line and crashed. As with Taj, the impression that the promoter left with Samuel is an ultimately positive one. "I remember Bill Graham favorably, I really, honestly do," he insists. "And not just since his death but prior to, also, although I never got a chance to express it to the man. I was on the road with my brother all the time, listening to him about what is not happening with his career. He wants to do more this, more that, and Bill's not doing this, not doing that. We're going back and forth this way. Management! I had a sense of the natural rift that occurs between entertainers and management.

"Bill exerted a lot of influence. Taj wanted to do more in different areas. One of the things Graham tried to do to appease Taj was get him a spot on *The Jerri Lange Show*. She was Ted Lange's mother, who was on *Love Boat*. Graham did some good managerial things. He got Taj on *The Flip Wilson Show*.

"But Graham was wearing a ton of hats – Bill Graham the promoter, Bill Graham the manager, Bill Graham the entrepreneur. As the entrepreneur, the booking agency and David Rubinson, the producer, were really all his. For some time, Taj and I suspected what was happening with double-dipping us. We discussed it with the attorneys. They actually did the real sniffing and figured out the angle. My mind doesn't work that way. After repeated meetings with Graham to get things changed, in terms of making Taj happier, we decided the best thing was to go on our own, but I was very, very, *very* hesitant about that. I didn't like it. I knew that there was so much that I didn't know about the industry.

"But we had some bottom-line disappointment with what was happening. When we found out what was going on, I didn't go to Graham. I didn't know how to confront him straight on with that. I didn't even talk the language that they talk. I just went after the artillery, the lawyers. That's how I was, then. If I had a real beef with a relative, we'd probably end up in court, because I won't directly confront that person.

"In the fall of 1972, we left Bill Graham's office and moved into our own space over in the East Bay, 3990 Telegraph Avenue, in Oakland. Graham didn't like the move. He didn't have a lot of dialogue with me around it. Graham might have thought that I wanted the power, since Taj was my brother, but I can tell you straight inside that was not what I wanted. I didn't want that whole cookie. I have enough of an analytical mind to know that I was in over my head. But I felt that was the only way to save Taj. Therein, again, is my Achilles heel – to save people in my family. That's how I ended up in management.

"We had meetings with Graham. This had been going on throughout 1972. Finally, Taj brought a lawsuit against Graham. The law firm Sanders & Tooks took our case. They were a very good, aggressive law firm, so felt that their job was to go after a high-profile situation and make a name. [The] time was right for a young, aggressive, positive, black law firm in the entertainment world. They were making their bones, making a name.

"They had a roster of entertainers, so knew their way around the business. These attorneys tipped us that royalties were owed Taj by Graham. The attorneys saw that there was a conflict of interest, and went after Graham because he managed the artist, but he also had controlling interest, or major interest, in the booking agency and in the production firm."

One of the attorneys, Lloyd Edward Tooks – now practising in San Diego – put the case in its legal perspective: "Graham represented Taj as his manager. In California, you have to be licensed as an artist's manager. Graham was not licensed in California as an artist's manager. The case was settled before it went to court."

Looking back on the experience, Taj says, "Winning that lawsuit had its consequences. Graham, being as powerful as he was in the business, was able to shut down a lot for me. I took a career hit. A *hard* hit. It wasn't subtle at all. If Graham was involved with a concert or show, I didn't work it. He kept me out of some big concerts, nationally; kept me from graduating up to a certain level; but he couldn't stop me from performing at folk festivals, in clubs, or recording. I started playing outside the country a lot – Australia, New Zealand, Fiji Islands, South America, Africa, Europe."

The problems of moving up to the next level weren't just caused by Graham. "For whatever reason," Taj continues, "I was not being heard in this country, because I wasn't coming through the beacon of the record companies/music business. I wasn't getting help from the record companies to see that my records got distribution, promotion, publicity. These are hardcore things. Looking back on it, what did I expect, a black musician out there? The record companies weren't used to treating black musicians, or other ethnic minorities, or women, in any way, shape or form other than what they wanted to, anyway.

"The public hears artists when the record companies are ripping the artists off, or when the artists are well protected. You hear Whitney Houston because she had Clive Davis and Arista Records, and she is selling a lot of records. She's got a protected situation. They ripped Tom Petty, of The Heartbreakers, after his first record that sold a lot. It took him time to get his bearings, reconstruct his program so people were looking out for him, and now he does well.

"You can't stop me from working, but you can certainly stop me from graduating up to *Rolling Stone*, Eric Clapton, the major national or international status. I'd go overseas and would be instantly put in the national celebrity spot.

"Around 1974-75, I wanted to play out ideas in my head for music that was more adventurous. A year before, I did a studio album – *Oooh So Good 'n Blues* – of things I wanted to record acoustically. My musical development was always going on. None of this was a sudden enthusiasm; these were ideas that I constantly, every day, thought about. It was all part of the energy that I brought back from Spain. Whenever I heard an idea, [I'd] go with it.

"I started to find different musicians I wanted to play with to form a band. I was looking for a solid niche to get into and just write. I wanted to be more like older bands, like Basie's or Ellington's, in solidly writing for the band you had. The real deal is that I'm a composer. Furthermore, I hear things coming in from the universe, whether in the form of light or sound waves or energy or color. I think everybody hears like that. If they don't, they have the ability to hear like that. I'm very happy that I make music, but I can't take that currency anywhere. That is the great architecture of the spirit world working through me. I can't take credit for that. I'm just lucky that I was able to get the hell out of my own way for the spirit to happen.

"So, I got busy putting The Intergalactic Soul Messengers together: Bill Rich on bass; Hoshal Wright, a really good guitar player; Kester Smith on drums; Kwasi Dzidzornu on percussions and congas; Larry 'Mongoose' McDonald on percussion; Rudy – Rudolph – Beacher Costa III as flautist and alto sax; Robert Greenidge on steel drums; and Ray Fitzpatrick on bass. We had a band that had a unique sound.

"I go back and listen to the album we made, *Music Keeps Me Together*, and I'm so glad that I recorded that music with that band. I'd go nuts having that music in my head and not be able to hear it in the world, or have anybody hear it. It allowed me to go onto the next level. I recorded *Music Fuh Yuh* in 1975. The next album, *Satisfied 'n' Tickled Too*, the next year, will always be, for me, one that was more than I wanted to do. There was tremendous pressure for us to get a commercial hit.

"The pressure was the record executives saying, 'We want a more contemporary feel, something that will get air play, something in the popular direction.' That was the end of the Columbia scene. I went over to Warner. At Warner, I did the soundtrack for the movie *Brothers* [1977]. That was a wonderful experience. It was put out by Ed and Mildred Lewis, who were involved with progressive, radical movies. The movie was about

George Jackson, the Black Panther, and Angela Davis, the radical black professor at UCLA. It is a love story between Jackson and Angela. The movie was controversial, because it expressed what was happening with the law enforcement and blacks at the time. The movie – released by Warner Brothers – got local, in-the-hood showings, but not national.

"This was a more settled time. We were working around the Bay area. Did a show with the Oakland Pop Symphony. But we were hitting the wall with Warner Brothers. They just didn't know what to do with the music, or how to market it."

Taj's current management company is Bill Graham Management.

17 *Mahal Meets Marley*

"My job is to link the past and the present," Taj says as we circle a block in downtown Berkeley in a borrowed Ford Taurus. He is looking for a parking place near the cigar store that carries the Matcan Maduro (band size 54, the big, fat ones) that he favors. "The past is very much here in our present – very present, in a lot of my songs. Not only in my songs but in the form and style of the blues and of jazz."

We circle the block four times, five times, past the cigar store, the newsstand, the coffeehouse, and the fruit store, with its open front spilling mounds of yellow, orange, and red onto the sidewalk. As we circle and circle, looking for an empty parking slot, Taj tells the story of how he met Bob Marley and The Wailers, a story about acknowledging the music of his ancestors. Taj is credited as the person who introduced reggae to mainstream United States.

"Sly Stone kicked Bob and The Wailers off his tour back in 1974. I couldn't believe it when I found out. *What?* That was crazy! Are you *serious?* Marley was starting to pull some interesting energy, and I think Sly was getting a little nervous, like, 'I'm the star here,' but his spotlight was starting to shine on Bob. So, Bob and his band were languishing around San Francisco with noplace to stay, no money, no gig, hanging wherever somebody could give them space.

"When I got wind of it, through other musicians, I sent my brother Samuel – who was my manager at the time – to round them up. We put them up in a motel on University Avenue in Berkeley. I had never met Bob, but I knew about him. Every now and then, over the years, some things popped in from the Caribbean, like a whole subterranean music scene that the mainstream didn't recognize, even though the people playing the music were stars. Bob was one of those stars, but the mainstream suits didn't see any money in it, so they didn't pay any attention. If there was anything I could share while The Wailers were going through that particular period, I would. Reggae is just Caribbean blues. It's music of the people and of the land, just like blues. The basic simplicity of the music is similar, and so are a lot of the scales, so I heard the blues in reggae.

"The first time I heard Marley and The Wailers was through the mail. One day in 1973, I came home from a tour and on the porch was a big stack of mail, the way the mailman always put it. In the stack was a package with an unfamiliar return address in England. No note inside, just the album *Catch A Fire*.

"I put the record on. My first reaction was, 'Too much bass.' Not too much for me, but too much for the record companies to put this on the radio. That bass was so authoritative. The energy was rebellious. It pushed through and scared the living shit out those record people. I realized that the record-company people would actively discourage this type of music, but I knew that, when I got ready to do a Caribbean-based album, I wanted Marley's input.

"After Marley and his band got settled into their motel digs, I drove down to visit. He and the band were playing soccer in the motel's courtyard. We shook hands. His touch was soft, but he was strong, a wiry guy. 'Hey, man, glad to meet you. I've been wanting to do some music with you.' Marley says, 'No problem, mon,' in his very sharp, gratey voice, that cut right across. He had an at-ease way about how he moved, but I recognized that Bob was always at a peaked energy. This man had things to do. He was not somebody who was a jokester or a trickster; Bob was a thinking person, a person very close to the ground, a real person, in terms of informing people of some alternatives to the way things are set up. And the other guys in his band had a natural reserve you find among Caribbean people, especially land people, who have respect for the work – like growing food – that makes something happen.

"Later, Samuel loads them into his old '68 blue Volvo and drives them up to my house on Tilden, in the hills above Berkeley. He and the guys came in, polite and friendly, and looked around at all the equipment – speakers, amps, guitars, all sorts of instruments – laying around the living room. I saw a bit of reserve go up in their eyes. I was a *have* in the Caribbean society, according to the amount of stuff I had. In the Caribbean, the *haves* make the *have nots* feel real bad. Bob saw that, with me, it didn't have to be about all that class attitude or color bar or wealth attitude. To him, it was pretty clear that I was genuine, and I really enjoyed what I saw of him.

"At the time, Marley was dealing with the issue that, as an artist, he shouldn't be making money. You know that trap: 'If I'm making money, that means I'm really pandering to the system.' Bob was dealing a whole lot with the social significance of coming by any kind of wealth by your art – 'Am I betraying the people in the slums of Kingston's Trench Town, the oppressed people my music champions? Am I betraying them by having a nice house up in the Blue Mountains?'

"When he came by me, he saw that you could be an artist and you could deal with money. Later, he said that's when the whole thing changed for him in Jamaica. He realized that he didn't have to give up his personal values to deal with material wealth. The wealth doesn't create who you are. It's the other things you have – the personal honesty and integrity – that is your wealth.

"We slipped right in with each other, talking music, musicians, politics. People with their brains on straight, that's usually what happens. Nobody put on airs or anything like that. Everybody was glad to be who they were, where they were. I felt that I was allied with Marley through the Caribbean connection in my own heritage. My grandfather and grandmother were from St Kitts. My stepfather is Jamaican, so I felt at home with them.

"Marley and his guys came up for dinner all that week. My sister Carole – who was living at the Tilden house then – fixed beans and Ambrosia. Inshirah cooked fish. We'd get loose with a little wine and smoke and do justice to the food. There was a lot of laughing, but not slap-happy humor. Bob took notice of the full-body acupuncture chart I had on the wall.

"After dinner, we'd go into the living room for impromptu jam sessions. I had a big bass sitting in the corner, a piano, guitars, lots of things to make music with. It was pretty spirited, a charged situation. Bob picked up on whatever I was doing. He was like the lightbulb of the universe. Whatever was flowing through, he put the light on it. We'd be up all night jamming away and the neighbors didn't seem to mind. Nobody called the cops, anyway.

"Bob wrote and wrote and wrote the whole time we were together. The Wailers' song 'Talkin' Blues' came out of those sessions. I watched that song 'I'm A Do You' – which is about me – come up in my own living room. At the time, I was mixing 'Slave Driver' – which Bob had written – on my *Mo' Roots* album at Studio B down on Fulsom in Berkeley. Bob and all the people with him – Skill [Alan Cole], Family Man [Aston Barrett], Wire [Earl Lindo] – came down and listened in to what we were doing. They'd go right to the mixing board and make suggestions how to make things different. Family Man – the bass player, the quiet one – donated a lot. He said to put more treble on the bass. He also played ska piano on the song to give it that offbeat deal.

"They were incredible musicians, very focused with the music. I got Wire, Bob's keyboard player, on my next album. He played with my band Intergalactic Soul Messengers for two years. He was a very, very inspirational person in the band for stretching out the chords and possibilities, in terms of arrangements. He was an incredible arranger.

"'Slave Driver' is a Bob Marley And The Wailers song. Jamaicans speak straight to the situation – they don't bite their tongues like Americans do. The song speaks out straight: 'Say it loud, I'm black and I'm proud/Slave driver, the tables are turning.' Anybody with any consciousness from the Afro-American theater understands this particular song, but it goes beyond that; it talks about somebody who's dealing with everybody. To me, when I was a youngster, it seemed like things were pretty well set, as how the society was run, and then it seemed like the tables started turning. I came through the '60s – that turned the tables. Now we're at a place where the tables have turned.

"Plus, on 'Slave Driver,' there are all these voices that are in me. They are voices that I grew up with and dialects that I speak. And also, for me, it was a praise song to Bob and The Wailers and that music for sustaining me so long and bringing me to a real positive point.

"That song completely freaked out Columbia Records. They looked at it as if I was ready to go into some pro-African, against-the-United-States kind of weirdness. The suits just didn't know what to do. 'How do we market this?' they asked. I said, 'This is just the truth. How come you can't take the truth coming from the people you step on?'

"That's how Marley felt, too. I could feel how his mind worked. If he thought something, he did it. It wasn't about what everybody else thought. His songs were about what he saw and the way he saw it. I felt that I had an ally in that. I found more strength in musicians from out of the country than I did with those in this country, who tended to be a little bit more worried about making a living and the heavy competition for record companies' favors. I didn't get that feel with Marley. He did what he did.

"After a week, Marley got it arranged to go back to Jamaica. Later, I sent a studio tape of *Mo' Roots* down to Bob. Then my brother Samuel went to Jamaica to make contact."

After the tenth circuit around the block, Taj parks in a loading zone. We walk around the corner to the cigar store. No one recognizes him, or at least gives any sign that a famous musician is standing next to them. In the cigar store, Taj is very knowledgeable about the provenance and quality of the cigars, in much the manner of a wine connoisseur. After buying a handful of cigars, he drives the few miles to Oakland, where Samuel's art gallery is located. As we walk in, Taj says, "I was just telling about you going to Jamaica to meet up with Marley."

Samuel is a soft-spoken, slender man with an attitude of great gentleness, patience, and fortitude. On looking at him, it's difficult to see that he's the brother of the tall, completely bald, barrel-chested man standing next to him. Samuel looks like a falcon alongside Taj's bald eagle. "It was one of the greatest and most terrifying experiences of my life," he replies with a warm smile. Then he tells the story.

"I stayed with the niece of our stepfather, Hughan. Family Man and Skill picked me up and we drove up into the Blue Mountains, where Bob lived. It was pitch black on that little switchback road, where sometimes two cars couldn't squeeze past each other. When they came around a curve, they'd blast the horn and flick the lights to warn whoever might be coming the other way.

"We get to the house and walk out onto the porch – nothing but black space out in front and the lights of Kingston way down below. There's Bob and all his other brothers, listening to the tape of Taj singing 'Johnny Too Bad.' Bob rolled a spliff and passed it. Everybody just really got into the music, enjoying the mountain air, just cooling out. After about a half an hour, a guy comes out of the back of the house with a glass of freshly-grated carrot juice with nutmeg in it and gives it to me. That was magical, because at that point I realized that I was accepted on their turf, that it was all right.

"We all kicked back for hours, chillin'. Pitch-black mountains, summer night. About three in the morning, Family Man and Skill drive me back down. We got caught in a roadblock. A 3am Jamaican roadblock is *real*, brother. If you're going to hire some people for serious stuff, you hire Jamaicans. Right. It was cops looking for dope or whatever else they could find. They ordered everybody out of the car and went through it like greyhounds after a rabbit.

"The cops looked through everything. I mean *everything*. I was carrying a leather satchel Taj had given me, and the cops did everything but cut the seams open. Family Man and Skill were arguing and explaining who they were, who I was, but cops are cops. They growled back. It didn't matter that Family Man and Skill were with Marley, or that Skill was well known in his own right as a professional soccer player down there. He was a star at the time, but he was also a true Rasta brother, so he got no slack. Those cops took the whole thing apart, but they didn't find anything, not even a roach. Still, being on that dark road with those cops was the scariest time I've ever had."

Taj smiles at the telling, and then turns somber. "We never got together with Bob again after Samuel's trip. I always wanted to collaborate on something with him, but we never seemed to be able to get to that before he died. He was a great writer and a wonderful poet. He was an incredible musician and a wonderful man. There's no two ways about it."

18 African Tour

In 1979, Taj and The International Rhythm Band (known as IRB) went on a West African tour, sponsored by the US State Department. "This went back to my father wanting to go back to Africa for a while to re-season our roots, to reconnect," says Taj. "For me, the final thing was wanting to reconnect. That tour was a big connection for me, a big circle coming back together, but still there was some part of this thing that was not correct. I had learned all these different styles of music – which was part of a huge fabric, here in the United States – but only on a couple of different occasions had I been able to get together one on one or two on one with African musicians directly with the stringed music that I was playing. On this tour, I wanted to play more with the local musicians, and we did that, but still I knew that I didn't completely lock in."

The tour held adventures other than musical ones. The band crossed from Zaire to Zambia during a border war involving Zambia, Zimbabwe, and South Africa. Half of the band's instruments were lost on the way to Kitwe, a copper-mining town near the Zambian border, where people had filled the auditorium hours before the band was to appear. Anticipation ran high. Every stop on the tour had been sold out. At outdoor venues, people hung off trees to get a better vantage point. Given all the gun smuggling, armed skirmishes, and border infiltration happening in the area, the tension was heightened that much more, so the promoter didn't want to disappoint the crowd. So, the band shows up, but with only a few instruments – some percussion, one steel drum, a couple horns. No bass, no traps set."

Taj's brother Richard, aka Seabreeze, was the sound man on the tour. "Taj didn't even have his guitars. What can they do? The promoter pleads, 'Oh, please, Taj. We beg you to play. We've been waiting so *long*.' Taj says, 'What can I do? We don't have any instruments.'

"Promoters, no matter who or where in the world, have only one thing on their minds: money. If the show doesn't go on, they lose money. So this promoter sends people to all the high schools and local musicians to round up whatever instruments for the band to play. They bring back this motley collection and say, 'Taj, please come see if you can play this stuff.' It was pitiful. Taj, being a trooper, says, 'All right, but if you guys [the band] say you can't do it, we won't do it.'

"Now, the band members, they're top-flight guys. Robert Greenidge, a famous steel drummer from Trinidad, who now plays with Jimmy Buffet; Bill Rich, bass; Rudolph 'Rudy' Beacher Costa III, soprano sax; Juma Santos, percussion; Kester Smith, percussion. Laurence 'Dr Che' Barksdale was the road manager. They look over the instruments to see what might work. 'Yeah, okay, maybe. Let's give it a shot.'

"They're pros, and maybe some sort of spirit came over them because of Taj's insistence, or because he took it in his stride like that. They go out onstage still trying to get the feel of the instruments. The people, they've been waiting for hours and were ready, *more* than ready, for the music. The band was down to basics, as far as what they had to play on, so the only way to pull it off was to get inside the musical vibe. They found that little niche where they could make the pitiful collection of musical instruments sound decent, and they nailed it. People loved it. It was a raging success.

"After the concert, the band takes a motorcoach from Kitwe to Ndola, about 20 miles. It was nighttime. Now, remember, there's a wartime mentality in the air. We get through a couple of checkpoints without trouble. At the third checkpoint, there was a long delay. We're not worried – we're Americans, no problem – but some of the local girls and men were on the coach with us. A soldier, who had been smoking or drinking, came on the bus to check identifications. His eyes were glazed over and he looked very angry. He looked like he wanted a reason to shoot someone. Everybody is starting to take this seriously and getting frightened. The more fright shows, the more this guy's vibe gets stronger and uglier. I recognized the mode from Vietnam, where I was in the air force.

"This guy gets back to the Africans in the bus. They don't have identifications. He says, 'I could shoot you now.' He pulled his revolver out and walked around like a terrorist. I decided that, if he started shooting, I was going to impale him with the umbrella I had. I was not going out like a pig in a slaughterhouse. He says, 'Give me a cigarette.' I said, 'Here, sir, have a cigarette.' I looked him in the eyes. I didn't look threatening at him, but [gave him] a look that said, 'I'm not afraid. I don't like this, but I'm not afraid of you.' I gave him a couple cigarettes for his friends. He says to the Africans, 'Next time I catch you, I shoot you. Now get out of here.' When you're on tour, you never know."

Everybody in the band has stories from that tour. For Kester Smith, the percussion player, music was the story. He recalls walking down the road in Kitwe and there were "two kids playing these things that looked like a bow and arrow, a one-string instrument, plucking on that simple instrument. And how they were using their voices was so nice to hear that I wanted Taj to hear, so I walk the two boys to the hotel and take them up to the room. I called in Taj, Rudy, guys in the band: 'Come on, check these two kids out.' Those kids, how they used their voices, blew everybody's minds. I found out that those two boys lived about 50 miles away in some small town and came to the city to sing and make some money.

"What blew my mind on the West African tour was hearing music that was almost like Cuban-Latin music." Kester was born in Grenada but grew up in Trinidad. "The calypso and Latin music has an African background. That's why the instrumentation of our band was interesting to the Africans. Taj with his blues, us West Indian guys, we had a mixture of a lot of African music roots. That was a big attraction. We did some workshops with African musicians. Growing up in Trinidad, I heard a lot of African-based music, so when I heard the music in Africa, I said, 'Oh, *that's* what it is.' I identified with it. The environment, the dancing going with the music – then it all made sense. Everybody was high on the experience of that tour. I always count it as one of my musical highlights."

"In Africa, we'd hear what musicians there are doing and incorporate it into our music," says Bill Rich, bass player with The IRB, who has played with Taj over many years on various projects. "It's just like telling stories – a little African, a little old-time blues. Incorporating the different themes into one musical story is what makes Taj. He's a storyteller.

"You have to be a little tasteful in what you do to make all the different music work. Taj has that. He's very tasteful about that. He had that tastefulness from the start, and then he'd listen to a lot of stuff I normally wouldn't listen to. I'd say, 'Why's he listening to that? What's he doing?' The more you get around different music, the more you keep your mind open, then you take it all in. Taj turned me on to that. Then I realized it keeps your mind open and your music more fresh.

"When working with Taj, you try to play the music the way it is. You don't want to add too much to take it out of character. I learned from Taj when to hold back, when to play the right thing. It's not how many notes you can play; it's how you play it and make the whole, overall. I learned from him how to lay back and to play it how it should be played, to play the right thing, to approach it in the right way.

"You play music the right way, have an idea how it should be done and how to do it, and then come up with an original type of music, making it different but keeping it in the same vein, where it should be. Taj stays to the authentic roots of the music and creates on top of that. That's a special talent, too. A lot of players play a certain type of music. They don't want to open up their mind. If it's not jazz or R&B, or whatever their thing is, they don't want to play it.

"Taj is a good guy. I respect him. There's something innately decent about the man. He's not any kind of saint. We've had our disagreements along the way. You be around anybody long enough – especially with the stress of touring – and that's bound to happen. When it happens, you just sit down and talk about it, yell at each other and get it over with, get it out of the way, and that's it, and keep on going. We've had a lot of those. He's spoken his mind and I've spoken my mind and we've made it through there. We're still tight, good friends. He doesn't hold grudges. He respects you and you respect him."

After Africa, The IRB went on tour to Australia and Fiji. "Our music made an impression down there," recalls Kester Smith. "We were playing a lot of calypso and reggae, which wasn't so popular down there at that time. Our band was one of the first to play reggae in the US. We took reggae to the colleges before it broke out big time, and we took it to Australia. Taj had this combination of musicians playing blues and reggae and calypso. It was different than anything else going on. To me, at the time, the blues represented the American original music. Calypso was the original music of the West Indies. Basically, that was a common ground the band hooked into.

"The blues and calypso share a lot of minor chord changes. The basic minor chords and the basic chord changes are similar, but you do different interpretations. Rhythmically they are different, but the changes are almost the same. Now, when I listen back to the old calypso, I can hear the blues in it. And calypso, like the blues, comes from an oppressed people. They line up the same way. It's basically the same background.

"In Australia, an Aboriginal band called No Fixed Address opened for us quite a few times. They played American music, but you could hear it wasn't that authentic. They also played their own music. I could relate to it in the sense that I could recognize the similarities to calypso, like chord changes. They picked up on Taj's blues. A lot of the bands and people could relate to Taj. He has a good, sincere way of putting over the music."

(On a previous Australian tour, Taj was shocked that no Aboriginal band was on the bill. "So I asked the promoter, 'Aren't there any Aboriginal bands that can open for us?' I clearly didn't realize that I was treading in some weird place. The guy says, 'Well, the Abos don't play any music.' I said, 'Black people? They don't play music? Who are you joking?' On the second Australian tour, a totally Aboriginal band, No Fixed Address, opened for us.")

"Basically, Taj is a blues player," Kester continues. "He understands the basic tradition or interpretation of music. If you got the blues down, it seems that everybody can recognize a portion of it. Taj to me is a spokesperson for that music. Every place I went with him, everybody was hypnotized by him. I never heard the raw blues, like Howlin' Wolf and BB King, until I was with Taj. Taj turned me on to the blues, which I can play now. He exposed me to musical stuff I wasn't aware of. I learned the structure of the blues from Taj. My head was in a Latin music space, and he opened that space more. When you hear the music from Taj, you finally hear it right. That's what makes him Taj Mahal. He has that inner thing. He's smart. His head is always open. He makes the music fit, and it becomes him. He understands what the music is, and it becomes his. He sings to the very basic human spirit. He knows how to get right to it.

"He always thinks about the music. From him, I learned the simplicity in music. I learned that the simpler you play, the sweeter it gets. He's got that. Taj helped me recognize where certain riffs and sounds come from, because he knows those roots in the blues. As soon as musicians – and the music – get real sweet, I don't care what kind of music it is; they end up playing the blues. Whatever they're doing, when it really gets good, it turns around to be the blues. The blues take over without anybody trying to do that.

"Taj is no big instrumentalist, but he gets the real music out of his instrument. It's not how many notes you can play; it's playing the right ones at the right time. Taj does that, and he gets more. He makes music. He's for real. You can't miss it. He can play a bad note and make that bad note make sense. There is no mistake with him. When he stumbles, he makes it roll, musically."

While with The IRB, Taj started playing more solo dates in order to support him and the band, financially. He'd left Warner Brothers and didn't have a record contract, and so to keep the cashflow flowing he'd go out for two weeks with the band and then go out for a week solo to make up the money he was losing by keeping the band together. Then he'd take a week off and start the cycle again.

Gradually, he cut back on the band dates and performed more solo concerts. By 1982, he was basically doing solo shows. During the '80s, he put out four albums: *The Best Of Taj Mahal, Volume One* (1981); *Taj* (1986); *Shake Sugaree* (1987); *Live And Direct* (1987); and *Big Blues* (1988), a live album recorded at Ronnie Scott's London jazz club.

"For most of the '80s, we were on the road and didn't have time to record," explains Carey Williams, Taj's tour manager. "We were doing five, six nights a week, two shows a night. It started becoming a grind for Taj. There were times when he didn't want to be on the road. He was going from place to place and not knowing where he was, really, because he was so depressed about touring so much. He had moved to Hawaii, so he had to fly back and forth to the mainland a lot.

"That was a hard personal time for Taj, too. His brother, Hughan, passed away. A lot of things were changing in his life. It was a rudderless time, in terms of recording, in terms of his career and the maintenance of his career. There weren't any career options for him. The '80s were weird, musically, anyway. It was more a dance, disco thing. He was getting older and beginning to wonder what his legacy in the music business was going to be."

A review of Taj's *Live And Direct* album in the March 6, 1980 issue of *Rolling Stone* magazine pronounced, "Taj Mahal made music that was a wonderful amalgam of Afro-American forms. At his worst, he's sometimes been an unconvincing ethnomusicological noodler... Taj Mahal has become the George Plimpton of pop, skimming through all his far-flung global-musical fantasies, never really going anywhere."

Taj agrees that the '80s were an off time for him. "People thought I had disappeared here, because the record companies weren't putting me out, but the magazine never went with me to South America, Europe, Africa, Fiji, Australia, and the Caribbean. The record companies had successfully figured out how to shut me down. I was no longer on a major record label.

The music industry is pretty much organized that you make a record, go out on tour around the record, then you're off the road. Then you make another record, and the cycle starts again. I was out touring on my own, in demand all the time in clubs, on campuses, whatever. So, as much as they thought they had shut me down, the record companies actually created this incredible situation where people wanted to hear me, since my music wasn't available on the radio or at big concerts. For many musicians, touring was associated with having product out. My touring was associated with my being an artist. My music was a re-affirmation of the individual."

19 *Treat Street*

Thanksgiving Day on the road, 1998. We take a ferry to Vashon Island, a 20-minute ride across Puget Sound from Seattle, where some of the West Coast Carlton branch of Taj's extended family live. Siena Riffia – the mother of Taj's 28-year-old twins, Ghamela and Taj Jr – is a Carlton. 27 people – family, neighbors, friends – mill about the open, airy kitchen-cum-living room, helping themselves to ham, turkey, mashed potatoes, spiced yams, six kinds of pie, five kinds of wine, and Haitian rum.

Taj explains his recipe for Thanksgiving turkey. Get a propane burner and a 20-gallon turkey cooker. Let the turkey thaw. Inject spices directly into the meat with an injector. The Jamaican jerk sauce Walker Woods is really good. (Taj also makes his own sauce, sure to perk up the tongue.) After injecting the spices, put the turkey back in the fridge to chill. Do not freeze. Pour five gallons of peanut oil into the turkey cooker and bring the oil to hot. Put in the turkey for 45 minutes. Then eat it.

After dinner, the tables are cleared and instruments come out: an upright bass, hand drums, a tambourine, and all sorts of things metal and wood upon which to pound out a rhythm. A neighbor, David Link, puts together his sax, which he plays professionally. A flute appears. Taj has brought the guitar that he plays onstage. Its case is battered, flaking, the stickers peeling off, the handle a thick twist of blue tape. Inside is his full-bodied National Dobro, which he depends on for more than making money; it's his emotional voice, his plaything, his intellectual stimulus, his partner in creativity. The guitar case can be seen as a metaphor for Taj's life and music: the real value is inside, no matter how the outside appears.

Wearing a dark-blue sweatshirt, Taj starts a song, his foot tapping out the beat while Siena's younger brother, Dick Carlton, plunks on the bass. Taj's 20-year-old son, Ahmen, picks up the beat on a hand drum. Siena shakes the tambourine and starts dancing in her stockinged feet. Others bong on marimba, clack sticks, and ping bells. The whole room becomes a jangle of music at cross-currents that mysteriously drift into sync and flow together tunefully. Bent over his guitar, Taj is just as intense as he is onstage, but he treats the amateurs with respect, calling out chord changes and bridges so that they can follow the song. The music stays in the groove, even when Taj launches into a polka rhythm and then slips into jazz, before ending in a calypso which leads him into 'Coconut Man,' from his *Sacred Island* CD. He closes his eyes and goes into the zone of music he often finds during a performance. Everyone sings the chorus: "Aya yai, aya yai, listen to me talking about the Hawaiian man."

All evening, music flows, stops, flows again – hands clapping, rattles shaking, sticks-on-sticks clicking – a conversation that words alone can't hold. At the end of one jam, Taj shakes the other players' hands with real sincerity and enthusiasm. He's having a good time. Music is music is brotherhood. A woman's wig is passed around as a party joke. Ahmen puts it on and goes from handsome to beautiful. He sashays around the room, doing a dead-on imitation of Flip Wilson's Geraldine – "You can see the traces of tears on my cheeks," he lisps. His pinkie draws an imaginary tear down his cheek. His sister, Ghamela, rolls on the floor in laughter.

Taj steps outside with Howard Koenig, our host, and his brother, Jim, Siena's brother-in-law. Taj passes around big, thick, Cuban cigars. They stand in the dark chill, puffing, balancing long ashes on the glowing tips, admiring the stars. Taj tells a story about elephants in Thailand playing soccer with a big ball. "I love the music coming off elephants," he says. His head bobs forward, his feet shuffle, and magically he produces an elephant. He hums two syllables and music comes out of the elephant movement. For that moment, the night stillness is transformed into an exotic sound. Then Howard tells a lawyer joke.

Taj links up with Siena during the evening for a private chat in the kitchen, balancing plates of food, then again in a quiet corner. They've kept in contact over the years, even spending a Christmas together when their granddaughter was a baby. In 1965, Siena was one of the original San Francisco Diggers, a core of perhaps 50 people, primarily actors of the San Francisco Mime Troupe and students at Antioch College (now University) on work-exchange programs from that liberal college in Yellow Springs, Ohio. A school with an excellent academic and intellectual reputation, in the '60s Antioch was infamous for its tolerance in allowing students to explore their self expression. One male student stripped naked in his classes. He was not referred to a psychologist until he added masturbation to his classroom exhibitionism. A female student once stayed in a large box in a dorm. She would occasionally emerge and have sex with as many boys as possible.

The Diggers grew into a loose family of hippies who established a series of communes, set up free-food kitchens and stores, and sought to bring about social change focused more on community and less on capitalism. The original Diggers were poor, disenfranchised English peasants who fought for land to be held and farmed in common, rather than being the private property of wealthy landowners. Their movement emerged in 1649, during the English Civil War against royalty. The Puritan Oliver Cromwell led the rebellion, and succeeded in taking over the government, after beheading King Charles I, but Cromwell's Commonwealth government was unable to stop the continuing steep rise in the cost of food, which had been a principal cause of the rebellion. People were starving, and they wanted land (commons) on which to grow food. The pamphleteer Gerard Winstanley led a group of followers to dig and cultivate common land, hence the name "Diggers."

This anarchistic act alarmed Cromwell's government and local landowners. Angry mobs attacked the Diggers and destroyed their tools, carts, crops, and houses. The Digger movement itself was destroyed. In his pamphlet 'Truth Lifting Up Its Head Above The Scandals,' Winstanley set forth the core beliefs of the Diggers: power corrupts; private property and freedom are mutually exclusive; and only in a society without rulers can people be free to act according to their consciences. These later became the basic tenets of the socialist tradition, and ultimately the guiding principles of the San Francisco Diggers, to which they added their special twist: anarchistic art.

The Intersection Game is one example. On one afternoon, at the intersection of Haight and Masonic Streets in San Francisco, wearing wearing on their shoulders seven-foot-tall papier-mâché masks of gargoyles and mystical-looking animals, seven Diggers handed out pieces of paper to passersby. On the slips of paper were random instructions: dance in the middle of the intersection; wait three minutes and cross the street; move like a tree. A huge traffic jam resulted from the Diggers' action theater.

Or take the time that Siena and other Digger women rode a flatbed truck with the band Cleveland Wrecking Company to the city's financial district wearing belly-dancer outfits. There they enticed suits to leave their jobs and "dance with the sun and the music." Some did. "We're all actors in the theater of life," Siena says when explaining her Digger days, and adds, "Emmett Grogan, a founding member of the Diggers and my boyfriend during those Digger days, described the Diggers as 'standing on a street corner waiting for nobody.'"

Siena goes on, "The idea was to let people wake up and see that there is another side of life that they might not have imagined, and to make the arts part of everybody's everyday life, so each day would be a creation. It wasn't, 'Okay, I've made a creation and everybody come look at it.' It was more like, 'Look, I'm creating. You can create, too. Let's create together.' It was done for people's benefit. We did creativity for creativity.

"One of the things I got out of the Diggers was that I could do anything I wanted. The only hard thing was to figure out what it was I wanted to do. Once that was figured out, I could do it. Being in the Diggers allowed me to develop a courage that came from within myself but that I didn't know I had. It saved my life."

Peter Coyote, now a well-known writer and actor but back then a hippie musician and member of the infamous San Francisco Mime Troupe, was also an original Digger, and Siena's friend. In his book *Sleeping Where I Fall*, he writes that the Diggers "was an anarchistic experiment dedicated to creating and clarifying distinctions between society's business-as-usual and our own imagining of what-it-might-be, in the most potent way we could devise.

"...We expanded the idea of freedom to include, first, anonymity (freedom from fame) and, second, freedom from money, as both a clear dividing line between us and the majority culture, and as a test of our integrity. By eschewing payment and credit for what we did, we tried to guarantee that personal acts were never unconsciously predicated on the desire for fame or wealth. After all, if we were getting rich and/or famous from our activities, it would be hard to say that we were doing them for free.

"Our hope was that, if we were imaginative enough in creating social paradigms as free men and women, the example would be infectious and might produce self-directed (as opposed to coerced or manipulated) social change. People enjoying an existence that they imagined as best for them would be loath to surrender it and would be more likely to defend it. If this were to occur *en masse*, it would engender significant changes in our society."

Siena's Digger name was Natural Suzanne, given to her by Emmett Grogan. Suzanne is her birth name. "That was one of the greatest names ever, man," Coyote says from his home in California as he recalls those days when he hung with Siena, Taj, and Inshirah. "It fit Siena, because she just won't lie. She is one of those people who are indisputably authentic and honest and spontaneous, besides having a great and heartbreaking regal beauty. She was extraordinarily real, and still is. There is something soft and receptive and non-presentational about her. At the same time, she doesn't miss a trick. She's a great woman."

After the Thanksgiving night on Vashon Island, Siena tells her story about Taj from her home in Sacramento, California, while babysitting her's and Taj's granddaughter. "In 1970, I went to Ibiza, that little island in the Balearic group, off the Mediterranean coast of Spain. I was sitting in an open-air cafe by the port and Taj came over and sat down by me. I had met him in San Francisco years earlier, but I don't think he remembered. When you're traveling, you get with someone who speaks English because it's easier to have a conversation. That's how it was with us.

"He seemed pretty nice. He was into natural foods and was very enthusiastic about being on the island. I was under the impression that he was going to stay in Europe. Taj said he was burned out on the United States and everything that was going on there. That's how I felt. I never wanted to go back to the United States. I didn't like the political scene. There was nothing about it that I belonged with.

"He told me that he had been divorced. We started seeing each other, but very briefly. We just didn't click. I don't think that he and I were ever the type of personalities that get along together. Our personalities were never really made for each other. I think I'm way too low-key. Who knows? I haven't spent that much time analyzing it. It wasn't that we fought or anything. Some people click and some people don't. He likes to think that the powers of that whole area around the island is what brought us together and it was beyond us. I have to agree, in some ways, because there really wasn't anything else that brought us together.

"I was living in a little house on the highest point on the island. It had been built strategically so that any warship or invaders could be seen coming from three directions. To get to town, I'd walk an hour or more down, down, down the mountain. I'd hang out there in the day and walk back in the evening. The house was painted white and was surrounded by flowers and had a really beautiful view. I was there in early spring – like, April – so flowers were growing everywhere. On the side that didn't face the Mediterranean were fields of wheat down below on the mountain. I'd sit on the stone wall of the house watching the farmers plant with horses and by hand – very rustic, old fashioned. Taj and I conceived our twin children in that house. Taj's theory is that, in Greek mythology, Zeus turned himself into a bull – the sign of Taurus – and procreated with a women on Earth, and twins were born. Taj is a Taurus."

Edith Hamilton writes in her book *Mythology* (New American Library, 1942), "Various mythological stories tell of an amorous Zeus and a cowardly Zeus and a ridiculous Zeus. The Zeus that fully emerges is a Zeus coming into being, as men grow continually more conscious of what is demanded of them and what human beings needed in the god they worshipped. Zeus is not a fact of nature. He is a person living in a world where civilization has made an entry, and of course he is the standard of right and wrong."

In mythology, Zeus was lord of the sky, the supreme ruler. Nevertheless, he was not omnipotent or omniscient. He is represented as falling in love with one woman after another and descending to all manner of tricks to hide his infidelity from his wife, Hera. Zeus was a dangerous lover for mortal maidens and completely unpredictable in his use of the terrible thunderbolt.

Zeus abducted the maiden Io. When his jealous wife tried to track them down, Zeus wrapped a thick cloud around the Earth so that day became night. He turned Io into a white cow to disguise her when Hera came upon them. After he restored her to her human form, she bore Zeus a son, Epaphus.

Zeus also charmed Europa, daughter of the King of Sidon. In the form of a bull, he lay down before her feet and she climbed on his back. Zeus took off across the sea to Crete, his home island, where Europa gave birth to Minos and Rhadamanthus, "Glorious sons whose scepters shall hold sway over all men on Earth."

After Ibiza, Siena went to Morocco alone. "I felt really at home there, in a weird way, because Morocco is such a strange place. I think that the strangeness made it so familiar to me. I spent time in the Rif Mountains, in northern Morocco. The people there are really beautiful. I just liked the idea that that place existed. I felt close to it. That's why I took the name Riffia, which means 'I'm from the Rif Mountains.' Siena is just a name that came later, as sort of a nickname.

"Mostly, I was in Tangier, by the water. In the morning, I'd walk down to the ocean and watch the caravans go into the desert. The Berber people were so incredible and beautiful. The most exotic place I went was Ouarzazate, right on the edge of the desert. It's a magical and incredible place. I really loved it there, but the people kind of scared me. They liked me a lot and they were, like, 'We're not going to let you leave.' The ladies wanted me to stay, because I was pregnant. They wanted to name my child Mausafa. I started to feel they were closing in on me and were going to keep me. I left and returned to the United States, to Grand Rapids, Michigan, where I'm from. I was in Morocco from about May to November, and the twins were born in December.

"From Michigan, I returned to San Francisco. Another friend of mine, Julie, was having a baby. Her and I and Phyllis Willner and Vicki Pollock got a house together on Treat Street, in the Mission District, between 17th and 18th Streets and between Fulsom and Harrison. We fixed that house up to have our babies, to make the house really special, a nest. It was a very loving house, built for babies. Everyone who moved into the house was totally into the babies. That was the whole *raison d'être* of the house.

"It was a long, narrow, two-storey, wooden, older house without the gingerbread or Victorian trimmings of picturesque San Francisco. On the stairwell wall leading to the second floor was a mural by Ahma of scenes from San Francisco – the carousel from Golden Gate Park, little children playing, the Golden Gate Bridge – done in bright, bold colors. To the left of the front foyer was a big room with three walls painted in Moroccan red. The fourth wall was covered with gold leaf. An old upright piano – a gift from a Hell's Angel – was in that room, along with hippie furniture – mattresses piled up, some found chairs, and a couch. An archway led to a smaller room with a fireplace and then the huge kitchen with a big table. Behind the kitchen were two bedrooms: one for me and the twins and the other for Phyllis. There were two bedrooms upstairs, also.

"I hadn't been in communication with Taj about being pregnant. Shortly after the twins were born, Taj was performing in San Francisco. Friends of mine – Vicki Pollock, Phyllis Willner, and Little Paula – went to the concert and told him."

Phyllis Willner is now a psychiatric nurse, and remembers delivering the news of Taj's fatherhood to him. "I had read that he would be playing at the Peppermint Lounge in Marino City, and thought it would be good for him to know about the twins," she tells me from her home, "so the night of his performance I put on a purple shirt and purple hotpants and went with friends to the show. Taj was playing with a big band – strings and winds and tubas. I didn't know how I would actually contact Taj. During the show, a friendly fellow in the band kept smiling at me. Then they dedicated a song to the lady in the purple shirt: 'She's Built For Comfort, Not For Speed.' I definitely was a big lady! After the show, I went to the guy guarding the backstage and told him I was the lady in the purple shirt that the band had dedicated the song to and he let us backstage.

"I searched out the friendly fellow, who was Howard Johnson, and told him how much I enjoyed the music. Taj was around talking to lots of people. I went to Taj and told him that Natural Suzanne was back and that she had twins and we thought that he was the father. His eyes got big. I gave him our address and split. A couple days later, he showed up at the house."

Siena recalls that moment: "One day – I remember this so much – I was in the kitchen at the sink washing dishes when all of a sudden I realized that someone was staring at me. I turned around and there he was, standing in the doorway between the kitchen and the living room. That was the first time I had seen him since Ibiza. He was pretty surprised about the twins. They were both asleep on the couch in the living room. He knelt down and was really quiet as he looked at them. My hope was that we would get together and raise the twins, but I don't think that he ever really wanted that. He moved in with me, but I don't know if it was a cheap place for him to live or to be with us. We lived together about a year. This was in 1971 and 1972. He was playing around San Francisco, not doing long tours like he does now.

"It was really fun while he was there. Every night there was music. I had a piano and he had all his instruments there. I had a lot of friends who were musicians. Whenever anybody came to the house, Taj would get them involved with music, whether they could play or not. Music was his main language. I would sit there and nurse my twins and listen to the music. It wasn't a party house, with people coming over to play music and drink and get high – it wasn't like that at all. It was serious music. And babies.

"Taj is a strange guy. I think he does love his children, all his children, but he doesn't relate well with children. Even in relationships with adults, he's more… You can talk about the big picture with him for hours, months, and years. He can get into the esoteric and everything that is big. But as soon as you start to focus down to today and who's around you and what is your relationship with the people who are near you, that's really difficult for him. I don't even know if he can do that.

"The one thing I have respect for Taj is that, when it became so painfully clear that he was never going to be a mate with me to raise our children, he still realized that we should not belittle each other, or put each other down, but [should] maintain a kind of respect for each other for the children. I think he did it to the best of his ability, and he did that consciously.

"After we had been together for a while, I realized that it was never going to happen between us. I really wanted to get away from him. Me, my brother, Dick, and some other friends decided to go to New Mexico, where I had friends living on a commune. Taj bought us this really incredible, great old utility truck – bright orange, with a huge cab. The seats were taken out in the back, and I bought Styrofoam pads to make one giant bed for the kids to sleep on. On the outside, the truck had all these little drawers for storage spaces. We kept all our food there. On top, it had a huge luggage rack. We had everything up there – trunks, my treadle sewing machine. I made tie-dye curtains for the windows. We were totally hippie.

"We spent a year living in New Mexico, in a place called Mora, up in the Sangre de Cristo Mountains, a little tiny, *tiny* town, where the San Franciscan priests who came with the Spanish Conquistadors first went. We were five miles up a winding road from Mora on Recondada, owned by Jack Nicholson, the actor, this huge piece of property he said we could live on. Taj came to New Mexico one day and went to a house where I wasn't living any more. He never told me he was coming and we didn't make contact.

"While in New Mexico, I met a guy who was wonderful with horses. My whole childhood dream was to have a horse. We – he, I and the twins – went to Canada – Fort St James, on the eastern side of the Canadian Rockies, in British Columbia – for about a year. We lived in a trapper's cabin 17 miles from the town and two miles from the road. There were moose and wolf tracks in the snow outside the door in the winter. Wild swans and geese were on the little lake nearby, where we got our water. Wild eagles lived in the trees. We had horses. But after a while I got my fill of it, as I always do.

"You can see how different Taj and I are. I'm always going off to the mountains somewhere and being with small numbers of people. He's very comfortable being by himself in front of huge groups of strangers, like when he performs. In one sense, he's always by himself.

"I returned from Canada when the kids were four years old. I went to South Dakota and worked on the Wounded Knee legal defense for a few months. My kids were with my mom in Michigan. Then I went to Michigan and got them and went back to San Francisco.

"I had been thinking of going back to college. I got a job as a paralegal for an attorney, Louis Hyman. He was the person who really got me started on a new path. He said I'd never be happy being a paralegal and that I needed to go to law school. He encouraged me to sign up for classes at San Francisco State. I started getting some college credits. I had gone to college, on and off – I had attended Antioch College and had one half of a credit in tennis on my transcript.

"Taj's first wife, Anna, was instrumental in my going to law school. She was going to Boalt Hall, the University of California, Berkeley, law school, and suggested I go there. I had no idea that it was this prestigious law school. Anna is amazing, so talented, but I never talk with her anymore. I did when our kids were little and we lived close by. I think I saw her once when I was going to law school. During those years, Inshirah, Taj's wife, helped me with the kids. During my first year of law school, the twins lived with them in Kauai.

"Taj is a good-hearted fellow. I really believe that, whatever his good and bad points, underneath everything he is a non-vicious, kind person. I can't ever think of him doing anything mean intentionally. In my value system, that's important. I like Taj in some ways, and in other ways I have feelings of disappointment. I don't want to leave the impression that he never did anything for my kids. He did."

(Taj did financially and emotionally support the children in private, non-traditional elementary school, despite his misgivings about those educational concepts, which ran counter to his traditional values of reading, writing, and math. Taj Sr paid for Taj Jr's tuition at Kauai Community College, from which Taj Jr dropped out to start his successful landscaping business. "I have the bills to prove it," says Taj. His daughter Aya attended Harvard on a scholarship.)

"He's helping Ahmen, so that's good. It's so amazing, what he's doing with Corrina now. I'm so happy about that. Really, really happy. Maybe if this had happened to any of his other kids, where they could not be taken care of by their mothers, he would have taken them. The fact that he is taking responsibility for her is wonderful."

(Taj won legal custody of Corrina, 13, after her mother proved incapable of caring for her. In 1998, Corrina left Hawaii and moved in with Taj and his lady, Dawn, in Pasadena. In less than a year, Corrina moved in with her grandmother in Seattle. She now lives with Taj's daughter Ghamela, who is known in the family as Mia. Corinna attends school in Sacramento and, according to Taj, is "doing great.")

Siena continues, "I've noticed that, in the past couple years, he's been spending a lot more time calling and communicating with his kids. He's more attentive and more aware. During the last few years it seems that his eyes are opening up a little bit.

"After law school, I came to Sacramento as a law clerk for a federal judge. I did all the prison cases – civil rights violations filed by prisoners without attorneys. My job was to research the issues and present the law and arguments to the judges to help them decide how they might rule. I did that for two years. Then I worked for a civil attorney. In 1989, I began work as a public defender, which I am now. Being a public defender, it's a love/hate relationship. I compare it to battered woman syndrome: you can't get away from the guy who is really mean to you, but you love him."

"The Treat Street house had lots of soul," says Siena's brother, Dick, who moved in with his guitar after graduating from high school in Grand Rapids, Michigan. "It was not so much a commune as a household, like a family. I remember Taj would get up in the morning, put his pants on, walk into the living room, and play the stand-up bass, which he was learning then. He'd stand in the corner, facing the wall, playing for half an hour or so, until someone brought him a cup of coffee. He faced the corner because he could get the best resonation. He wanted to hear the intonation of the instrument. Sometimes he and I'd play guitar together. I remember once him spinning around and saying, 'Tune your guitar, boy. That's impolite.'

"Peter Coyote was very dear and close to the people at Treat Street. His Hell's Angels friends were part of the extended family that showed up at Treat Street. They were a fairly dangerous lot. Packed guns. Some were criminals. This one guy kept calling the house to harass someone. Taj's reaction was very brave, very straightforward. Once, when the guy called, Taj took the phone. 'I'm the man of the house. What do you want?' There was no hesitation that he would take control of the situation in a second.

"The Hell's Angels were fairly racist, but once, one of them looked at the twins and said, 'These are the most beautiful babies.' There was a lot of transcending going on at Treat Street. This one Hell's Angel – Pete, a good friend of Vicki's – admitted to her that they didn't take a visit to Treat Street lightly. The four main women there were a force.

"Taj and my sister were like apples and oranges. She's kind of hard on men, period. She's just driven. Taj seemed very generous, took good care of her. He would spin his daddy magic with the twins. It was never a struggle for him. He'd get the babies to laugh. He was strict, too. Sometimes one of the kids would be crying, and he'd go, 'SPO, SPO, SPO,' and haul them off and put them in a room and let them scream for a while. He didn't pacify them. SPO was some sort of family code meaning 'spoiled,' something he grew up with.

"With my sister, I don't know what happened. Taj bought a cute little black Volvo and left it with her when he was on the road. He'd haul us around to his local gigs, taking anybody in the household who felt like going. One time he took some of us to the East Bay area to play in some borderline high-school gymnasium. Taj sat on the stage with his banjo case on his lap, opened it, and started to tune his banjo. Kids in the front row were going, 'Let's boogie-e-e-e! Let's boogie-e-e-e!' Taj put the banjo back in the case, hooked all the latches, stood up, and walked off the stage. He looked at me, like, 'We're out of here.' He made such a bee-line for the door that it was all I could do to keep up with him. As he was going through the crowd, this older woman gave him a compliment. He stopped and was very courteous. 'Well, how do you do, madam? Nice to see you this evening. Glad you enjoy my music so much. All the best. Goodbye,' and we were gone, in the car, home. One of his favorite phrases was, 'I'll pass on that,' and he did. He felt like it wasn't going to work for him.

"The Treat Street house was a home, really settled, but my sister had this idea that she wanted to travel. The trip to New Mexico was her idea for a road trip to see some friends. She asked Taj if he would buy a vehicle for the trip. When she saw that one-ton orange truck with a big steel utility van on it, the type a survey crew used, she said, 'That's it.' She didn't want anything conventional. It was a combination Winnebago, hippie bus, survey vehicle, and chuck wagon. Taj did come to New Mexico after we were there, but my sister, she didn't miss him. She didn't want to go out of her way to see him.

"Later, I did commercial fishing in Alaska and along the West Coast. I eventually made my way back to Seattle, where I settled. Now I'm a 47-year-old grandfather, an electrician by trade, and manage the Escola de Samba Seattle, the only samba school in Seattle."

Peter Coyote, who knew Taj from the early '60s at 47 Mount Auburn Street in Cambridge, played music with Taj at Treat Street. "I was friends with Tom Rush, Geoff and Maria Muldaur, a bunch of people who were part of the Cambridge folk scene whom I knew from Martha's Vineyard. This was a time when a lot of white kids were getting into blues and black music. Not so many black people were playing it, to tell the truth. Taj burst onto the scene with his extraordinary talent and voice, rooted in that music. He was a living exemplar of the music available to us, and he could talk about all the contemporary records. He was an urban guy, sophisticated. He tended to disguise himself a little bit, disguise his formidable intelligence and insight behind the kind of folk he personified.

"Jump eight, nine years or so to San Francisco. Natural Suzanne had gone off on holiday to Ibiza and got tied up with Taj, ol' ladykiller that he is. She came back pregnant. I don't know what the financial arrangements were, but Taj certainly accepted paternity. I guess I'd consider Taj part of the Digger family, but like a distant cousin, in the sense that he really didn't participate in our kind of visionary-orientated politics. But he had two children by Natural Suzanne, our sister, so, to the extent that he was on the scene, he was part of the family. He'd come stay at Treat Street or Willard Street or one of the houses. He just showed up. I can't claim to be a real intimate friend of his, but I always felt comfortable when he was around. I never felt that he was bringing attitude, or mau-mauing anybody. He was real as a nickel. Sometimes Diggers can be a little snobby, a little cranky, but I don't remember any of that with Taj.

"Music was something we did. I was flattered that Taj accepted my music. It was something that was important to me then. I jammed with Taj once or twice. It was a feather in my cap that I was good enough to play with him and that he would let me play with him. Phyllis Willner played a tape of my music over the phone to Taj. He said – and this was important to me – that I had picked the words out of time in just the right places. He was talking about my sense of time. I used to be a drummer, so that was important to me. That was a lot of approbation from somebody who was a professional and much more talented than I was.

"I really don't play blues anymore, because of a curious little rigidity of my own. I started thinking one day, 'How would I feel if I saw a bunch of German Catholic kids singing songs from Auschwitz?' Those songs, that music [the blues], comes from such a particular reality. There are so many white kids who can play all the notes and they just don't have the juice. Then you see a guy like John Lee Hooker play, who's like a *griot*, who has no technique but he's got so much *ju-ju* that he sets the whole room shaking. There are guys like Taj and Alvin Youngblood Hart and Keb' Mo', who are really, consciously honoring their tradition. They got the notes *and* the *ju-ju*.

"Back in those days, I had an incredible crush on Inshirah, who was living with Taj. She was so beautiful. Inshirah is a virtuous woman, as far as I know. I could never seduce her. I tried my best. I was a dog. I didn't respect any kind of relationship or anything. I think she enjoyed my company. We certainly had a flirtation, but that was as far as it went. I thought she was an extremely elegant woman, very smart, and a good match for Taj. I felt she would have made a better match for me. That was not to be. Looking at myself now, as I must have appeared then, I was, like, a big, tall, skinny, white-boy junkie. I think she had too much sense to get involved in that.

"I could feel the ambivalence in her and Taj's relationship. She and I once spent the night together lying on a couch, fully clothed, talking, half sleeping. Nothing happened, just two people who were attracted to each other. She was married to Taj, his woman, and she was not going to give it up; but the fact that she would get so close to me, and we would talk so intimate... Well, she alluded to some things that were difficult. Any number of women – Digger women – might have talked about such difficulties if they were with rambling, ambitious, sexually avaricious men.

"Those Digger days still influence my life. I give a lot of my free time to environmental issues, like changing our species relationship to where we live and how we treat the place, also in trying to extend the consciousness that there are other forms of life other than human life that have an equal right to their evolutionary destiny. That's a big one. I give time and money, narrate a lot of documentary films, write, do things every way I can for environmental causes.

"I've been involved in a lot of Native American issues, primarily having to do with sovereignty issues and the releasing of the Native American rights activist Leonard Peltier, an old friend. I'm one of his two non-Native advisors. He has been in prison for over 20 years. Unjustly in prison."

(On June 26, 1975, Leonard Peltier was involved in a shootout in which FBI agents Jack Kohler and Ronald Williams were killed, along with American Indian Movement [AIM] activist Joe Stuntz. Peltier escaped and was concealed at Crow Dog's Paradise on the Rosebud reservation in South Dakota. On November 25, 1975, Peltier and three other AIM members were indicted in the FBI agents' deaths. Peltier was arrested at Smallboy's Reserve, in southwest Alberta, Canada, on February 6, 1976. A year later, he was convicted on two charges of first-degree murder and sentenced to two life terms. Peltier has consistently maintained his innocence. The Leonard Peltier Defense Committee was established to support his case, attacking inconsistencies and improprieties concerning the government's treatment of evidence and witnesses. The case has attracted international attention, but Peltier remains in prison.)

"Also, as a general area, Buddhism and Buddhist practice is an interest. I've been a Zen student since 1975. The intrusion of Buddhist values is going to be one of the agents, I think, that will soften and sensitize white people in the United States, so I support that as an extension of my political work."

20 Hard-Lovin' Truth

Taj has had 15 children, three of whom died in infancy. The first, Cybelle – who would now be about 41 years old – was given up for adoption, and is referred to by the family as "the lost sister." Next came Aya, born in 1967 by Anna de León. Then come Siena's twins, Ghamela and Taj Jr, born in 1971. Inshirah and Taj had seven children: Kali, born in 1975, died in 1975; Fatimah, born in 1977, died in 1977; Ahmen, born in 1978; Deva, born in 1982; Nani, born in 1984; and Zoe, born in 1991. Zoe's twin sister, Sachi, died two months after her birth. Yasmeen Mahal Montgomery, now 16, born of Victoria Montgomery, lives in Kauai. Joseph Binch, now 18, lives in Cornwall, England, with his mother, Caroline, a well-known children's author and book illustrator, and Taj and Theresa's daughter, 13-year-old Corrina, now lives with her grandmother. His youngest child, six-year-old Micah Celine, lives with his mother, Valerie.

Taj got together with Cybelle's mother, Suzanne, before he was 20. She was Caucasian, and her father talked her out of keeping a white/black child, so she gave the newborn up for adoption. Taj and his mother tried to adopt the baby but were denied. Suzanne had stipulated, as terms of the adoption, that Taj should have no access to his child. Back then, the law didn't give even a passing nod to a father's rights, so Taj had little chance of reclaiming his child.

"I think that is a key to an understanding about Taj," says Inshirah, his estranged wife. "I think, after losing his father, and Cybelle, and our two babies, he decided not to allow the bonding, the parenting. It was something he let go of."

When Cybelle was still a child, Taj traveled from California to the East Coast with the intention of finding her. He was married to Anna de León at the time, and she made the trip with him. "But he gave up," Anna recalls. "He said it was too painful."

Meanwhile, Taj Mahal Riffia (Taj Jr), one of Taj's twins by Siena, lives on the Hawaiian island of Kauai, where he runs his own gardening and landscaping business. He plays and writes music and sings, although he is not at present pursuing a career in music. It's six in the morning, and he's just gotten out of bed. He has to travel up to the North Shore for a landscaping job, but insists on taking time to talk about his father. "Once I get going, I can really talk," he warns. "I inherited that from my dad." His voice is light and clear, unburdened, and you can hear the shimmer of joy just under the surface.

"My dad has gotten a lot of bad press along the lines of his family commitment. A lot of controversy and disapproval has been focused on him around that issue. I want to share something about that. It's amazing how much my dad has taught me, shared so much with me on so many different levels, and how much influence he has had on me, considering how little he has actually, in the flesh, been in my life. One of the most intense lessons for me has been learning to be in the moment, be with my life, and make the most of all my different experiences with my father.

"Comparing my dad with other fathers, or comparing my family with other families – especially comparing them up against the United States of America social norm – definitely made me feel that I was lacking something. There can be so much big charge around so many things with my dad, even my name. My name is Taj Mahal Riffia. Taj is me. Mahal is my twin sister's name at birth. Riffia is Mom's last name, that she chose for herself, and Taj Mahal is my dad. That's the way it makes sense to me. I refer to myself as Taj Jr, mainly for clarity between my dad and I. I refer to him as Taj Sr. Taji is my family name among people who really know me.

"I've always had good times with my dad. He came into my life when Ghamela and I were five and a half years old. We flew out to California from Michigan to be with him. I remember expecting to spend all this time with him. As it turned out – as it's been my whole life – he was gone most of the time, working. Inshirah was there. She had just lost two of her babies, so it was an intense time for my twin sister and I to go live with them.

"I remember the couple of times my dad came off tour and actually showed up. Like, wow! He really is here! Oh my god! He drove us around in his jeep, really being a character, driving real fast, saying he was a speed racer, and getting the two of us cracking up. His joking around and acting silly was the intense point of connection between us. We were kinda scared, too. Who the heck *was* this guy? He was so full of personality and expression and drama. Later, he traded in the jeep and bought a new VW van and took us – with our older sister Aya, by Anna de León – on a camping road trip. That was really fun.

"My dad and I were into model airplanes and remote-control airplanes and cars – hobby kit-building stuff. He is famous for giving gifts that are way beyond the age of the person. I still have all these awesome Exacto knives I got when I was eight.

"When we were eight or nine years old, we moved to California with our mom. We would visit dad and Inshirah every other week. Those visits could get sort of uncomfortable. In 1980, my dad took everyone to Fiji – Aya, me and my sister, Inshirah, and Ahmen, who was just a baby then. Carey Williams, Kester Smith, and The IRB band were along, too. That was neat, an incredible experience. Around 1988, Ghamela and I lived with Taj Sr and Inshirah on Kauai while my mom was in her first year of law school, the hardest year.

"When I was eleven, I went on tour with my dad for 30 days. That was the one single most bonding experience that he and I have had. We had an awesome tour. I met him in Jamaica, where he was playing at the Sun Splash Festival. Then we toured all over the United States, by road and airplane, and ended in Canada. It was cool to really be with him. That's the first time I got to be at his side.

"I learned what my dad did, and realized how difficult that was. I got to see what was involved with just showing up for a gig. Not just showing up for one gig, but showing up for *all* the gigs, and [living] a life that is about showing up for all these gigs. It's not as glamorous as a lot of people might think. There were a lot of things about it I didn't like. It was fun to be on the move and meet so many people, but Taj Sr set a pretty good pace. He didn't want to tire me out, and I did good, in terms of keeping up with him, but as an eleven year old I didn't want to go to his shows in smoky clubs, bars [and] auditoriums night after night.

"Energetically, it's amazing what's emotionally required for that job. I definitely get that feeling that, once he was done giving all that energy, the people want more, right away. They don't even think he's a human being and wants a break. They think that he is a never-ending source of inspiration and energy, and they can keep tapping him for it. Sometimes he gets remote. I think that is to protect himself, to re-energize.

"On that tour, I got an understanding of what his life was like. He wasn't home, because of work. That was the main excuse. His work is a totally involved process. His only time to check in was after the gig was over, when he's finally back in his hotel room and he gets a chance to pick up the phone for a minute and talk to the people he loves. Then it's on to the next place, on to the next place, on to the next place. Then he gets this short window of time when he comes home, but there was always another tour coming up. He'd have half a week to come home and get it together to go back on the road for another couple of months.

"It was always like that. I got used to seeing my dad, on an average, once a year. Twice a year was a bonus. If I didn't see him at all in a particular year, that was something that could happen.

"And then, in those short times he was home, he was supposed to be the disciplinarian and hand out corporal punishment in the form of spankings. It was his job, because he was our father. He had been gone for months on the road, and he comes home and his wife hands him a list of disciplinary actions to take against these two little kids he hadn't seen for a long time. In some ways, I'm still healing from that, emotionally.

"His whole thing was, he was just spanking us with his hand. That was supposed to be the big break we got. Physically, the guy is huge, and we were just little kids, so it was overwhelming, from our view, just that feeling of, 'You did something wrong and now you're going to be punished at 12.01, so go wait in your room for a half hour until I'm ready' – that came out of his childhood, where physical discipline was there. Yet he could have this totally fun, friendly, silly side. So it was really weird, like, who is this person?

"When he was gone, Inshirah was the disciplinarian. She was into it. She would use a spoon or a hairbrush or a comb or something. That was the first time me or my sister had ever received spankings or beatings. Some of the reasons I ended up getting a spanking for was bullshit, some of the most rigid, orthodox training. Inshirah and Dad were really young, and hadn't been through child-rearing before, so we got to be, like, guinea pigs for the rest of the family.

"My relationship with Inshirah has changed from one of a hated nemesis, an arch-rival, to the present friendship. My greatest challenge in life, as a kid, was to mentally overcome her. She is very intelligent, so it didn't happen. Now, the friendship she and I share is deeper and more true than anything I could ever imagine. It is my greatest dream come true. She has said things to me that I felt I would never hear from her, in terms of apology for some of the experiences she was directly involved in with my upbringing. I have incredible respect for Inshirah. She is a world-class beauty, and has a world-class mind. It's interesting that my dad was able to tune into her as an incredibly unique individual.

"But now, physical punishment to the kids at home just doesn't happen. When I look at Inshirah's techniques of child-raising with the three kids at home, I see they are so different, so much more relaxed.

"Looking at Inshirah – my mom – and Anna de León, Taj Sr chooses incredible women. They are my examples of how to be, what it means to be an adult. I'm so proud of my mom. Once I get started on it, I can go on and on about how much I love her and respect what she's done with her life, even way back to the days with the Diggers. When I think of what my mom contributed to the world through her involvement with the Diggers, the political vision they had and acted out with integrity, I get so much inspiration from her. Those shock waves are still going out into the universe.

"Fishing was, and is, another bonding experience for me and my dad. I first went fishing with him when I was about six, when I stayed with him in California. I remember the experience to this day – getting up super early in the morning, way earlier than I wanted. It was so early only the yellow lights on the stop signs were flashing. I had never seen that before. We went salmon fishing on San Francisco Bay. I remember catching eight-pound and ten-pound salmon. I gave them names.

"Fishing is one of the most intimate things my dad and I have shared throughout my life. We go fishing in Hawaii when he's here for a few days. It's a time when I can hang out with him. We don't talk a lot when we're out fishing. It's all about just being together, being around each other, being in each other's energy, and not exchanging a lot of words. It's a place of relaxation, a place of quieting down the self. As soon as we touch dry land, there are people in his face.

"When fishing on the ocean, he shuts out all the other influences so he can take in being on the water. My hit is that's the place where he gets to just be a man. He doesn't have to be Taj Mahal out there. The fish don't know who he is. Being out on the ocean, surrounded by all that water, that's the time he feels that he is safe. No one can bug his trip. No one can call him.

No one can come into his world. It's, like, this really safe place for him to go and be on a real basic level. Fishing is much like a parallel world to his music world, a safe place for him to create and be.

"Here is a story he loves to tell. One of the first times he got into big trouble, as a boy, he was watching his younger siblings and got this great idea to take them fishing at a pond. They went on bikes and walking, and were gone for the day. He got in trouble for not letting the older folks know what was going on. That little fishing trip was a bonding thing, something he shared with his brothers and sisters.

"Gardening is also a connection to my dad. It's natural for me to love gardening, to do the physical work. My dad always has a garden wherever he lives, even if in a rental. I've had my business full time for six years now. The idea of creating a job and making it work, creating the business – I got that inspiration from my dad, in terms that I'm creating a life for myself. My dad is big on independence, and so am I.

"Gardening is a common ground we both share that doesn't have anything to do with music. On a musical level, we talk and relate, but he's way ahead of me. On a gardening level, with landscaping and plants – especially as I've been educating myself on tropical plants – it's the one place where I absolutely meet him man to man. I know more about landscaping than he does, and he accepts that. He has genuine curiosity and questioning on his part, which is rare, because he usually has the answers when we talk. I get a lot of respect from him.

"I've always looked up to my dad. I've idolized him in some ways and emulated him in a lot of ways, too, but also I've always had things about him – especially in the past – that I didn't know how to handle, things I could really make him wrong about and make myself wrong about. I've definitely been through a lot in my younger years about him.

"One of the difficult things for me, growing up, was having a dad who was so different than all my friends' fathers. I couldn't even prove that he existed to my friends, because he wasn't there. I remember this one kid, whose parents listened to my dad's music. The kid heard that Taj Mahal was my father. He got in my face about that was a lie. I argued that he was my dad, but I realized that I couldn't prove it. It hurt. I almost doubted it myself. This was in eighth grade.

"I had a lot of pent-up feelings and thoughts that I didn't know how to express. The last five years or so have been really a transformation. It's pretty neat to finally get to the place where I don't feel angry at my dad about anything anymore.

"A lot of his kids don't feel like I do. It's interesting now, at the age I'm at, to see some of the other kids growing up, experiencing the same exact kind of thoughts and feelings and emotions that I went through with my dad. At times, I've been able to help the younger brothers and sisters understand what's going on and not to feel so alone, to see the cause for separation. I feel sad seeing my other family members – even the younger kids – hating him and feeling dissed by him and feeling that they're not getting enough from him.

"My relationship with music and musical instruments has a lot to do with my dad. He's always been very supportive of me, musically. Any time I've ever asked for a musical instrument, he's always found it for me. That's one of the places where he does play an active role in support. If I want an instrument, it shows up; but in terms of *him* showing up, he's never been there to teach me. I've definitely had issues about that.

"I've loved music since I was really young. I think it's genetic, because, before I ever really knew my dad, I loved music. I started playing banjo when I was a kid. I've always been totally afraid of the guitar. That was my dad's instrument. There were so many instruments in the world that I was going to play anything but the guitar.

"Many years ago, Taj Sr gave me a bass. I never got it together to get the instrument in my possession until about five years ago. Then I shipped it out from California and started to learn to play. I got hold of an acoustic guitar. Somehow it came into my life. I've been teaching myself the guitar and the ukulele. I'm in many ways self-taught, just like my dad. I got that from him. He taught me that the way to play music was to just play. It's easy to pick up a lot of musical information from him.

"I've had thoughts of going public. When I look at the music industry, I don't like it. That has been a central conflict for my dad, the business of music and the making of music. I've always respected his stance of staying true to the music, first and foremost. With the financial and family pressures he's endured, he could have gone out and made hit after hit. Not doing that is the kind of sacrifice he's made that no one even knows about. I feel people don't respect him for staying true to his path.

"His staying true to the roots, that's all coming back around. Years ago I knew that he was going to have a resurgence of popularity that would rival his high peak back in the early 1970s. Instead of going for the glitz, glamour, and short-term big cash, he said, 'I'm going to stick to my roots. I'm going to stick to playing music for people.' He did it the hard way, basically being a hardhead. I can see the wisdom in that. Now, there is a chance for all that to come back around.

"My sense is that his music, through the songs he sings, is his way of expressing his inner self. It is a gateway into who he is, intimately. The songs he chooses to sing are ultimately about him and his life. I can hear that within the lyrics.

"Being in Hawaii influenced his music a lot. He had heard a lot of Hawaiian music that hadn't turned him on much. When he heard some of the master Hawaiian musicians, he decided to pay attention to that music and listen to it, the slack-key sound. That has become more part of his music.

"I jammed for the first with my dad at the family Thanksgiving on Vashon Island in 1997. I played a song I had written. My dad heard me, and was attracted to the music. He picked up his guitar and started playing. It was really beautiful, because we had never actually jammed together before that. We were playing the first song I had written and composed on the ukulele. We played three or four songs after that, so it became a full-blown performance. Later, he complimented me on the song, said that he had never heard anything like that before. To me, that was the greatest compliment I could ever, *ever* be given.

"I've been thinking about what could I say about my dad, overall. I definitely, totally idolize him and love him so much. I have such a respect for him. In the past, I've stuffed my emotions about him. In recent times, I've been learning to express myself more and free up my own experience. Still, I've not created the space where I feel absolutely spontaneous with him. That's something I can feel bad about, and I've been doing a lot of work to get that spontaneity. Things have been shifting a lot, but I realize that I'm just not there. I still have an intense charge when I'm around him.

"In 1996, I realized that I had a lot of incomplete communications with my dad. For many years, I would have conversations in my mind, arguments with him, or just heart to heart. I didn't have a dad there, so I had to project it in my mind. They weren't always pleasant or cosmic thoughts. It really started to bother me a lot. I realized that I had a truth that I needed to share with him.

"I wrote this landmark letter to him where I opened up and shared the thoughts and feelings I had been repressing, mainly how I could feel cheated and ripped off and like I didn't even matter to him, that I was a tokenism in his life. I also shared with him that, years before, as a kid, I had stolen some things from his house. Usually small, little things. I admitted to it all – that I could remember, anyway – and sent him $300 for the things I had stolen.

"He got that letter the day before he was coming to Hawaii. I didn't know that he was coming. He calls me up: 'Hey, this is Dad. I'm on Kauai.'

"'You are?! Did you get my letter?'

"'Yeah, I got your letter.'

"I could tell that he didn't want to talk about it. I could tell how deep it was, and that it was embarrassing stuff. 'Yeah' was all that he could say. He knew that I had to get the ghost out of my head.

"That was a real major turning point for me. It had an incredible effect of bringing my dad and me closer. The voices stopped in my head. I stopped having those arguments with my dad, for the first time in my life. It's been different between us, in terms of me feeling that I'm on the same level with him.

"I'm really proud of my dad. In the face of everything that he's had to deal with, he's done great. He's got a lot of room for growth, which is so cool that, at his age, at his level of completion, he's got so much more, a whole world of relationship to keep learning about.

"I am constantly amazed by Taj Sr and his intelligence, his openness. He is more tuned in than people give him credit for. He's been fighting against being misunderstood for his whole life. What he's needed has been support and the space to feel that he's okay. Maybe in his own mind he has to deal with feelings of 'I'm doing it wrong,' or 'I'm not enough.' When he starts to hear that from other people, too, I hope he can handle it. I have a lot more to learn about him. Even though he's my father, and has been a presence in my life, he and I still have so much relationship to look forward to. It's exciting.

"I think my dad's work was, and is, difficult for him in two ways: one, to be on the road so much; and second, to want to be on the road, because that is a safe place for him. My sense has always been that, if Taj Sr could make the same amount of money being a farmer, having a big farmhouse where all the kids could live as a giant family, and just do farming and take the kids fishing on the pond, that's what he'd want to do. Because he can't, he does what he has to do the only way he knows to support his family. He's definitely comfortable, doing what he's doing. He's comfortable in the role of the father that's gone, and only checks in every once and a while, kind of shows up, and it's a real big deal. Then he takes off again.

"I don't think that is the life he prefers. He has created his own reality for a reason. Obviously, there is some kind of major payoff for setting up the situation the way he has."

Ghamela, Taj Jr's twin, who in 1999 legally changed her name to Ghamela Lhela Mahal-Riffia, has a strikingly beautiful face. In all truthfulness, she doesn't look anything like her father, except if you look at photos of the younger Taj, and then the family resemblance is apparent. Her energy embraces everyone, friends and strangers, with enthusiasm for jumping into life at that moment. An aspiring actor, she works as a project director for an international software company. As her four-year-old daughter, Khalili Lei Ann – Taj's only grandchild – plays in the background, Ghamela tells a tale about her dad: "I went through most of life believing that he didn't think of me the same as he did his kids by Inshirah. No doubt that he liked me, even loved, but I felt it wasn't the same. When I was about 17, I had my first inkling that my dad really liked me.

"I had invited my dad to my Davis High School graduation, but I didn't think he'd fly from Hawaii to California. The graduation was held in the University of California Davis Football Stadium. I'm sitting there, nervous, looking out over the crowd, and see this flash of unusually bright colors. There was my dad, Ahmen, Deva, Nani, and Inshirah, in their Hawaiian shirts.

"Then, in 1992, I came close to dying. That was a huge change in my relationship with my dad. It was the first time I ever saw my dad openly express emotions to me. It was so shocking that I didn't know what to do. I had gotten crepitus from a SCUBA-diving accident in Hawaii – too much carbon dioxide got into my bloodstream – but after diving I went home thinking everything was all right. In the middle of the night, I woke up with a blinding headache. I lived on my own in a duplex. I went to my neighbor and said, 'I think I need to go to the hospital.' I remember getting into his car and rolling down the window because it was too hot and thinking the cold air felt good, then waking up three days later in the hospital. I had gone into a coma. The ambulance had called ahead and said I was coming in dead on arrival.

"Dad was booked to do a European or South American tour, and was due to leave. Historically, my dad has never missed a tour. No matter what tragedy is happening in his life, he will always go to work. That's the way he handles the tragedy. When I awoke from the coma, with my face swollen and a breathing tube down my nose, I looked up and saw my dad. He was holding my hand. He said, with this heavy, heavy sigh, 'Baby, I've never been so scared in my life. Don't ever do that to me again. I was supposed to be on a plane today, but I'm not going. I'll stay here until you're out of the woods.'

"To understand that it was more important for him to be with me than anything else was the most awesome thing in my life. I couldn't believe it. He was there every day. When they moved me out of intensive care, he asked me if it was all right if he left. If it wasn't, he would stay. That was phenomenal for me. It was like an awakening. I felt that he really loved me, that he was really proud of me.

"Inshirah was with me the whole time. I remember coming into consciousness and hearing her cry, which threw me off, because at that time we had a very, very volatile, high-energy relationship. Neither of us really believed that we loved each other. At the bedside, she was reading me books that she had read to me as a child. Then she'd stop and cry and tell me how much she loved me and how sorry she was that she didn't always treat me well.

"Recently, I was diagnosed with a serotonin deficiency. I was in the hospital's mental facility. Wow! Mind funk. It was very, very frightening. I had this automatic fear that my dad was going to reject me because of this. No one else in our family has a history of mental illness. I was afraid my dad would be ashamed of me.

"Dad called me at home. He was real quiet, then said, 'Baby, I'm so worried about you.' My first thing was, 'Daddy, are you mad at me?' He said, 'That's not the question you need to be asking me. You need to ask, "Daddy, no matter what happens, are you always going to love me? Will you always be there for me? Will you always be proud of me?"'

"He was on the phone with me for 45 minutes, telling me incident by incident what he was proud of around my parenting skills and how I've raised my daughter. He said, 'Every time I watch you with her, it brings tears to my eyes. I feel that I'm the luckiest man in the world. Baby, I'll always love you. You're so important to me.'

"Sometimes I call him to tell him that I love him. Sometimes he'll call me out of the blue – 'How's everything going? I love you.' He'll call from the set of a movie, or from Zurich. Not all my brothers and sisters have that relationship with him. It takes time and a matter of accepting. Dad is who he is. You need to open up and allow him to be your dad in the way that he is your father. As long as you can do that, you can have a mutually respectful relationship.

"I never needed my dad to be anybody else but my dad. There is the comfort – to the sense of equality and commonality and safety – in that. I think that's what has generated the kind of communication he and I have. My dad has taught me that I am completely capable of doing anything I want. It's a matter of deciding to do it, and that's it. It's invaluable that he brought me up to believe I can always hold my head up high, no matter what people say about me. I knew what kind of people my family were. They had integrity.

"There were several talks my dad gave us kids, such as the 'dollar talk.' The dollar talk came whenever any of us wanted some money and we had been hitting him a bit hard to go to the mall or movies. He'd tell how his father gave him a dollar to take his brothers and sisters to the movies and buy them candy. He would have 15¢ left and he would give it back to his dad.

"[Our] relationship further deepened when my daughter, Khalili Lei Ann, was born. She gives him the freedom to be relaxed, more so than I do. My daughter is very reserved, but when Dad comes to visit she's chomping at the bit: 'When is Grandpa going to get here?' She hears his steps coming up the stairs to our apartment and she goes, 'Oh my gosh. Oh my gosh. It's my grandpa.' I open up the door and she peeks around the corner and screams, '*Grandpa!*' He comes running to her and she jumps into his arms. She's petting his face, kissing him. I watch my dad and all of his reservedness melts away.

"We get packages from Taj for her when he's on the road, pretty little dresses from India, Mexico, Europe, the Caribbean. Having a granddaughter has brought about a real change in him. He attributes it to having a grandchild.

"She made a card for him on Father's Day. 'But it's really Grandpa's Day,' she explained. It shows her and Dad with fishing poles over their shoulders. She wrote, 'We going fishing, Grandpa. Just me and you.' She doesn't see Grandpa as a musician; she sees him as her grandpa and king of the universe, as far as she is concerned.

"Fishing – especially on the ocean – has a cleansing effect on him. It's an opportunity for him just to be Henry, the little boy hanging out at his favorite fishing spot. When he goes fishing, it's even different than when he plays music. When he plays music, he puts on his best aspect of his persona; but fishing on the ocean, he has a freedom. He doesn't have to worry about being the man of the house. When he's fishing, he can be free of all his problems."

Aya de León, Taj's daughter by Anna de León, is an articulate and accomplished woman. A Harvard graduate, she describes herself as "an Afro-Latina artist, writer, youth worker, and trainer." She is the director of the Mothertongue Institute for Creative Development in Oakland, California. Her memoir about her relationship with Taj, 'Hitting Dante,' appeared in *Children Of The Dream: Our Stories Of Growing Up Black In America* (Simon & Schuster, 1999). Speaking from her home in Oakland, she seeks the fine balance between telling her truth and being fair to her dad.

"My dad is a wonderful and successful musician and cultural historian. He has not been a wonderful or successful father. This is a painful and difficult truth about my dad.

"Love is a verb. An active verb. Loving children requires that a parent be there. During my childhood, years would go by without a word from him. The hardest part was when I'd run into people who had seen him perform. How could I tell them that the magnificent artist who had touched them so deeply didn't pay his child support? How could I tell them that, when he came into town to do that show, he hadn't even bothered to call or visit me?

"I grew up with two dads: the public hero and the private disappointment. I don't question that my father loved me, but his love was generally a private experience, a sentiment that went on between him and the image of me that existed in his head. My dad liked the idea of being a father. He just wasn't up for behaving as a father.

"After I graduated from college, I met a guy who told me he had sat next to my father on a cross-country flight. My dad had spent most of the flight talking about how proud he was of me. It was like a *Twilight Zone* episode. My father had not contributed to my college education, hadn't made contact with me in a year, and yet would talk about me as if we'd spoken just yesterday.

"When we did interact, he had a hard time listening or having a regular conversation. He often spoke in long, abstract monologues. I wonder if it's because he's a star and used to being around strangers who hang on his every word. I think the saddest part is that, for most of his life, he chose the adoring strangers over his family. A life on the road suited him, because, when anyone made emotional demands on him, he could just move on.

"However, my dad has gotten a lot better as he's gotten older. He still forgets my birthday, and has a hard time listening and following through, but he seems more present and more settled. He's also a lot less defensive. When I tell him about the impact in my life of his neglect, he hears it without making excuses, like he did in the past.

"I am like my father in some ways – I also perform, as a spoken-word artist, and I sing. I can see how easy it is to get caught up in a stage persona. All that attention, applause, and adoration can be intoxicating. After performances, I need to be with close friends, who keep me grounded.

"I've learned that real love doesn't happen between a performer and fans in the audience and in the dressing room. Real love happens between people who know each other and are there for each other in the many moments outside of the spotlight that make up the fabric of our lives."

21 *Hawaiian Hurricane*

Tonight, Valentine's Day 1999, we're at the Boulder Theater, an authentic 1930s art deco showcase, where Taj is taping a broadcast for *E-Town*, a nationally syndicated radio show. Taj sits on a sofa in the changing room talking to an American-Asian woman about hay farming in Massachusetts. She seems genuinely interested. "As a little girl," she interjects, "on my dad's farm, my job was to ride on the machine and make sure each onion seed dropped into its hole. Now I do desktop publishing."

In the adjoining room are three Hawaiian slack-key guitar masters: Cyril Pahinui, winner of several Na Hoku awards (Hawaii's equivalent of the Grammy); Dennis Kamakahi, one of Hawaii's most prolific composers/songwriters, who writes lyrics in the Hawaiian language; and George Kahumoku, who won Hawaii's State Pork All-American award in 1992, which followed his 1982 Young Farmer Of The Year award. He is also an artist, with a degree in fine arts (bronze sculptures), a songwriter/composer, teacher, storyteller, and winner of the Na Hoku Hanohano award for the Best Traditional Album Of The Year. Cyril, Dennis, and George are considered Hawaii's foremost "roots musicians," not too far removed from the Delta bluesmen of the mainland. They are a perfect musical complement to Taj, who lived on Kauai for twelve years. His 1997 album *Sacred Island* is a tribute to Hawaii and Pacific island cultures.

In 1977, George played behind Taj at a gig at the University of Hilo. "His American blues and our Hawaiian slack key blend well," George says. "Taj plays with a twitch to itch in his music. He's mischievous. We have that in our music, too. Slack key has been described as 'the blues and soul of Hawaiian music.' It is the music of the land – cowboy music. My great-great-grandfather was one of the six original cowboys who learned to play the guitar from the Mexican cowboys, who first brought cattle to Hawaii, in 1843. Traditional Hawaiian music had no string instruments. It was all sticks, stones, bamboo flutes, and bamboo mouth organs. This is very mystical, spiritual music, in that it's soft and soothing. It's like when you're half awake, half asleep. That's when Hawaiians believe you are the most creative, between two and six in the morning."

George gives an impromptu lesson in the slack-key technique. The solo finger-picking style is called *ki ho'alu* in the Hawaiian language, literally "loosen the key." The keys are slack and the tuning is almost always based on major tonality, which often has a full major chord, a chord with a major seventh note, or a chord with a sixth note. The unique sound derives partly from the technique of plucking a note and immediately fretting on that string to produce a second note. Another part of the technique is the "pull-off," produced by plucking a string and immediately pulling the finger off that string, sounding a second note, which is either open or fretted by another finger.

Taj's journey to Hawaii had its genesis in 1973, when he met Inshirah, who was born Beverly Ellen Geter in Bridgeport, Connecticut. She was 21, a senior at Scripps College, majoring in dance and English. Taj was 31, playing a gig at the school. Inshirah was (and is) tall and slim, with a beauty so striking that Sean Connery once crossed a room to tell her that she was the most beautiful woman he had seen in his life.

"The night I met Taj, I was turned completely upside down," Inshirah says from her home on Kauai. "In my mind, I had written of this moment, when I'd look in someone's eyes and I'd recognize them for some important event, the right connection. I saw that connection in Taj's eyes. Far out! I stayed up all night and danced around a park. I knew I was going to see him again, but I didn't know when. That was the moment I had dreamed of all my life, so it had to happen again.

"I finished school and went home to Bridgeport. A few months later, he played Bridgeport with The Pointer Sisters. I went, and was totally enthralled again. He claims that I was the only person he could see in the audience. He was watching me, and I knew he was watching me, but I pretended like I didn't. After the show, I felt that, if he leaves and we don't meet again, the moment would pass. I sat in my car – actually, my grandmother's car – not knowing what to do, and I couldn't get the car started. It was an automatic, and I was used to an stick. I had the gear in drive instead of neutral, so it wouldn't start. I felt it was an omen from God. I got up to Taj and asked him to help me start the car. He got it started immediately. He looked at me – 'Oh, this is a new one.' We kinda met that night. I left the hotel before he woke up, and I thought of leaving a lipstick message on the mirror, but I changed my mind, so he didn't know how to get back in contact with me.

"A couple months later, a dear friend in LA passed away. My grandmother gave me enough money for a one-way ticket to the funeral. I had a metaphysical experience, with the passing of my friend Kojo. He was one of God's angels. After the funeral, I was on the highway, figuring out which direction I was going to go in life. I headed for San Francisco, where Taj was living. I was there a couple of months when I called Taj to tell him I was in town. He came over within an hour. That was in 1974.

"We started seeing each other pretty regularly. He had the big house up on Tilden, in Berkeley, the place where, later, we hosted Bob Marley and The Wailers. I started living there. We were pretty much married, in my mind, from that point on. One day, he put his hand on my stomach and said he wished that we had a baby, so we did.

"Kali was born April 11, 1975. We changed her name to Raven because of Peter Coyote. While I was still in the hospital with her, Peter sent some women from Treat Street to visit. They told me that Peter had said that the name Kali was invoking the Hindu god of life and death. The women told me that Peter was channeling through the Hopi god the Raven, and that I should change Kali's name, so I changed the name to Raven.

"When Raven was two weeks old, she went through – in her sleep – a series of very precise *muderas*, hand movements, as precise as a dancer in an Indian temple, not uncontrolled flailing. In that one moment, she was functioning as an ancient spirit, not as an infant. I sat there – a new mother with her first baby – in amazement. My vision at that moment was like being on a high mountain in Tibet communing with ancient sages. The channels were wide open to other realms of existence.

"Raven suffered from metabolic acidosis. She had too much acid in her blood. Metabolic acidosis is a biochemical definition, not a diagnosis. The doctors don't know why there is too much acid in the blood, so they say, 'Well, it must be genetic,' but they don't know what it is. That's why it was so academically challenging to them, and they put a lot of mind to it with Raven."

The causes of metabolic diseases are complicated and, in some cases, not well understood. Hundreds of human hereditary biochemical disorders – termed "inborn errors of metabolism" – have been discovered, and are continually being discovered, according to the *Textbook Of Pediatrics*, 15th edition. Children with inborn errors of metabolism may have one or more of a large variety of signs and symptoms, including metabolic acidosis, persistent vomiting, failure to thrive, development abnormalities, and elevated blood or urine levels of a particular metabolite – for example, an amino acid. Most inborn errors of metabolism are inherited as autosomal recessive traits. This is true of non-ketotic hyperglycinemia. The majority of patients with this disorder become ill during the first few days of life. They suffer poor feeding, failure to suck, and lethargy. Convulsions – especially myoclonic seizures – and hiccups are common. This disorder is usually fatal. No effective treatment is known.

"That baby was in great pain. She screamed a lot. For months I walked her all night. I was on 24/7 on that one. There was no relief, except from Phyllis Willner, one of the women from Treat Street, who stayed side by side with me through the baby's suffering. Raven was my first baby angel. She died November 4, 1975. She was born on a full moon and died on a full moon, exactly seven moons later.

"After Raven died, I attended the University of California Berkeley School of Education. Taj and I talked it over and planned it so he could pay the tuition and expenses. For one and a half years I did student teaching and substituted at grammar schools in Oakland and Berkeley and at Berkeley High School. At Berkeley High, I did a six-month 1950s-'60s retrospective of US black history. I covered the prison system, the women's movement, Black Power, the civil rights movement, the American Indian movement. I loved it.

"Taj and I got legally married nearly two years after Raven's death, in late January 1977. I was six months pregnant with our second baby. I was surprised that he asked me to marry him. When we got the marriage license in Richmond, California, the clerk gave us a bag of household cleaning products. We laughed about it. Then we had to figure out how to get married. He was going on a road trip with a big band, so he said to come along and we'd figure it out from there.

"On the way down to Santa Barbara to a big gig, we stopped in a health-food store/restaurant run by the Brotherhood Of The Sun, a farming cult. We told them that we were looking to get married. They said, 'We'll give you a wedding. We'd love to marry you.' As we drove out to their land for the ceremony, a flock of hawks circled above the van. Hawks, by nature, don't circle or flock. This was very interesting, because Taj and I always noticed hawks and eagles. We were very much into the predator birds. That was part of our connection.

"I wore a red dress and Taj wore a white-lace African shirt. We had, like, 300 people at our wedding and didn't know a soul. In the middle of the ceremony, I said, 'Oh, excuse me, I have to pee,' being pregnant. This huge hawk swooped down and escorted me down the long path to the toilet.

"After we got married, we went to Mexico for a honeymoon kind of thing. We bought a cheap silver ring in a little store. When I first got together with Taj, I gave him a silver eagle bracelet. That bracelet with the open wings was more a wedding band than the ring. The wedding ring exploded off my finger after about four years, because of all Taj's infidelities and lies in the spiritual space. I took that to mean, in the long term, that the closed bond symbolized by the ring wasn't what we were about. The open wings of the eagle were more symbolic of our relationship.

"I see it that two people have to be whole. People can come together and be one. The book [The] Celestine Prophesy talks of how marriages worldwide are falling apart at this time. The reason is that two people try to come together and there are two heads trying to govern one body. It ends up a struggle. That's why people have to separate and become whole beings. The psychic movement for the human population is that, when two heads can be whole persons in themselves, then relationships will come into a different order. I think this kind of spread-out, crazy relationship of Taj and I manifested that new order.

"In the long term – being that he lives up to ten months on the road, and he is a musician – there is no way to judge our relationship by traditional standards. There is dissolution of traditional values and traditional marriages, but I think there is a way to be whole with someone, to be united.

"Our second daughter, Fatimah Desiree, was born on April 7, 1977. Because I had named Raven twice, I told Taj he could name this one. We did home birth, and when she came out I heard the word 'Fatimah' as clear as if it was spoken. It wasn't a name I would have selected. I said, 'Oh, shoot, I said that Taj could name her.' I said, 'Taj, what do you want to name this baby?' He said, 'I don't know. Fatimah or Isis.' Of all the names in the universe, we both heard Fatimah.

"She, too, suffered from metabolic acidosis. She lived exactly four months. She went through a lot towards the end. She suffered beautifully. She communicated to me on a spiritual place.

"Our son, Ahmen, was born in 1978, and a couple years later we sold the Tilden house after it suffered minor earthquake damage. This was the start of our move to Hawaii, although we didn't realize it at the moment. First we moved to Norwalk, Connecticut, for a year. One day, Taj came home and said, 'How about let's try Hawaii. Let's try Kauai.' We flew out to look it over. Deva, our next child, was conceived on that trip. We returned to Connecticut. In nine months, we moved to Richmond, California, to home-birth Deva, because I was more comfortable there, with Taj's family around and people I knew – I didn't know anyone on Kauai. When Deva was three months old, we moved to the small town of Poipu, on Kauai, in 1982. Later, we lived in Omao.

"We had bad luck almost from the beginning. Our real-estate agent talked us into investing $450,000 – much more than we had on hand from the sale of the Tilden house – in 13 acres, with the idea to build a subdivision. While we were in possession of the land, I went through the county engineers and designed the subdivision. Then a hurricane hit and the real-estate market dropped. If we could have hung on until the real-estate market came back, the land would have been a wise investment, but it took greater amounts of money than we had, so we weren't able to sustain the investment. We suffered heavy financial losses. We were into a $10,000 note every three months, and nothing was selling. It was also a low point in terms of Taj getting gigs. There was a foreclosure and tax liabilities and everything was lost. From then on, we lived in rentals, one nice rental after another. I live in a rental right now.

"In 1984, Nani was born, and in 1991, the twins, Zoe and Sachi. Sachi had metabolic acidosis, too, and lived only two months. Taj left for a gig one day and she died the next day. It was four days before I could find him and tell him she was dead. Her body was preserved so he could see her before she was buried. I punished myself, and him, by going to view her corpse when he came back for the funeral.

"The reason our first baby, Raven, suffered so was because it was my first time experiencing metabolic acidosis, and I wanted the doctors to save her, so I let them do anything, but there is nothing that can be done with that disease. With the second baby, I was less willing to let the doctors interfere. With the third baby, I didn't let them do anything. It was more important that Sachi have a quality of life, rather than be tormented for experimental purposes.

"Taj was very *there* for Fatimah's illness. We slept at the hospital together. He was very there for me. When we had Sachi, he had already met Dawn, the woman he lives with now in Pasadena.

"Our relationship was, most of the time, very intense. We were very deeply bonded, bonded for many past lives. We embodied eternal struggle between the male and female entities of the universe. Over the years, we've both been trying to find a way to heal that rift between god and goddess, man and woman. It is a long process, and it's not quite completed yet. Taj's life is the road, and my life is now Kauai, but we are learning to be friends.

"I was one of five children, and I don't think I ever felt loved. I didn't have really high self-esteem. I didn't have enough self-esteem to be able to turn away from the great love of my life. But I've learned that God is the greatest love of my life. I am God. I stayed in a difficult relationship for a long time, 24 years, and endured hardships that [see] most marriages nowadays disintegrate. I don't intend to marry again, so I haven't found a point in breaking my word to the marriage. I am still raising the children. To me, marriage serves as a nest for young birds, until they fly away.

"But I didn't have the strength or character to leave him. I informed him that I was going to make my own independent sexual choices, but I would tell him, not betray him. I made a couple of choices that drove him fucking insane. He was quite stressed by it. It was all about control. We acted out the whole male/female control issue drama to the extreme. We are both very dramatic, theatrical people.

"I've tried, through most of our relationship, to create the space for him to feel honest and safe, but I don't think I've been totally successful. And I haven't always made him completely safe with the truth, either.

"Our relationship has always been pretty charged. A lot of the volatile incidents were around infidelity. He'd always be, 'Oh, I stopped. I'll never do it again. It's over.' But it never was. He doesn't like to be cornered, even by himself. The violence is why he ultimately left. It was dangerous for both of us.

"I've always had compassion for him being unfaithful. I can imagine ten months out of the year on the road, alone, and coming from the stage after all that adulation, walking to the hotel room with nobody, to sit there and pick up a cold telephone and call me. Why, when you have 30 women in the front row saying, 'Take me to your hotel room. I've got a joint here. I'll make you feel good'? Adulation is such a drug. Look at the reflex. Your kids are angry at you, disappointed, not getting what they need, and then you go onstage and 10,000 people shout that you're the best, most wonderful person in the world.

"We mulled over the option of a second wife as some kind of solution. The whole idea was to be up-front and honest to what was going on, as opposed to going into denial. We talked intellectually about it. I said, 'For once, please, let's see if we can live with truth here.' At my request, he brought his new mate, Dawn, to Hawaii and introduced us. He brought her to my baby shower when I was nine months pregnant with Zoe and Sachi. His timing was not the best. I was not pleasant to Dawn. She was not suitable for me. I told him right then that he'd have to choose. He said he would choose me, and then he tried to go on living his double life. I told him, 'Six months of celibacy and an AIDS test. That will show you're committed.' I guess it wasn't worth it for him. That was in 1991.

"He left me and the kids in 1995 to live with Dawn. I decided that I couldn't blame Taj for this horrible relationship, because I stayed in it. If the rabbit bites you once, it's the rabbit's fault. If the rabbit bites twice, it's your fault. I got bit a lot. I kept feeling that I would bleed to death if I cut off the relationship. I thought he was the only one who did love me and, I felt, the only one who could. I thought I was too large of an entity, too passionate, for most people to love. We matched, in some kind of crazy way.

"I stayed in the relationship so long because he became my whole family. I didn't have a successful relationship with my family. I didn't have a successful relationship with myself. I did not love myself enough to go into the world and be who I was meant to be. I know that. I didn't trust my own abilities to be a fully realized human being. That's why I stayed.

"I am pretty happy with our separating. It has, step by step, given me time to grow. I don't know why we're still married, but we are. I know that the bond between us is deeper than traditional values. The relationship had to expand, had to stretch out over a space of time. Trying to conform to traditional standards was impractical. We were living two separate sets of values, two different realities. None of it works, but in the long run it exists because it exists. When it's not necessary to exist in that form, then it won't exist.

"I haven't divorced, because in my mind I just changed the terms of our relationship. We're co-parenting. The marriage is about securing the future of all of his children. I will protect the rights of every child of his line. I thought that, if I divorced him, then the children would lose him in every single way.

"His children are very strong, very beautiful, very creative. In that, they have inherited his legacy. Every one of his children is phenomenal. A lot of kids doing this emotional yo-yo of a not-present father would go down, but his kids don't go down. They go up. I think Taj is trying to teach them a lesson about emotional independence, even though it's a painful lesson. There is also a lesson about not stopping in what you're doing until you're on the top of your game. They get that, too. I give them a lot of credit.

"He hasn't been there emotionally or physically, but he's there financially very well with all his kids. His idea is to make sure that all of his kids are supported. He's done very well, keeping up the pace with what he needs to do by them, financially. I give him credit for that. He's a brilliant human being. He has flashes of insights into the issues where he knows it and he sees it.

"Taj has a spiritual direction, and music is his spiritual practice. He reads a lot of spiritual-guidance materials, but he just can't come from top to bottom. He has too many shelves. He separates his conscience and can tuck things in the shelves. He's not able, at this point, to be spiritual from top to bottom. It's in his head, and I think it's in his spirit, but he's got a lot of closets he needs to clean out. That's hard for him, because of what he does for a living. Most of us can stay in one place and work through these things point by point. The difficult part for Taj is that he always has to get on the stage, catch the next plane.

"I consider Taj my friend. I have to trust that his heart is ultimately good. I still love him. I'll be his friend forever. He's a great person. There is so much good about him.

"As for what's going on in my life outside of Taj, I had an art gallery for a couple of years. Now I teach and practice Ashitanga yoga. I'm working with the Department of Education in Hawaii to rebuild my teaching credentials. Right now, I'm teaching art, music, social studies, and physical education to first- and second-graders. Plus, I have my invalid 92-year-old grandmother – who needs a lot of care – living with me, and I have my three girls here. At this point in my life, I'm in a service mode."

*

Personal relationships are commonly seen through prisms. People's loves and hates are colored by their point of view of their self, as well as the other. Caroline Binch, mother of Taj's 18-year-old son Joseph, sees her relationship with Taj through an artistic, rose-colored facet. She listens to Taj's *Mo' Roots* album while working on her latest book illustration and takes a break. She sits in a rocker, looking through the windows at the big sky that bends over the Atlantic Ocean a short distance away. Her cottage is six miles outside Penzance, a village on England's Cornwall peninsula, which points vaguely toward the Caribbean, one of her favorite places on Earth.

"I was 34 when I met Taj at the Glastonbury Festival in 1981, where he was headlining," she says. "He just knocked my socks off. He was all those things you dream about, and he still is. I purposely wanted to have Joe, who was born in June 1982, even though I knew that there would be no chance to spending time with Taj, because of his gypsiness. I didn't know at the time that he was married. Looking back, it was a very wild thing to do, but it didn't seem wild to me; it seemed inevitable. The man is so extraordinary, of course I fell in love with him. I think that he complements his music in person. He is a larger-than-life bloke. I am thrilled to have known him, to know him, and to have an extraordinary son by him.

"When I first met Taj, at the festival, I didn't get close to him, as I was with someone else. He went on to Ireland, and I caught his next show in London. He was over here for a month, so I got to spend quite a bit of time with him. Now, I see Taj sometimes two or three times a year, or there can be whole big stretches when we don't see each other.

"What can I say about Taj? He is striking, curious, soulful, beautiful, intelligent, inspiring, instinctive, enthusiastic, humorous, and charming. He is a hell of a good-looking guy, which is why he has so many children by so many ladies. There's no point going into the false side, because I'm not involved enough in his life, and there's no point, anyway. It's easy to keep the magic with him, because I live in a different country than he. No, it's not so easy, either, but it's nice to be positive.

"Taj is a real explorer. He's on the move out there and wants to communicate. He listens and gets excited about what he's hearing. He's like a beacon – the energy he has shines when he's performing and as a private person. Taj is a bit of a gypsy, isn't he? That's how I thought of him at Glastonbury, as being a gypsy, and music comes through him from all kinds of places. It's such a positive, honest music. His music is rooted in the land and sea, and that part appeals to so many people, because they have that same sense of being connected.

"I love how he adores cows. That comes through Joe, too. Joe loves cows, quite independently. He didn't know about his dad loving cows. A man who loves cows – you know you're on a winner. And he knows so much about everything. There's not much he doesn't know something about. I think of him like a sponge: he absorbs as he travels about. One of the best good things [is that] I like listening to music with him and talking about it. He's interested in music the whole time. You get the politics coming in, but that is just what's happening around him at the time. The music is a wonderful journey that he's on. He just such a good person to have in the world.

"Joe's a very unique chip off the old block. He's been playing the drums since about six and is self-taught. Joe is a damn good drummer. He likes a lot of his dad's old music. In 1990, we had a big family reunion – instigated by Inshirah – at Anna de León's restaurant in Oakland. It was unbelievable, so much fun. But even getting there was difficult for me, because Joe – who was eight – was so angry at his dad, because he hadn't had contact. In the airport, Joe ran down some chute into the security area. Oh, the drama. He's meant to be onstage, like his father. Joe and Ahmen have become really good buddies. It would be great to put together all the siblings who are into music and see what happens.

"I love Taj's talking and all his stories, and his sense of humor, and how he improvises. You have to listen close to get all the things going on. It's lovely, how he plays with words and the languages. He speaks in a kind of poetry. And then the singing! His voice is the thing for me, so expressive and beautiful. He reminds me of a king. That's the African thing. He must have come from some king line. He's so great, because he's so vital and so creative.

"He was such a darling when he met my mum and dad, so charming to my mum. [He] took her arm, and my mum loved it. He made her feel really nice."

Victoria Montgomery was 17 years old when she met Taj. They had an eight-year-long relationship before their daughter, Yasmeen, was born, in 1982.

"My girlfriend talked me into going to this club in San Jose," Victoria says from her home in Hawaii. "I didn't want to go. I didn't even know who Taj Mahal was. But during the show, he made eye contact with me. During the show, we were staring at each other a lot. I would have never initiated meeting him, but after the show he sent out a band member to invite me backstage to meet him. Boy, therein began this whole change in my life.

"It was an immediate hook-up. There was always this struck tone between us, something about his music. It was so different. It hit me in this place where nothing else had ever touched. I really connected to that. I thought that anybody who could do that and make people feel that way has really got to be exceptional.

"He was living in Berkeley, and used to play the whole Bay area a lot. We just hung out a lot. I was really young, a party girl who wanted to have fun. We went all over. We went to Canada together and hung out at the Queen Victoria Hotel in Vancouver. I went to LA with him. That was *so* exciting and fun, all these big stars all around all the time. Very impressive. I remember when he was making an album in Oakland at the Blue Bear Studios. It was fun to be there.

"At the time, when we met, he wasn't married, but then he did marry Inshirah, except no one told me for a very long time.

"We 'enhanced' ourselves quite a bit back then. There were some Jamaicans in the band, and they had quite a bit of spliffs. They basically rolled a whole lid of weed in a joint. We smoked a lot of weed and snorted a lot of coke in those days, dancing and partying and having fun. It was all kind of fuzzy.

"I was pretty wild, and was really into drugs a lot. I got real crazy out there for a while. In 1979, all that ended for me. I went into drug recovery, and have been clean ever since of all drugs and alcohol and everything. But before that, it was insane. There was a lot of drugs going on. I was majoring in drug addiction.

"Taj will tell you that he and I was real. Once, he told me that I saved his life. He felt that he was going to die, out there in the world. He and I were very close at one time; we totally connected. We've always been able to really talk. I remember, in San Jose, he had this old beat-up van. He'd come and pick me up. We went out after one of his shows in San Cruz and parked at the end of the wharf. We sat up all night long in the back of his van, talking and talking and talking until the sun came up. He poured out everything, his whole life story, and Taj is not that kind of man. He does not talk about feelings real comfortably. He's not real in touch with that whole part of himself. But he told me everything about his mom and dad and about the accident that killed his dad and what that did to him.

"Everything changed, at that moment, with us. Before that, it had always been, 'Yeah, let's go party and have fun.' After that, we were real bonded in a whole different way. He used to call me from the road and we'd have long heart-to-heart talks on the phone. He'd tell me about how lonely he was there out on the road. I can imagine that that is really a tough life, in a lot of ways.

"Of course, many years later, I came to realize that he did that to himself a lot. He didn't need to have that happen. He could have stayed connected to family and had a lot more of that in his life. He has made choices. For whatever reasons, he's chosen not to do that.

"It was a long-standing relationship, but there were periods when we won't see each other for several months. He'd be gone on the road. It wasn't like it was a committed relationship, or we were a couple and that's that; we'd come together whenever he was close enough to do that.

"I knew the moment I became pregnant. I even told Taj – 'Oh, we just made a baby.' He said, 'Okay, yeah, right.' Of course, I was right. We were in the lobby of the Doubletree Hotel in Monterey when I told him. While I was pregnant, I found out that Taj was married. It was clear that I was probably going to be on my own having this kid. While I was pregnant with Yasmeen, I hooked up with Arvin, the man who was to become my husband. We got married when Yasmeen was two months old. He and I stayed together for a long time and then got divorced. Now he's here again, and we're back together and have a three-year-old daughter.

"Yasmeen was about two years old when Arvin and I split. Then Yasmeen and I were living in Santa Rosa. I was working in a methadone clinic. We lived in a good neighborhood, but there was still drive-by shootings. One night, a bullet went through our living-room window, right where Yasmeen had been sitting moments before. That's when I decided, 'I'm out of here.' When you've got to teach your kid to hit the floor, it's time to go.

"I took Yasmeen to Hawaii to visit with Taj and Inshirah for two weeks. Inshirah and I have shared a lot. Boy, we've been through it! She and I have been pretty good friends. We live on the same island. I totally fell in love with the place. A couple days before I was to leave, it occurred to me that I could live there. I'd like that. We were all horseback riding, and I told Taj, 'You know, I wouldn't mind moving here.' Taj was just thrilled that we would move to Hawaii. He was real supportive of the whole idea. I prayed about it, and it seemed like a good move. A real motivation for me was that I really wanted Yasmeen to be around her dad more, for better or worse. I wanted her to know him more.

"We had some falling out over Yasmeen and his not really coming through. He would send her things from the road – his music and lots of things – but he didn't show up for her functions. He didn't show up for her graduation. He's just not flat showed up – not called on her birthday, not done a lot of things. That really caused some serious pain. He's kind of hurt her quite a bit. Not only her but all the kids. What can I say? He's a bluesman.

"Taj was paying child support, but it was sort of a battle to get that going. Over the years, I've had to track him down, but not too much. I have to say that, all in all, I've been lucky. I've known a lot of women who've had to fight tooth and nail for every $5 bill in child support. Yasmeen was able to go to a private Christian school, and that would have never happened had Taj not been responsible in that way. I may have a lot of personal feelings about things he didn't do, but what he did is nothing to spit at. Many, many men walk away from that, and he didn't. For that, I really do admire him.

"I was able to raise an incredibly wonderful daughter, a real go-getter, a brilliant, incredibly intelligent human being. She's real clear about her goals. Real clear about no drugs, thank God – that's a miracle in itself. She's now a freshman at Santa Rosa Junior College in Santa Rose, CA, majoring in theater arts with interest in teaching high-school psychology. She is very talented, and has a great voice. It must be the gene – not only from Taj, but I used to sing in a band for a long time, and took piano for years. Yasmeen had the lead in her high-school production of *Hair* and now has the lead in *Tommy* at her college.

"Taj is Taj. He's one of a kind. He's difficult to communicate with in a lot of ways, but I think that his heart is in the right place. He's a real unusual person. I have a whole lot of feelings about Taj, and a lot of them really conflict. I know that, overall, we have said to each other that we are very close, and we always will be. He always used to say that any two people who can do something like make Yasmeen have got to be something good. She's just awesome.

"I don't want to bad-rap him. I really don't have anything bad to say about Taj. I think he's got a really good heart. I love Taj. I'll always love Taj, no matter what. He'll always love me – I always know that, too. Maybe not in a romantic way, or in a couple way. We've moved past that. We're good friends, and we have a real bond. I resent a lot of the pain he has caused his kids, but I think he did the very best he could do with what he had. He went through some traumatic stuff in his childhood that contributed a lot to who he is today."

Yasmeen doesn't want to bad-rap her dad, either. "He's done a lot for me," she says between classes at Santa Rosa. "It's been difficult not having a father, and Taj is a hard guy to get to know, but he's helped me when there was no other help. In the summers, I went to the Omni Camp in Poland Springs, Maine, because we did a trade-out for Taj playing concerts and giving workshops there. Without Taj, I wouldn't have all these wonderful brothers and sisters.

"I listen to Taj's music and really, really like it. Even if he wasn't family, I'd listen to it all the time. There are so many influences in his music that it's hard to categorize, and that makes it a learning experience."

Valerie Celine, mother of Taj's youngest son, six-year-old Micah Martin (after Dr Martin Luther King, Jr), is also positive about Taj, although with a harder eye on reality. She is a professional psychic consultant who works with individuals and corporations, and has helped the police on a couple of cases. "I wear many hats," she says, sitting in the enclosed sun porch of her home in Minneapolis. "I teach psychic development; I'm a clairvoyant and a medium, which I've been doing full time for 13 years; I'm a spiritual trainer, where I work with kick boxing and different types of movement to build people up, spiritually; [and] I do kick boxing."

She pauses to look out of her big windows. It's winter, but inside the sun porch green plants flourish and hanging crystals reflect darts of rainbow colors. Outside, the leafless trees are dark, skeletal sculptures – nature as rendered by Giacometti – so Valerie can see the nearby Mississippi River.

"I was 24 when I met Taj, in 1984, when I worked for a local radio station. My job was to go out into the field and interview different artists when they came to town for a concert. I was assigned to interview Taj Mahal. The concert was canceled at the last minute, so we met at a private party and did the interview at a person's house.

"When I first saw him, I was really taken aback by his presence, which seemed bigger than everybody else's. I remember thinking, 'God, who does this guy think he is?'" Valerie lets loose a delightful, full, ready laugh, which often punctuates her conversation. "At the interview, I said to him, 'You are an incredible person.' He looked me right in the eye and replied, 'Everything you see in me exists inside of you, or you couldn't see it.' He's the very first person that ever gave that context to me, of people being mirrors to each other. We talked about every philosophy under the sun. I was instantly aware of a heightened state of awareness in his company. I'd think, 'Why can't I have that feeling when he's not around?' At that time, I didn't know that it was available to myself and within myself. As a result of meeting with him that evening, and hanging out at the party after the interview, I began a relationship with him that is very unique.

"Taj has been the most powerful teacher in my life, opening up new worlds to me that I had never experienced. I've learned from Taj that life doesn't always go the way you think it's supposed to go, especially in the area of love and why people meet. That doesn't always follow the straight-and-narrow track. I learned a lot about my spirituality through knowing Taj. He was the first person who actually understood what I was talking about when I shared my psychic experiences, and that was very powerful for me. He was the first person who said, 'Oh, yeah, I know what that is.' I definitely connected with him on a soul level that went beyond reason or explanation.

"A lot of people put Taj on a pedestal. That not only separates and isolates him from people but also sets him up to be their savior, like in, 'Being around him, everything is perfect, so I need to be around him.' He helped me understand that the ability to be my own savior was within myself. It wasn't him so much I was experiencing but that I was given the opportunity to experience a part of myself. That was, and still is, quite a gift.

"I've written many songs about Taj. One is about breaking my heart open to a whole new existence. I've been a musician since I was a young girl, and have had a deep love for music. I feel that music is one of the tools that can open other dimensions for us. Music is a very powerful healing tool. When Taj plays his music, he does the same thing I do when I do a reading – that higher energy comes through. He's a channel for that.

"With Taj, there are two things going on all the time. First, there is the part of him that is comfortable in opening up his heart onstage to an audience. He has the most incredible heart I've ever known in a person.

Inshirah in 1990

Taj's sister Connie with brother Winston

Performing at the 1991 Bearsville concert

Taj with Tim Duffy, founder of the Music Makers Foundation, on the Winston Blues Revival tour

Taj playing at the 1991 Bearsville concert

Taj backstage at the
1991 Bearsville concert

Left and below: Taj
and Michelle Shocked
in concert at the Ulster
Performing Arts
Center in Kingston,
New York, 1992

L-r: Dawn; Marie "Sweet Mama" Janisse; Marie's daughter, Desiree; and Taj at the San Bernadino Renaissance Fair in California, May 1998

Ozzie holding his newborn child

Taj Jr and Ghamela in Sacramento, 1997

Taj performing at an outdoor concert on Catalina Island, California, 1999

Etta Baker (left), Alga Mae Hinton (center, on comb) and Taj playing old-time blues in 1999 as part of the Music Makers Foundation

Performing at an outdoor concert on Catalina Island, California, in 1999

Taj with old-time blues player Aunt Lydia in her kitchen in Lebanon, Maryland, in 1999

Taj, Inshirah and Taj Jr in Hawaii in the late '90s

The Winston Blues Revival tour, 1999. L-r: Chris Uhler, Taj, Danny Dudeck, Macavine Hayes (seated), Beverly "Guitar" Watkins, Ardie Dean and John Schwenke

Taj Jr in 1999

Deva in 1999, the year of her high-school graduation

Taj playing on the Music Makers tour in 1999

Second, in his personal life, he has difficulty with that kind of intimacy on one-to-one relations.

"I was challenged a great deal around trusting that my love for Taj was more than others thought of the situation. Like, 'Oh, she's just a groupie. She just this young thing he has in Minneapolis.' Our relationship didn't fit in accepted modes. It was constantly challenged by what I felt in my heart for this man. I knew the relationship was very old, like I hadn't just met him for the first time. I had memories and sensations like, 'Ah, I know you.' There was no rational reason why I should feel that way. He lived a totally different world than I did.

"Throughout my years of knowing Taj – before I had our son, Micah, born in 1994 – there were times when I thought, 'Maybe, yeah, this is just one of those things, that he's got a woman in every port. I don't mean anything to him other than convenience.' That was easier to accept than what was really happening.

"How to describe Taj? I think of a line by Kris Kristofferson in a song about Johnny Cash: 'He's a walking contradiction, partly truth and partly fiction.' I think people see a reflection of their higher energy in Taj. They attach a whole lot of expectations on what he is going to do for them, instead of acknowledging that it is an energy available to everyone to do for themselves. A lot of times when you're a star, when you radiate light like he is able to do when he opens up to play his music, people want a piece of that. They want to attach to that, because they don't believe they have direct access [to it] within themselves.

"People constantly tell Taj, 'Oh, you're incredible.' I've seen that move him farther away from being able to just be human, to have that human connection. He is a human being, just like you and I, here on Earth to learn.

"I've learned first hand with Taj that we don't run from our fears. We run from love, and we run from ourselves. It's not fear we run from but the light, the power within us, our divinity. Taj and I were both running. Part of the safety in knowing Taj was that I knew he would leave, and part of his safety was knowing that he could leave. He wrote a song about that, '21st Century Gypsy Singin' Lover Man,' on the *Señor Blues* album. He wrote that his palm starts itching if he doesn't have that airline ticket in his hand. But that song has a lot of longing and sadness, in that he has to say goodbye. That is what he has to walk with, every single day of his life. There is part of him that doesn't want to keep running, but he keeps running. That's what has allowed me to have the depth of compassion for him I do, after what we've walked through.

"There is an enormous amount of loneliness in him. I think his loneliness is one thing I had in common with him when we met. I was very alone with my way of viewing the world. He was the kind of person who wasn't in the textbook, and neither was I. There wasn't any way to say, 'This is what I do,' without people being suspect.

"Taj never denied Micah, who was a miracle in and of itself. I was told that I could not physically have children. Taj always talked about this soul he would see floating around whenever we were together. I'd say, 'No. Ain't going to happen, honey.' Then comes this child. The universe couldn't have picked a worse time for either Taj or myself. It was really a struggle for me to go ahead with the pregnancy. I really questioned it. The whole time I was going through that decision, I couldn't make contact with Taj. He was just not responding.

"The whole time I was pregnant, I put headphones on my stomach and played Taj's music to the unborn baby, and I continued to play Taj's music to Micah after he was born, so he constantly heard his father's voice.

"I felt a sense of abandonment when Micah was born, to put it mildly. Kicked to the curb and left for dead was how I felt. Adios, amiga. It was really deep, very hard. During that difficult time, I wasn't allowing Taj to be human. I had all these 'shoulds.' He should have known better. He should have done that. He should do this. I didn't cut him any slack. I couldn't allow myself to see the human aspect of where he was really at. I had all these judgments.

"I never really dreamed that we would talk again, after Micah was born. I couldn't conceive of it, at that point. I hated Taj with such power that I was killing myself inside. I ended up in a hospital from hating him so much. It was the most painful thing I've ever gone through. Thankfully, today, I've been able to heal that. We now have a trusting and understanding relationship, which is very humbling.

"The day Micah met Taj, when he was two and half, Taj and my relationship was like troops facing each other across the front line. We were not in a very good mood. We had yelled at each other on the phone, which we had never done. I was very angry. I didn't even know that he would show up. I didn't tell Micah that we were going to meet his dad, in case it was a no-show. Taj pulls up in the car with Carey Williams. If it hadn't been for Carey, bridges would have been burned between Taj and I. Micah leans out of my arms towards Taj and says, 'Dad.' At that moment, everybody was in tears. Even Taj had tears in his eyes. Micah just held onto his neck and would not let go.

"One minute I had wanted to slice Taj in two, and the next minute my son said, 'You can forget all about that.' Children shall lead the way. Micah figuratively took Taj and me by the hand and said, 'Okay, this is how we're going to do it. We're all committed to this. None of us are victims here, so we might as well get along.'

"There isn't a day that doesn't go by that Micah doesn't think of his dad. He hasn't seen him in almost two years, yet they are so connected. I've had to learn not to judge what isn't happening and trust that this unfolding is exactly the way it's suppose to be. My job is to make sure that Micah doesn't grow up thinking that he is not loved by his father. I have to trust that there is a divine order here, and that my son is not going to grow up lacking in love.

"The first time Micah heard *Señor Blues*, when he was three years old, was with Taj, who was here visiting. After Taj left, Micah kept saying, 'Mom, play the magic. Play the magic.' I kept saying, 'Micah, honey, what are you talking about?' 'Daddy's magic.' Whenever he heard *Señor Blues*, he'd say, 'That's the magic. That's the magic.' So, the day Taj called and said the album was nominated for a Grammy, I knew instantly that he would win, because that was the magic.

"Taj is a crowd-pleaser. He doesn't like to say no, because he doesn't want to hurt anyone's feelings, but he ends up hurting them more because he can't say no. He wants to please everybody. I think that's why he is so good at what he does. When he works the stage, he makes everyone feel good, even if you don't like his music. You can't help but smile in the presence of his music.

"He loves to please and hates confrontation with people. He disappears out of people's lives if he can't follow through with what he said he was going to do, because he feels so bad about it. If I could be so presumptuous to speak for him, what I've seen is that a lot of that stems from the unresolved pain from his childhood around his father's death. There was such a feeling of abandonment, on so many levels, and Taj had to grow up so quickly. He has continued the pattern of abandonment, and if he doesn't resolve them within himself those patterns will continue.

"Sometimes I've seen Taj get on this self-pity thing, where, 'I've got to do all this for everybody and everyone's dependent on me.' Well, hello! You signed up for this. I don't see Taj as a victim; I see him as a very blessed individual with a lot of people who love him, a lot of people who hang on him, a lot of people who don't want to do anything for themselves. They want Taj to fork over the money. I don't envy his situation, but at the same time he is truly blessed by his beautiful children.

"I was never treated by Taj in a disrespectful way, except when our son was born. That's why it was so devastating for me, when he disappeared those two years after Micah's birth. That was so different than what I had known him to be. What healed our relationship was Micah. When I saw how much my son loved his father from the git-go, that it was in his soul, I knew that I would have to deal with my feelings.

"That's why it was very hard to bring legal action against Taj. At the time, Micah and I were living in a basement one-room apartment. Taj has always wanted to tell the story, in his own mind, that he did what he was supposed to do, financially, for this little boy; but, the truth be known, the only reason that happened was because I hired a sheriff to go to Taj's concert and serve him papers. He owed me, at the time, nearly $40,000 in back child support. It was the hardest thing I've ever done. I was scared to death. From that point on, things have been straight, financially. I've hired lawyers to maintain the account. That's removed it from the personal to the business.

"I still love Taj. I wish him all the best."

Taj now lives with Dawn Perryman in a modest house on a quiet, leafy street in Pasadena. On most mornings, they take a brisk, two-mile walk, part of their regime to stay healthy. Taj has given up cigarettes and his much-enjoyed cigars and eats a primarily vegetarian diet. After the walk this morning, Dawn settles down in the kitchen and talks about her life with Taj.

"I first met Taj in 1990, after burying my father, to whom I was very close, and his death was traumatic for me. I was flying home from Jackson, Miss[issippi], to LA. I was very, very, *deeply* depressed, and in a fetal position in my seat. The plane was full, and this last person rushed onto the plane with a big boom box and sat next to me. It was Taj. For a long time we didn't say anything, then started talking. He helped me come out of the shock I was in over the loss of my father.

"Over the next year or so, we talked a lot over the phone. He helped me get through my father's death, and we became really good friends. My dad had a degree in horticultural and animal husbandry, just like Taj, so there was an immediate bonding. We'd talk about farming. We loved family and cooking and basic, country, simple things.

"Taj was touring most of the time, then. We were just friends, and would talk on the phone maybe two and three times a day. Taj also was having a lot of pain at this time. As I got to know him, he explained his situation – working non-stop and the issues *that* caused with his kids and Inshirah. Their relationship was supposed to be over, but they were staying together because of the kids. That was very painful for him. He would talk about it, purging, venting, and getting rid of a lot of things. He doesn't like to hurt people; he tries to make everybody happy, tries to take care of things for everybody else.

"We became friends first, and that's what really has made our relationship work. I was so in shock and pain, and Taj was in pain over his things. I think that slowed us down to one another at that moment we met. We embraced one another in pain. Fortunately, we grew beyond that. Our friendship blossomed into a romance. We finally acknowledged that we were in love in about 1991.

"We stopped seeing each other for about a year, because I wanted a monogamous relationship and Taj was seeing somebody else. We still had contact. He'd call if something important was happening, or when he'd be on TV, and let me know. We got back together when he said that he wasn't going to see anybody else, he really wanted to be with me. We really got closer and cemented our relationship. We decided to build a life together, especially after he said that he was going to start a new life. You get what I'm saying? This was 1995.

"We had a lot of trials and tribulations, because we had multi-lives going on – his children, his making a shift in his marriage with Inshirah and a shift in his career. He was terribly frustrated. This guy worked so hard that he hasn't been able to do a lot work on himself, because he was providing for the kids and Inshirah. In his pain, he didn't make the right choices, because he was so busy working. That constant working is part of his pain. In a lot of cases, I wouldn't say that he did the right thing, but I'm not in judgment of him. Basically, he tried to do the right thing.

"We're working our problems out and finding solutions. We've learned to talk and talk about things, even though they hurt. What really makes it work for us is that, when he goes on tour, I get busy with my career. I design clothes, and have a passion for it. I've been designing for 21 years. I had a studio and design wedding and prom dresses, eveningwear, and suits. I started doing wearable art. I've done a few special projects on movies. I love making people look really cool. I'm interested now in retailing and mail ordering. I've been making the transition from a shop to a website.

"I'm finally getting my blessings, after all this time. I see Taj blossoming and dreaming again. I think he's going back to that freshness that was there when he was a teenager. He's going back to opening up again, of not being afraid to open up a little bit more.

"For example, he's more introspective now than before. He'll say, 'I know that I don't do this or that, and I don't do it because of my past experiences.' Just recently, he said, 'I know that I don't communicate, sometimes. I know that I cut off from you. That's because, in my previous marriage, I was very communicative, and then my communication would go nowhere. So now I'm numb with that and just shut off sometimes, but I'm learning not to do that.' He'd never apologize, but then he'd go deeper and say, 'I realize that I shut down, and I'm not going to shut down. I'm going to communicate more.' The lesson we're learning now is [to] soften up. We don't have to be so powerfully energetic or bombastic. We're learning to solve problems instead of whining and being a victim. It's been painful, but we're doing it.

"Taj is reading more spiritual books, like *Seat Of The Soul*. It talks about your addictions and why you have them. I think that Taj's singing is a form of meditation for him; he transcends and totally connects to that source. The key is not being afraid to allow your heart to open, to be vulnerable. There is such a sweetness there. I know that the reason we were put together is to do the spiritual work. There is work being done with Taj on the spiritual plane."

22 Well...

Well, Taj?

"Everybody has his or her story, and there is truth in that story. I don't mind being called out on the line, but the others should acknowledge their part, too. They have to smell the skunk that is on their side of the line. The rules of engagement are, you are responsible for whatever it is.

"Like with Siena. She doesn't mention that there was another man in the delivery room thinking she was giving birth to his children. Then out comes these tan babies. The wrong color. Clearly I had spent intimate time with Siena, and then I didn't see her after that. Months later, I'm back in the United States and I get word about the twins in January. I count up the months on my fingers and the numbers didn't add up. But I wasn't figuring in premature birth, which is what happened.

"I made it my business to go over and see the kids that this woman was claiming to be mine. As soon as I looked at them, I said, 'Sure, fine, they're mine.' I didn't go through, 'No, now I'm going to take you downtown and we're going to get blood tests.' I put in the best support I could at the time, considering where I was. I paid the rent on the Treat Street house. Whenever Vicki asked for money to buy food or whatever, I gave it.

"As far as supporting the kids' education, I always didn't agree on the type of private schools Inshirah wanted for the kids. I believe in the basics – that is, you learn reading, writing, and arithmetic. So, some of this modern approach, I questioned if that was the best place to put my money. Now, I admit, the support money wasn't always there how it should have been. At times, when Inshirah was handling my personal business, things didn't get taken care of always in the best possible way. Carey and I took over and got things spread out evenly. When the kids hit 18, then it's their responsibility.

"Whatever it takes to be responsible, you have to be up to it. In my case, that meant that I had to be gone to earn the money to support the family and kids. I accepted the responsibility. The mothers and kids are not going to see that it's a good thing. They're going to go, 'Wow, my dad ain't here and I wish he was.' Well, the set-up is, if you want to eat pancakes, somebody has to go out and get the means for the pancakes. That's what was there for me. With Monday-morning quarterbacking, we can come up with some reason why I could have been something different.

"Kids who have fathers who travel a lot, be it a professional athlete or IBM executive, the dad is gone. The kids start to understand why Dad is gone when Mom walks the kid into the into the kitchen and opens up the refrigerator and says, 'You see all that food? This is what your dad is hard at work making sure we have.'

"There is the kid's point of view and the parents' point of view. There is a time in the child's life that, whatever you do as a parent, you are wrong. Every parent knows this. I knew that there was a time when I'd always be wrong with my kids. I knew it was coming. But if the parents are really connecting together, Mom swings over what she can do because she is that particular kind of softness, the embodiment of the beauty, the heavens themselves, come down to do a part of this thing on Earth. That's her job. It's Dad's job to set the pace and cut the line and say what's got to be. That is not something everybody is always going to enjoy. My mother knew how to smoothe my father down without making him [aggravated]. She could do it without chopping him down or disemboweling him to get her way. I really appreciated that.

"I think the kids…it's their job to piss you off from when they are ages eleven to 25. They are having the most rapid growth in their lives in those years. All kinds of things can happen at that point. The only thing you can do as a parent is be a friend. The problem for parents is when you are not willing to be disliked by your kids.

"I feel that I'm lucky to have the job I have, of being able to go out and do this thing that really charges people up with energy to continue on and have positive lives, to look at things better. It's costly as hell to be this guy, in all kinds of ways. There have been people who have supported me when, at various times in my life, I've been so focused on what I've had to do that they suffered. I know this. Whatever I need to do in my life to reconnect with those people, I've been on a movement toward that reconnection. One by one, little by little, we've made the connection.

"I want to see all my kids be personally successful. I'm not worried about them being movie stars. Not that they couldn't be! I want to make sure that my kids can handle all the danger that is out there, and there is a lot of it.

"Inshirah is the mother of my children. We have made a family together for many years, and I owe her that respect. I'm just not a person who can talk about private pain. We did have some rough-and-tumble stuff, no two ways about it. I just don't think that needs to be in here. The highs and lows are ours, really, and they just don't belong to the world.

"When Inshirah and I first got together, she came with me on the road, and it was fun, traveling together. We went to England, Switzerland, France, Spain, Italy. She traveled around the States with me as I toured. She got to meet a lot of people. We had fun times.

"Within six months of getting together with Inshirah, we were pregnant. Although the woman carries the baby, it definitely is a *we* – that's the way it really is. Then Raven was born and was ill for seven months and died. This was a difficult time for us. Then Fatimah was born and she was also ill. Even with sick babies, I had to work. This was my reality. That was really crazy, because I couldn't just stop the business. I was working on the road for much of that time. I had just got everything balanced again towards the end of the '60s, after years of being crazy. In the '70s, we came around the corner and got the finances in balance and got ahead. A certain amount of nudging it along had to happen in order for it to happen, and that nudging was my working.

"With the babies, something was wrong, that the chain of protein breaking down into nutrients wasn't happening. Ultimately, with all the work that the doctors did, they couldn't put their finger on a specific cause. They never did know what caused it, the map on it, after doing biopsies. We started thinking of all sorts of things, like we have relatives from the same state, all sorts of things.

"I don't blame Inshirah for the death of the children. What I said to her was that I didn't understand this. 'Why is this happening to us? Why are we being visited this way?' It would make anybody question what was going on. Not one baby but *three* babies. If there had been a better meeting of the minds between us, we would have looked at this as a lesson that we have to work through. It was never meant to be that. Not for me.

"I've never been one to talk about my personal life. It is difficult for me to share my feelings about painful things. The death of my three baby daughters was extremely painful for me. No words can describe the pain, really. It felt like I could never really grieve the loss, because I had to go out to work to support the family. Basically, because of the path I took with music, I was a journeyman working musician.

"Inshirah says that our relationship was the struggle between the sexes. Therein lies the problem she has and she'll have with anybody she decides to be intimate with or want a relationship with. The real problem comes from her not being supported as a child, so when that is placed in front of her she doesn't know what to do with it. The whole point of a relationship for her comes down to, 'It's got to be a struggle.' I don't see it as being that. I don't see being in a relationship as being in a struggle between a male and female.

"When a relationship goes into that kind of male/female power-struggle level, that makes me really suspicious of a person's personal motives in a relationship with another human being. When it comes down to issues of control, there is something wrong. I do not see a male/female relationship about struggle and control; I see the relationship about co-operation and collaboration and about synergism, where you put two people together and you create so much more incredible energy and possibility. I thought that was, and is, the value of getting together with somebody.

"This is the bottom line on this. My idea is two people working together. Her idea is that there is the war of the sexes going on. So, whether I did good or did bad or didn't do, it would still come up in the frame of the war of the sexes to her. That's her truth.

"My parents had incredible synergy in their relationship. Perhaps it is naïve or unfair of me to expect that from everybody, but that is what I see a relationship between a male and a female is about. It should be very complementary. I've known some of my women friends for years before we became intimate. It was like, 'Allah, be willing.' *Kaboom!* It wasn't some game we were playing. It was never, 'Okay, I got them, but I won't take care of them. I'll disappear.' When I hear all this disappearing stuff, I say, 'Hold on. You got to go for what was really working.' What was working was financial support, and when that's working, then I try to give as much emotional support as I can.

"With Inshirah, it got to the point where I started to doubt the truth about how things could really be with us. It was so impossible to convince myself that there was a good side to all we were doing. I don't see, being in a relationship, that is a struggle; I see it as being where you can completely soar. And not a co-dependency thing, either. It's like the song says: 'You got a line and I got a pole.' All right, let's go have some fun. After the day is done, we walk back home with a mess of fish and talk about how it was. I don't know why people don't want to go there. Like, maybe that's a little too easy. Like, we need a little drama to make life really good.

"I did not leave her for Dawn. I left Inshirah to get away from a relationship that, after seven or eight years, wasn't good for either of us. I left because the relationship had fallen to a point that seemed to be unredeemable. I really didn't want to leave at all. That was a hard decision, because I knew that the kids would be played in the balance of that.

"Our traveling together was interrupted by the illness [of] the first two babies. After Ahmen was born, we could travel together as a family, even some after Deva and Nani were born. Ahmen, Deva, and Nani went to France, Italy, Spain, and Fiji with Inshirah and me. We traveled all around the States, too. We did it all the time. It had gotten pretty much into a rhythm. During the summer, when school was out, the kids would leave California and go back east to visit family. When my tour would end, we'd spend two weeks on the East Coast visiting relatives. The kids would stay on there and visit with Inshirah's family, then go to Springfield and visit my mother and Poppo. Then up to Boston to visit Inshirah's sisters and their kids. We visited relatives in Brooklyn. We traveled as a family a tremendous amount.

"It was hard with the kids when touring, moving from place to place, sometimes every day. I couldn't really parent while I was working. It was just too frustrating for everybody. It was a lot harder to get soundchecks and interviews and get to all the places I had to be with a wife and children, especially little children. After a few kids, it was pretty impossible. I just didn't make the kind of money that would have paid the salaries of other folks to travel with us to make it easier.

"I tried to set up touring so that I'd work hard for a week, to make some money, then we'd have a couple weeks to visit and move around with the kids. That happened for a bunch of years, but the kids got tired. Ahmen just finally got tired of always leaving his friends, and that became an issue. They missed their own lives as they got older, missed their friends, so it was not easy. Hard on the family. Hard on me, too. After years of trying, I mostly stopped trying to travel with the family and brought them to one place awhile, like in Fiji.

"Being on the road working did make it hard to get home, or stay home for any length of time. Going on the road was not an escape from domestic responsibilities for me. It's a major legacy with me that my grandparents – particularly the males, and my father – would pick up their lives from where it was not working and move to where it could work. They had to do that to support their family. Whatever it took. I've been able to take that kind of energy and put it on the stage.

"There were times when I'd just as soon stayed home if someone else could have held up the financial end. I had no problem there. I would have been really happy staying home. There was a time when Inshirah went traveling for a couple of weeks in Europe, and the kids were fine with me running the home. I wasn't on the stage for the adoration. I can't do anything about the adoration fans give. I have to put adoration in context. You can get sidetracked from your work with the music by the whole adoring fan community. How does one work that out? My answer was not to go for what was in vogue but for what was true for me, staying the course, being strong and resourceful enough to do it. There is a spiritual, metaphysical, cosmic force to do what you set your mind to. In the music, the lesson was not, 'Look at me, I'm onstage. Ain't I grand?' I'm saying, 'Look at us as examples of what we can be as human beings if we put our minds to it.'

"In Hawaii, when I was home, I'd take the kids down to the beach and go boogie-boarding in the surf, or go to the mall, as kids like to do. I'd take them to school in the morning or come to their school and play music. I *wanted* to do those things. Parenting was a regular part of life, when I was at home. I went to their soccer games, and I was hollering from the side like everybody else. I'd go to their school plays. That's what helped ground me and not be so hung up in what's happening with the career, which can be taken away.

"I like to cook, and made breakfast for the kids, particularly on the weekends. I developed different kinds of pancakes they liked, with coconut and a little pineapple. I'd make home-made ice cream. They didn't like onions or garlic, but the way I learned to roast chicken with garlic, they'd eat the whole thing. I'd make fish, chicken, turkey, Mexican dishes, different kinds of curry for the kids. I'm a good cook. I make seriously good bread. I learned to cook from watching my mom. Poppo was a good cook, too, especially with the West Indian curry flavors. I'm always trying to stretch everybody's imagination of what to eat. My food centers around rice; taro; chicken; gravy; curry; stream, smothered, or smoked fish; grilled vegetables. I've developed an orange/pineapple meringue pie, which is like a combination of a key lime pie and a lemon meringue pie.

"At home, I like to maintain the grounds around the house, although in the last few years I haven't been able to maintain a high level of gardening. When I'm on the road, I miss gardening. After the late '60s, when I started changing my diet around, I realized I missed certain foods I grew up with, so I wanted to grow them in my garden. And I don't know if I'm going to do this touring forever. If I do settle in and do less traveling, then at that point I don't want to start learning the things that I want to do. I want to know and be able to start at that point, so I've taken in the agriculture information, how to deal with the soil without chemicals, how to return the organic matter. For me, fishing and gardening represent honoring what the earth has to offer and making your living that way.

"I like a domestic life, I really do. Even on the road, I have – in a strange way – a domestic life, with an extended family. I wash my own clothes. I don't ever send my clothing out to be washed, except for a specific dry-cleaning.

"It's a great concern to me what I eat on the road, so I try to go to Indian, Asian, Italian, Spanish, Cuban, African, or Caribbean restaurants, if they are available, and health-food stores to maintain energy and vitamins. I carry dried fruit supplements with me. I really work on that level. I try to stay healthy. I'm putting out a tremendous amount of energy. Traveling in different places, water is different, so I usually take bottled water. I'm very minimal in terms of intake of alcohol, although it's a little different in Europe, because they usually have wine with meals. In Europe, I also try to buy fresh fruit daily.

"I often travel with a large bus, especially in Europe, set up with a kitchen, lavatory, sleeping accommodation. When you're traveling by bus, everyone gets up for breakfast: 'Good morning. Hey, how ya doin'?' Good morning to the people who serve you breakfast. In the summer of 1999, The Hula Blues Band and I did a tour of Europe. We'd play full swing on the bus going from city to city. Those guys liked to play and sing. Everybody was swapping around tapes of Miles Davis, old Hawaiian music, Bob Dylan and The Kingston Trio, Duke Ellington, Ella Fitzgerald, Louis Armstrong, Cassandra Wilson. We were listening to everything. It was a full scene of music. It was very wonderful. I had along Smithy [Kester Smith] and Rudy Costa, guys I've played with for 30 years. These are my friends. It was like family. For me, a bus is a lot better than airplane travel. Airplane travel is usually the pits. In a plane, I leave Frankfurt and I'm in LA the same day. It's like an Alley-Oop time machine.

"When I'm on the road, it's very important to me to hit the same restaurants that I've gone to for years in different cities. In Austin, Texas, there is a place called Los Manitas, a great Mexican restaurant run by a group of Latinas. These are way hip ladies. They've been running this restaurant since I'd been going to Austin in the late '60s. They know, when they see my name as playing in town, that I'll come around and hug all the ladies and have a great meal and buy a couple of their T-shirts and bumper stickers. I just love the stuff they've got. And they're right next door to this store that has great folk art from Mexico and Central America.

"I've seen the kids of those ladies grow up. I've seen the ladies mature. The thing that makes Austin really great for me is that my day will turn around and I'll walk down to Los Manitas and they'll get Lila in the back to come out and I'll invite them all to the show, and they always come.

"This type of extended family, I've known for years and years, is a connection to real people really in the community. These are seriously politically oriented people, into stuff like gay rights and local Chicano rights. They have the support of the community, so I plug into the information that's really going on in Austin. It's all right there, in Los Manitas through the Hispanic community, so I know exactly what's going on. I'm not walking down the street thinking that everything is really cool when it ain't. That allows me to be part of a community life, even though I'm not there every day.

"There are lots of places – especially in the States – where I've hooked myself into. I'm not just from airport to hotel to club to hotel to airport; I've got friends in these towns, long-time friends who know that I'd appreciate a real good meal, so they invite me and the band over. Some of these people go back 20, 30 years. This is what my parents did for traveling musicians when I was a kid. There is a black family who has five restaurants around Albuquerque, so if I want barbecue chicken and rice and greens and black-eyed peas and all the stuff that goes along with the Southern diet, but

Western style, they've got it. If I'm up in Santa Fe, I'm going to be at Josie's: blue corn tortilla, pear pie – they're going to throw that down on you. Josie will always come out of the kitchen and give me a big hug.

"It gives me a kind of stability, having these on-going relationships with real people. I'm actually interested in all these people. I don't want to be sitting in a hotel; I want to meet people who are interesting, who carry real life with them. When I did the film *Sounder*, I did a lot of fishing with a local man, Ted Lee. I got to know the local people, go out and party with them on Friday night. On one level, they were thinking, 'Here's this guy from the movie,' but on the other hand they're just people who want to talk. Being with the local people, you get a real feel for where you are. The hotel and TV is just not for me.

"It feels like an extended family to me. I'm coming into that town, making money, and sharing that money with the people who are giving service to people. I'm careful where my money goes. Lots of time, people will serve you but they don't really care two farts in the wind about you. I'm in showbusiness, where people have to be 'on' all the time. I don't mind the 'on' part of it, but I'm real critical about the territory that 'on' exists in. Like, in that transition between coming off the road and hitting home, I always stop at a Cuban restaurant, the Versailles, not too far along Venice Boulevard and Motor Avenue from LAX. It's a familiar place for me to cool, re-adjust my head. The night before heading home, I don't eat anything. When I get off the plane, I head straight for the Versailles, have a meal, then go outside and smoke a cigar and let my food digest. When that's settled, I'll walk around the block, then maybe visit some friends on my way home to Pasadena. Some people at that restaurant have been there the ten years I've been going there. We know each other. I don't have to be 'on,' so I can ease back into my home self.

"When I'm off this summer tour [1999], I'm going out to hang out with Etta Baker at her house – a most wonderful place in Morganton, North Carolina – and play music with her. Two of her nine children live next door to her. She's real great, and I've gotten to know her grown kids. When I'm on the Winston Blues Revival tour, I hang with Cootie Stark, because we can't go into no city where he doesn't have relatives. Neal 'Big Daddy' Pattman, the harp player on the tour, brings his wife on the road. He's in his 70s, and she's probably coming into her 40s. They have two kids. She wears short skirts and high heels and gets down and boogies when he plays. They have big fun when they travel. It's like a family, being with these people.

"And being on the road with my son, Ahmen, is being with family. It's a lot of fun. We have the time to talk, and I find stuff he likes about the music I'm playing. I've realized that he has quite a bit of knowledge about it. He is really a solid bass player, in that, when we're playing, he anticipates where I'm going next in a song. I was really shocked that he knew that much about what was going on. He can play anything.

"Yeah, I like a domestic life. I try to create it wherever and however I can."

23 Phantom Blues

We're at the Janus Jazz Festival in Snowmass. Glam Aspen is ten miles down the road to the west, over the shoulder of Ajax Mountain. The festival is in a flat field down the narrow, winding asphalt road from Snowmass village and the ski lifts. About 8,000 people sprawl on the grass in front of the stage under a bright-blue Colorado sky. Crosby, Stills And Nash, Bonnie Raitt, and Keb' Mo' are on the bill. Onstage, Taj is fronting his Phantom Blues Band, with which he won the 1998 Grammy for the Best Contemporary Blues Album, with *Señor Blues*. This is the last stop of a three-month tour that included Scotland, France, Germany, and Sweden. Taj has let his hair and beard grow in. Tiny white curls give him the look of a village elder.

When he arrived backstage, carrying a freshly pressed Hawaiian shirt on a hanger, Taj acknowledged that he was tired after being on the road continuously for the last 90 days and nights, but onstage the fatigue is not apparent, as the band blazes through their opening instrumental, 'Honky-Tonk.' This R&B classic starts deceptively, with Taj on the guitar. The intensity builds as the sax puts some fire under the kettle. The drums, rhythm guitar, and bass punctuate the beat until the audience collectively feels that it's being given CPR, a direct pound on the heart. The band wants to jump-start the people onto their feet. They know that, once they have the audience dancing, they own the crowd. People closest to the stage are up and waving their arms in the air. The band jacks up the intensity to another level, and the middle of the audience rises, hips swiveling, shoulders twisting. Just when it seems that the music can't be sustained at that intensity, that the rhythm can't go any faster, it goes faster, and the people in the back are up and clapping. Then the song is over. For a split second, the audience is left suspended in the echo, their bodies still dancing to the vibration, still surprised at the power of the music, and then they laugh and shout in delight.

Taj leads the band into 'Down Home Girl.' Directly behind him sits Tony Braunagel on the drums. To Tony's left stands Denny Freeman (rhythm guitar) and Larry Fulcher (bass). On the other side of the drums, Mick Weaver sits at the keyboard. Slightly in front and to the side of Mick are the horns, Darrell Leonard and Joe Sublett.

A couple of measures into the song, Taj starts to dance, twisting from one foot to the other. This is no Michael Jackson choreography, more like something at a family barbecue when good feeling has everyone well lubricated. When Taj is on the move, he can throw the music into an unexpected direction just to see what will happen. Miles Davis did the same with his band, making unexpected key changes in the middle of a tune to jar the musicians out of their groove and make them improvise into something new. Taj likes to spur that spontaneity, too, forcing himself and his musicians to stretch. If he or they stumble, then that's all right, because they might stumble into something deeper, different, fresher. That's what makes it fun.

The musicians are extra alert, anticipating a challenge. Tony keeps a steady beat on the drums. He knows that, at any moment, Taj might throw out something unexpected, a snatch of quick musical conversation, and Tony must signal this with a little lick, like a flashing neon arrow pointing to a new direction for the band to follow. Like all drummers, Tony is the leader behind the music. He sets things in motion and holds them there, and then, in the conversation of the music, sets the next guy up for his solo, and then taunts the player during the solo, or appeases him, or makes him feel secure. Sure, go ahead, do whatever you want and I'll back you up. No problem. He's the engine of the band, driving it forward. At the same time, he's the anchor that keeps the band from getting lost when the music becomes perhaps too spontaneous.

He listens closely to Taj's vocals for his cue to play louder or softer. The song moves toward an eighth-note section, and Tony starts a drum fill in an eighth-note pattern so that the band glides smoothly into the new section, as opposed to falling into it.

Keeping time on Tony's left, on the hi-hat side of the kit, are Denny Freeman and Larry Fulcher, on rhythm and bass, respectively. Denny keeps an ear close to Larry's rhythms, adding a high-pitched riff beneath Larry's low notes, like running water under thunder. Together, they try to make "musical gumbo" happen, with Denny adding the seasoning to the basic stock ingredients that Larry puts in the pot. They support each other and counter each other to keep a churn going, throwing in a verb or an adjective to each other's sentences. Denny hits the seventh chord on the two and four downbeats to give the music a pulse, as steady as a heartbeat. He believes in the minimalist approach to this song, making a little bit go a long way. Then, just when his two-stroke pattern blends into the music, he adds four unexpected notes, a dash of color, the same as a painter might add a highlight to make a still life jiggle a bit.

Standing next to Denny, Larry plays with that inward look of bass players, the "brains behind the music," as Larry describes his role. The bass player is the interpreter between the band and the drums. He produces the musical result of the percussion. The bass sets up a foundation, a musical structure, in which the other instruments operate. "The bass player is the secret controller," Larry confides after the set. "My job is to make people dance, to hit people from the waist down, to make their bodies react in a certain way."

He stands close to the hi-hat and the snare drum, because they produce a higher pitch. That leaves more space for his bass, the lowest-pitched instrument in the band. He simultaneously plays rhythm and counter to the drums, paying special attention to Tony's bass kick drum. He times his notes with the kick drum so that the resonance adds impact to both of the deep bass notes, doubling the depth of the boom. He accents a chord by fluctuating a note section without going counter to the drums. Taj throws him a quick smile. A bass player himself, he knows how Larry operates. He drops his voice and Larry softens his playing. On the next line, Taj sings powerfully and Larry answers back. Taj is conducting the band, using melody, rhythm, and intensity as his invisible baton.

In front and to the side, Darrell Leonard and Joe Sublett add color and texture, complementing Taj with the horns. They listen for opportunities to put in swells, long notes, licks that double whatever Taj plays on the guitar. They blend, rather than overwhelm, refraining from doing that *DA-da-ta-ta* thing to announce that "The horns are here!" Larry and Darrell are very aware of Taj's experiment with the Howard Johnson tuba band, so they know that he welcomes something out of the ordinary and yet in harmony with the band. When Darrell throws in a riff of dissident voicing with his trumpet on some songs, Taj acknowledges with a smile and extra-wide-open eyes to let Darrell know that he has heard and appreciates.

The song is winding down. Joe, on sax, hears something in the rhythm of Taj's singing that alerts him. Taj likes to sing in B flat or A flat, which are good keys for the horns, musically. On some songs, like 'Sophisticated Mama,' Taj plays a kazoo solo using trombone phrasing, so Joe knows that the guitar man has a horn inside his head. Joe listens for a set-up. Taj starts to improvise vocally, moving away from the structured ending, opening a different rhythmical pattern. Joe hears it and adjusts to get in stride, then adds his own color to tell Taj, 'I'm with you. Let's go.' Taj sings a four-bar measure and Joe takes the next four bars. They do it again, like a saxophone and trumpet in a jazz song, with Taj's voice the trumpet. They do this call-and-response routine for four verses, a basic blues chorus but with jazz instrumentation. Joe blows his coolest New-Orleans-style licks, jazzy and R&B at the same time. Snaky. This is new territory. The band doesn't know exactly when, or how, this will end. Neither does Taj.

The band has become lost in the music, at times. When that happens, "we all just hold on and breathe – exhale, inhale, exhale, inhale – until something starts to catch on," Tony explains after the set. "It's always Taj who finds the way out, because he's the leader. Then we all grab and go with him. He has the absolute sense to know how to build the music, be dynamic with it, be entertaining, and get that across to the audience. It becomes so infectious that you know what to do, because you hit on the whole spontaneous, creative force. It's an enormous adventure."

'Down Home Girl' can end differently every time the band plays the song, depending on how Taj ad libs the ending. Now, bent over his guitar, he calls out, "Sock it to me, sock it to me," and then utters such sounds that it's unclear, lyrically, if they are words at all, some out-of-the-mind energy responding to the blasting, white-hot band, the music rocketing away from words and into spontaneous emotion. Joe and Taj are locked in the pocket, making music happen, their only focus. The whole band is in the groove with them, not knowing where it's going to end, not trying to control or direct this "magic." The audience is jumping up and down, leaping into the music that they sense can spin out of control. They want to go out of control with it, to be taken out of themselves. That's why they've come to the concert.

Joe gives a nearly imperceptible nod to Darrell, who raises his trumpet and steps up to the mic. Tony knows that his next drum fill must introduce the penultimate phrase. He raps it out and Darrell starts the passage that leads to the ending. The band knows where they are now. They play the closing phrase several times to make sure that everyone's in sync and that they finish exactly on the same beat.

For the audience, the performance sounds like a rehearsed-down-to-the-last-note professional job. They stomp and whistle and clap and call for more. The band members look nonplussed, but they're breathing a little extra hard. They pulled it off. They just took a side-trip down some unknown, white-water rapids and didn't tip over. Taj nods to his musicians. "That was good."

For the final song, Taj calls out, "I spotted my favorite redhead and asked her to come up and sing a song." Bonnie Raitt walks onto the stage wearing bib overalls, her hair pulled back in a ponytail. Without the Big Hair of her publicity photos, she looks small, which she is, slim and small of frame. She starts the song and Taj calls for the people to get on their feet, swooping with both arms, exhorting the people to rise up and dance. It's as much for his benefit as for theirs.

After the set, Tony says, "To have a roomful, or a fieldful, or a stadiumful of people digging you and handing that energy back to you – here I'm going to get a little cosmic – that is really incredible healing energy. You can go out and work 30 days in a row and do things that defy human nature, in terms of not getting enough sleep or proper meals, traveling all the time, changing time zones, being sweaty when you come off the stage, being cold while you're sweaty and not get sick, not ever give up. There is a healing energy from the music and the audience that allows you to go through all that. Taj knows that energy. It's one of the reasons he is able to do what he does. It's very healing and wonderful energy, and he lets it come back to him."

It's like a school reunion behind the outdoor stage. "I remember David Crosby when he was just a kid sleeping on our floor," Taj says. Tony, Joe, and Darrell were once part of Bonnie Raitt's band, so they fall to catching up with her, and they all played on Taj's *Phantom Blues* album (Private Music, 1996). On that album, Bonnie shared lead vocals with Taj on 'I Need Your Loving'; Eric Clapton played lead guitar on 'Here In The Dark' and 'You've Got To Love Her With A Feeling'; and Mike Campbell, of Tom Petty And The Heartbreakers, contributed a twelve-string guitar to 'Lovin' In My Baby's Eyes.' Reviewing the album in *Blues Access*, Bryan Powell wrote, "50 years from now, when blues lovers are investigating the late 20th century with curiosity and nostalgia, Taj Mahal likely will be acknowledged as one of the most memorable, diverse, and consistently entertaining musicians of our era. *Phantom Blues* is simply the latest stone in the musical monument that will survive him."

Taj sits at a table with a plate of food, but he doesn't get to eat much. Every few minutes, someone comes up to talk, ask for an autograph, just to shake his hand. Two 13-year-old boys approach timidly. "You're my hero," one stammers out. Taj is polite to everyone, but he wants to eat.

The band members fill plates from the buffet and settle around a table. This is their last scheduled gig with Taj until a summer tour in 1999, so they talk about their experience with Taj as if reviewing the details of a fabulous meal that they've just eaten.

"Remember that time on the Caribbean Blues Cruise, when we did a late-night set that started about 3am?" Joe Sublett's eyes light up as he starts the story. "Taj turned the set into a 1955 after-hours blues joint by pulling old R&B songs off the top of his head. He'd say, 'It's in B flat,' and he'd play a lick. He knew that we knew the idiom and could follow him. Then he'd start throwing tunes out. It was one of the most incredible sets I've ever experienced. You never know what Taj is going to do, and he has so many things he can do."

"Taj doesn't come across as particularly sophisticated, or having even studied the music that much, but this is part of his no-air approach," joins in Tony. "He's not trying to go above the audience's head. There's no noses-in-the-air kind of thing with anybody in this band. Nobody is trying to go, 'Hey, listen, man. I can't play this kind of shit, because, like, I'm a Coltrane fanatic.'"

"Taj keeps his music simple, elegant, interesting to listen to," adds Larry. "Sometimes, that's the difficulty, making it sound easy. It's like religion: if you've got a religion you can't explain to a six year old, I got doubts about your religion."

"Taj said, when we first got together, 'Cool. You guys speak the vocabulary. You know the language.'" Joe again. "I had always thought in terms of riffs and licks that musicians had in common, but the word 'language' gave a new twist – language in that we had all listened to the same R&B, blues, jazz records over a period of time. We know a common language. So when we play, it's in a conversational sense."

"Once you learn the parameters of the language," adds Larry, "and where the adverbs and pronouns and all those things go, that makes you more proficient in the language. Then it's easier for people to understand what you're saying."

"With Taj, as long as you're speaking the language, and it's something that is right, he basically allows you to do anything you want to do," Joe says. "He's happy to hear you go off on a different direction on a solo. He's really happy when you take a chance, even if you fall on your face. At least half the time you might do something really brilliant. When someone in the band takes their solo out a bit, does something a little different and strange, that's when he really lights up. For Taj, it's all improvisation."

Larry: "The only direction he has ever given me, in the six years I've played with him, the only thing he said was, 'Once you find a part and it grooves – by whatever definition you put on "grooves" – play it strong and play it loud. Play it like you mean it. Don't sound like you're in doubt.'"

"He paints with the blues, and we paint, also," Joe continues. "There are all these different colors and different types of paints you use with the blues. Taj has never been afraid that the purists will criticize him about what the bluesman should be about. To that, he says, 'Oh, yeah. You guys just want me on the porch in the rocking chair with the banjo. That's what you guys think a blues guy has gotta do.' He has a totally different concept, because of his background with music from the West Indies and the South. He never had any boundaries to paint himself into a corner with. For Taj, music is like a paintbrush. It's an artistic thing. He says, 'I can take a little paint from here, a little from there, and come up with my own concept.'"

"In Taj's music, there is jazz influence, reggae, ragtime, soul, the blues of the late 19th and early 20th centuries, Caribbean and African music," adds Larry. "You won't find Taj doing the standard shuffles. He consciously tries to stay away from that and goes for the unique. It's a meditation, a joy, to play with Taj."

"He's so secure about himself and who he is that he's not threatened by somebody onstage." Tony pushes back from the table. "He lets you really go into your thing, digs what you do, sees you sweating and seething and huffing and puffing and going for it, and he's right there with you. His energy is right there. When you see him work, he's the same way. You get behind a guy who performs like that, you're going to play your ass off every night. That's why I think the band is so strong every night.

"Taj always gives his best. Taj now has a band of guys who always give their best. When you put that combination together, you have a great band. It's like, before the Chicago Bulls had Michael Jordan, they were just contenders. When the team got the right guys, you couldn't beat the Bulls. Same with this band. It's the chemistry. It's everybody's thing. If one night one person is not on, or kinda down, nobody allows that. It's like, 'I'm sorry, man. We take no prisoners.' When we go onstage, we go up there to tear it up."

"The key to this band – besides understanding the same musical language – is respect and trust." Larry's voice drops softly in sincerity. "We respect every other guy's musical ability and personality so much that it's a joy to get onstage together. I cannot even measure the amount of respect we have for Taj. Even if you make a mistake, you have trust in yourself that you can recover, and you have trust in the other guys to cover for you. That gives a good deal of freedom. That raises the level of what you personally can do. After you respect and trust someone and love what they do, you form a bond with that person. You become a unit. Then, traveling, this band is its own little invading army. We learn to rely and depend on each other, onstage and offstage. That's the key to the whole thing. That's the energy we all feed off to do what we do."

Since the Snowmass gig, Taj and band have toured Europe and released the CD *Shoutin' In Key* on Kan-Du and Hannibal/Rykodisc. Although The Phantom Blues Band has no immediate project scheduled with Taj, they have plans. "We've talked about doing an acoustic jazz record, because of our love for Horace Silver – who wrote 'Señor Blues' – and for Barry Harris and other great jazzmen," says Tony, "and we'd like to do a project of Caribbean stuff, that Taj loves to do. I think that, when Taj finds the right time and feel for signing another record deal, the tunes and compositions will come forth from Taj. I think he's been... I don't know if 'holding back' is the right word, but it hasn't come forth yet. He can go anywhere, given his knowledge of music. He can put together different musical traditions flawlessly in the same song. How many people can do that? Rural blues, African, Caribbean references in the same song and they all sound like they belong there, naturally? Take 'Queen Bee.' That song has influences from Mali, the Caribbean, and the South. I don't know many musicians who can do that."

Taj sits at the next table over, not joining the discussion. He finally has a moment to eat, so he eats. During the conversation, Keb' Mo' has been at the far end of the food tent eating with his keyboard player. Later, when he has a chance, he talks about Taj. He wrote the song 'Henry' with Taj in mind. "All the bluesmen are important to me, but Taj is important because Taj – especially when it comes to acoustic blues and culture and roots and heritage – had been out there preaching it when no one was preaching it. He was out there all the time when not a lot of people were listening, but he stayed true." Keb's speaking voice is much like his singing voice, soft and melodic. He laughs frequently during the conversation, inviting the listener to share an easy spot with him.

"Taj says to listen to the call of your ancestors, that your ancestors are with you. When you make the call for help to your ancestors, no one can override that call – no body of government, no person. That's a heavy call. It's a call of faith and belief in you and in who you are, not only ethically who you are but who you are as a soul.

"The song 'Henry' is not only for Taj, Henry being his given name; it's also for Henry Townsend, the dean of St Louis bluesmen, who played with the legendary Robert Johnson, and all the other great blues guys who played the steel guitar. I wrote the song with John Parker. He was on the piano doing a minor chord and I was humming a melody when I came up with a chorus: 'I can hear the Delta calling/from the light of a distant star/I can see my future, and I can feel my past/when Henry plays his steel guitar.' The phrase 'when Henry plays his steel guitar' just came out like butter. I started the song in early 1997 and finished it when my album *Slow Down* came out, in 1998. That album won a Grammy. I won the my first Grammy in 1996 for *Just Like You*.

"The song is about that feeling the blues gives you. It's about knowing who you are, of you having a sense of oneness, of hearing your own voice, hearing what's inside of you. It's about forgiveness. The second verse is the forgiveness verse, talking about the things that have made the blues, of releasing the blame and then moving on.

"The line in the chorus 'I can see my future/and I can feel my past' applies to everyone, not just blacks who might sing the blues, given our racial history. We really are one thing. That sense of unity comes through. And those like souls are also just like the souls of all the souls, just like you and me and everybody making that connection. That's what the blues does more than anything. That's why so many people around the world like the blues – it's honest and it makes that connection with the personal experience. It's not trying to be pretty. It's just what it is.

"I first came upon Taj musically in 1969, when he played at an assembly at my high school in Compton, near Los Angeles. I was attracted to his music right then, but I didn't have enough background, or know what I was or was supposed to be doing, to really grasp it in any kind of way. It definitely had an effect on me. Then, I was playing in a Top-40-style band at the school and playing the French horn in the school orchestra. I was dabbling in music and thinking about what I was going to do when I grew up. I wasn't too sure about the music thing. That Taj concert didn't set me on the musical path, but it made a big imprint on my psyche. It made a very important impression on me. I always remembered that show because I really enjoyed it and felt that nobody was with me on it.

"After high school, between the ages 17 and 18, I went to Los Angeles Trade Technical College, where I studied architectural drafting. I didn't play a guitar at all for a year; I just concentrated on my studies. After a year in school, I got a call from one of my high-school friends, who asked if I wanted to play in a band they were putting together. So I came on, went back to my mom's house and got my amp, brought it to where I was living at my father's house, got my guitar, and started seeing if I remembered anything. I was going to school, playing, and going through some juvenile-delinquency issues at the same time.

"That second year when I started playing, a friend gave me a tape of Taj's *The Natch'l Blues*. I must have listened to that thing umpteen thousand times. I guess the blues was in me, but I was in big denial. I started music professionally somewhere between the ages of 19 and 21, [although] I don't know if you could really call it professional. There were people really making a living at it, and there were people trying to make a living at it. I don't know when the pipe dream becomes a reality.

"I enrolled in computer-repair school, but after a while that idea didn't thrill me. All the time, I'd been a part-time arranger at A&M and playing, sitting in with a local club's house band. I was about 35 before I realized that my music was a gift from God so I may as well get with it. That epiphany came when I played a part of a Delta bluesmen in a stage production of *Rabbit Foot*.

"Somewhere along the line, I picked up the nickname Keb' Mo'. It comes from my real name, Kevin Moore. The connection is easy to hear if you say Kevin like 'heaven.' Kebin. Keb'. Mo' is from Moore. When I started getting into the Delta blues, in the late '80s and the early '90s, I went back to the *Natch'l Blues* album. I started studying it again and doing some of those tunes with my band.

"For me, Taj was hard to get to know. It felt that it took a long time for him even to acknowledge me, probably because I felt entirely too close to him. I was probably too enamored by him. I was very patient. Basically, I'd hang around him like a groupie whenever I got a chance. But I maintain my own relationship to who Taj is to me and who he is to himself. I am very, very secure in having my own identity. I'm not him, and he's not me, but at the same time he is.

"I know that people call me the young Taj Mahal. That's just something people have to say. I've got no connection to that stuff. I always thought Taj Mahal was a whole lot older than me, but he's not. He's 57 and I'm 48. I was 17 when I first heard him and he was 26. There's a world, a whole *ocean*, between 17 and 26; but at 48, I feel like I am part of his generation.

"My biggest interest outside of music is spirituality and development of the soul. I had a formal Buddhist practice for 14 years. That's what cured me of organizations. Inevitably, when you're around so many people, they start doing your thinking for you, telling you how you should interpret things. I don't have a formal practice right now. I like to go my own road, read and read and make my own connections, listen to what I'm getting."

When she has a quiet moment, Bonnie Raitt tells of her nearly 30-year-long friendship with Taj: "I first heard him play live at the Club 47 in Cambridge in 1968. I was a college student at Harvard, where I was majoring in African studies. I was very much into politics. Social relations was my major. I thought [that] what he was doing – to take blues to another level, his charisma, his voice and range – was great. It was as astounding then as it is now. I'd been a fan, very enamored of his first couple of albums. I got a record deal in my senior year at Harvard, so I left. I said I'd be back, but I guess I didn't go back. I became Taj's friend soon after I started playing myself. I started opening for Taj in 1970, and we've been friends since then. He co-produced my third album in 1973.

"Taj is probably the most important bridge that we have between blues and rock 'n' roll and modern contemporary music. Taj was the first one, before there was ever a connection with the younger black generation to the older blues. He was there in the mid '60s, when there was a great revival and appreciation for blues. A lot of the older bluesmen were being discovered in the South after many, many years of doing other jobs and being neglected. There was a resurgence of interest right around the Newport Folk Festivals in '64, '65. The folk-music craze swept across the colleges, especially the centers like Berkeley and New York and Boston, but mostly the Eastern Seaboard.

"And in England, there was a big appreciation by The Rolling Stones and The Beatles covering R&B. The Rolling Stones basically re-introduced blues to young, white audiences in America in the '60s for the first time. So there was this whole interesting cultural phenomenon that was basically young, white, middle-class kids discovering music that had been invented by older black people in the early part of the century.

"And here was this young college student from Amherst, Taj, who happened to be black and was totally authentic in his love and portrayal of the music. He sung the music with complete authenticity, and meant it. When you really want to get moved, you've got to get into the music that is deeply of the soul. The blues doesn't get any deeper than that. The blues is about pain. I doubt there is a person alive who hasn't experienced the feeling of being abandoned or broken-hearted or bereft or lonely or angry or sexy. All the things that the blues sings and celebrates are universal. Taj sings all that with authenticity.

"So for me it was fantastic to see the torch being carried by somebody from the black community. I wanted blues to be something other than an ivory-tower, hip, college thing. It should be a living, breathing, appreciated part of American history and taught in schools. People of all colors should know where rock 'n' roll came from and where the music they like today comes from, which is basically the blues.

"Taj was, and is, a living, breathing link. Early on, he was stepping into world music way before other people. With his Caribbean background and his love for different kinds of jazz, he had a very deep and broad appreciation of other kinds of music. He was the renaissance we needed to get the music across. He's stayed fresh and vital and growing and stretching the whole entire multi-decades of his career. As a musician, he's never ceased to amaze me with the number of new things he comes up with.

"There has never been anybody like him, in that he's shepherding a lot of the younger black bluesman as well, like Cory Harris, Curt Fletcher,

Eric Bibb, Keb' Mo', and Alvin Youngblood Hart. A whole generation of bluesmen have been influenced by Taj. I don't think there is anybody more significant than Taj. He is an avatar. A bridge and an avatar. He is not restricted to the blues. He lives and breathes music without any categories. I think he is that way as a person. I admire him so much. He's been a really good friend to me, always really generous and supportive. He's as bad as they get."

24 Soul Singing Blues

Tonight – April 15, 1999 – we're at the Casino, a club in Denver's Five Points, once a notoriously dangerous inner-city neighborhood but now rejuvenated and made spiffy by urban redevelopment. This is the penultimate stop on a 16-city Winston Blues Revival tour for Taj, who returned a couple of weeks ago from an Australian tour with his Hula Blues Band. He's well known Down Under; he's toured there several times and does Just Juice commercials on New Zealand television. In Fiji, where he often stops over to give a concert and to fish, he is recognized as the dancing man on those commercials, as well as a musician.

"Life is fast, right now," he says backstage, watching Neal "Big Daddy" Pattman open the show. Pattman is a one-armed harmonica player who lost his other arm in a wagon wheel when he was nine years old. The club is packed with 400 fans, 98 percent of whom are white, ranging from early 20s to mid 50s. Onstage, "Big Daddy" Pattman is resplendent in a brilliant white suit, the empty right sleeve tucked into a pocket. During his second song, Taj walks onstage unannounced and plays back-up on an upright bass. Pattman sings straightforward street-corner blues. You can damn near see the red dust of some back-creek Mississippi town between his toes. By the third song, he and Taj have moved into revival picnic blues – foot-stompin', sweatin', get-up-and-shout-the-glory blues. The audience is up and shouting.

Taj stays with the upright bass as the second act is led onstage. Cootie Stark – blind, dazzling in a red suit, red shirt, and silver tie – settles on a chair in front of the mic. Cootie spent 50 years going from juke joints to small clubs to bus stations, playing his music, and nobody knew his name. Since he joined the Winston Blues Revival tour, though, he earned a name for himself. Within a year, he performed at the JVC Jazz Festival in Berlin and at the Newport Jazz Festival, he toured Europe three times, and he released his first album, *Sugar Man*.

Like Pattman, Cootie Stark is from the generation of bluesmen who didn't come to the old roots blues. They came out of that music culture like heat comes out of the sun. They know those blues like the body knows its blood. They don't live without it. They came out of the soil into which Taj sunk his roots. Taj is as content as a diving duck in rich water to be in the background playing the bottom line for Cootie Stark.

Taj is introduced for his solo set. Somebody must have hit the Eject button, because people come flying out of their seats to welcome him. Young girls rush the stage. He settles behind a synthesizer, does a five-song set, and then moves out to make room for Beverly "Guitar" Watkins. No one in the audience is quite sure what to make of her, a short woman in a maroon pants suit with carefully coiffured hair, short on the sides and a pompadour wave on top. She has a dour look – no smile for the audience, like she doesn't want to be messed with, like perhaps she disapproves of foolishness. Without a word, she goes on a tear with her electric guitar. She stalks across the stage, laying down red-hot licks. She plays behind her head. Who came first, Beverly Watkins or Chuck Berry? She sticks her guitar into the people crowding the stage, her face immobile. The crowd jumps and screams, as if they've just discovered the latest blues rock 'n' roll sensation.

She's coy about her age, but somewhere between 50 and 60 is a good guess. She's been playing as a sidewoman since 1952 – most notably with Dr Feelgood and Piano Red – until 1969, when she dropped out of sight. Tim Duffy, the force behind the Blues Revival tour, found her playing on the street in Atlanta. Now she is the star of the show.

At the show, it's easy to see the lineage from the old blues to Taj. He knows the spirit and life of that music in some ineffable place within his being. Joe Sublett, of The Phantom Blues Band, once said, "Playing with Taj, I feel that I'm playing with one of the guys who is a living link from the very old blues to now." Many people link Taj directly to 82-year-old John Lee Hooker, one of most prolific bluesmen in blues history. And John Lee acknowledges the continuity.

"I always was a big fan of his," John Lee says when asked. "He's different. He's a nice person. I don't think you could find a nicer person than Taj Mahal. He's a good bluesman, but he sings it different than anyone else. He mixes reggae and Caribbean and African and blues. It's not the hard blues, but it's good."

In 1999, John Lee received the Lifetime Achievement award from the

Rhythm And Blues Foundation, which provides emergency assistance to needy artists. He returned $20,000 of the award, saying, "I'm glad to be part of helping out by returning the funds from this award to help those who need the help right now."

Tim Duffy had the same idea when he founded the non-profit Music Maker Relief Foundation (www.musicmaker.org) in 1967. The foundation (of which Taj is a partner) raises money to assist older blues musicians. The Winston Blues Revival show – sponsored by the tobacco company RJ Reynolds – is part of that effort. After the show at the Casino, Tim Duffy finds time to talk about the Music Maker Relief Foundation.

"In the first year, we raised about $20,000 to $30,000 to help the musicians. In the past few years, we've been raising over $100,000. We have low overheads, so most of the money goes directly back to the artists, in the form of emergency relief. If someone has a house fire and they need something, or there is a cold snap and they don't have any heating oil, then we get that. Or if someone is on a fixed income of $400 a month, and their medicine for heart problems is $200 a month, we provide the check for medicine every month. We buy guitars, or a car if someone needs one to get to a gig. Whatever it takes to help the musician get back into the groove, we provide the life necessities.

"We got George Connor of Aliceville, Alabama, a new Fender Stratocaster and a Fender amplifier. Taj picked out an Epiphone Howard Roberts guitar for Precious Bryant. Precious' trailer burned and she lost everything. We plan to help her get a new well dug, a septic system put in, and buy her a new hot-water heater. We helped Essie Mae Brooks get her leaking roof fixed.

"Basically, the musicians have to be 55 years or older, make less than $18,000 a year, and be rooted in Southern musical traditions. They don't have to have recorded. We feel, just because Robert Johnson was recorded, doesn't mean that a musician living in the next county – where the record-company field scout didn't come – makes that artist any less important. We deal with people 87 years old living in the same county and never left, but how many people did that musician influence? Who knows? Right now, we give aid to 78 people. We can do more; it's just a matter of raising the funds.

"Taj is perfect to headline the show. He can explain on the guitar the music of the world and play it every different way. He can go through the South and play every different style of the blues. He can play what South

African music does, relate it to the chords and the eight different chord riffs of Southern blues. He can talk about Indian music and its scales. He's well versed in Native American music. It goes on and on and on.

"Taj is very much an academic, but not a trained academic," continues Duffy, who has degrees in folklore and ethnomusicology. "He's not an academic in the sense that he has a degree in musicology, but in a very academic sense he's done his research, done his reading, gone off and done his field work. He knows the academics behind the music, and he can execute it. That's the difference between him and his academic counterparts. He can hold forth amongst any of those guys. There are very few people in the academic circle who have the breadth of understanding of world music, African music, and the blues more so than Taj. Intellectually, he knows about it; and musically, he can do it all. I can't think of anyone who knows more than he does on this music or the importance of it.

"I think he's an inspiration to young kids coming up. He's a shining star, leading them into other worlds of music – blues music, stuff that's not heard on the radio. He's pointed three or four generations of kids in the right way."

Taj's 1998 release, *Taj Mahal In Progress And In Motion, 1965-1998* (Columbia Legacy), is an affirmation that Taj is a musician's musicologist. The 54 cuts – including the previously unreleased 'Sweet Home Chicago,' live with The Pointer Sisters – on the three-CD box set is a superb compilation of Taj's range. Josef Woodard, writing in *Down Beat*, said, "Raw, bone-deep funk and sweetness flow naturally from Mahal's fingers and mouth. [His] teasing licks have nothing to do with virtuosity and everything to do with taste. Mahal is unmistakable, a musician without precedent or peers." Meanwhile, Tony Scherman, author of *Backbeat: Earl Palmer's Story*, wrote in *The New York Times*, "Taj Mahal has about the deepest and widest roots of any pop-music performer today…" *In Progress And Motion*, wrote Scherman, "amply shows he's pop's Walt Whitman, an optimist endlessly proclaiming his oneness with the world's vernacular music."

Although Taj is the headliner for the Winston Blues Revival, he doesn't do the star trip; he stays in the background, playing for the older musicians and not stealing the show with his solos. Taj has always had a soft spot for the little guy, the individual who goes for his vision full speed ahead and damn the corporations. When Leib Ostrow wanted to start his own record label, Taj signed on and helped to turn the dream into a successful business.

When two young filmmakers wanted to do a film about a pig riding in a motorcycle sidecar, Taj said he'd do the music, just give a call when the film is ready for the soundtrack.

"Taj and I had a common friend, Cocoon," says Leib Ostrow from his home-cum-office in the redwood country of Northern California. "My company then, Music For Little People, was mostly mail order, sending out artists' records. I am a big fan of Taj's, and thought he'd be perfect for a children's album I wanted to produce, so Cocoon put us together. This was in 1987. Taj jumped at the idea. He was between record companies, and I think his career was at a low point. We recorded *Shake Sugaree*, a really cool album that's sold over 200,000 units. Taj's version of that Elizabeth Cotton song, 'Shake Sugaree,' has become a classic.

"On *Shake Sugaree*, Taj wrote 'Funky Bluesy ABCs,' a kids' rap song to help them learn the alphabet. It's a very catchy blues song. Underneath, I think Taj is a teacher. He always has information about how the blues came into the United States through Africa. He's always learning about how it all ties together. He's a teacher to those from one year old to those 80 years old. He's always trying to turn people onto music in different ways.

"Taj was pivotal in the starting of my company. After Taj did his record, we got quite large quickly. Warner Brothers came in, and we did a partnership with them. They bought half the company. Then, about four years later, changes happened at Warners, so we left and became independent again. Our catalogue has 90 releases, counting our adult label, Earthbeat. We're sending out 1,000,000 units and have got two Grammy nominations. One of the nominations was for *Shakin' A Tailfeather* (1997), a collection of songs featuring Taj, Linda Tillery And The Cultural Heritage Choir, and Eric Bibb.

"When doing *Shakin' A Tailfeather*, Taj put his baseball hat on sideways and was dancing around like a kid, laughing and coming to life. *Shakin' A Tailfeather* had a lot of old rock 'n' roll stuff, like 'Willie And The Hand Jive' and 'Rockin' Robin.' He had everybody on the floor laughing. There is a certain childlikeness about Taj that comes through in his music, that delights children. They think that he's one of them. He doesn't do condescending things for kids. He really gives children credit for being sophisticated listeners. He gives them the real stuff. His love for music comes through in everything he does.

"Inbetween *Shake Sugaree* and *Shakin' A Tailfeather*, we did *Smilin'*

Islands, in 1993, which we recorded on Kauai, where Taj was living at the time. We had Bob Marley's mother, Cedella Marley Booker, on that one, along with Taj's brother Winston, who did a great voice of a Caribbean grandmother. Winston also did some work on the *Shakin' A Tailfeather* album. Also new with Taj is 'Hippity Hop' rap, for children."

When the Hanson brothers, Geoff and Chris, had an idea for a film about a pig, a Colorado ski town, and hippies, they heard Taj's music in their heads. "I'm an old Taj fan," said Geoff, a former music promoter who co-wrote and starred in the film *Scrapple*. (Scrapple is a hodgepodge of cornmeal mush made from different parts of a pig. It was a delicacy of the Pennsylvania Dutch at around the time of World War Two.) "The first film project my brother and I conceived of was a film about Taj Mahal. Our idea was to make a film called *Taj's Garage*, an idea inspired by the work he did in LA in the '60s, when Taj was hosting all the legendary blues musicians at his house in exchange for them teaching him what they knew about the blues.

"I first met Taj when I was a reporter for *The Telluride Times Journal*, in Telluride, Colorado, which is the model for the town in *Scrapple*. Taj came in for the Bill Graham Midsummer Music Festival in 1991. There were The Allman Brothers [Band], Joe Cocker, all kinds of incredible musicians. When The Allman Brothers played the closing set of the weekend, they brought one musician up onstage with them, and that was Taj Mahal. He played a set that blew the roof off the place.

"I did an interview with Taj when he was in town for that show. I was so inspired by it, I wanted to make a film about him. Here, let me read you part of the interview. This is Taj speaking: "'My music is roots-force music. It deals with a lot of pan-African and pan-American elements. Basically, in terms of my own progression, blues is a color I paint with. It's something you have to study. The object is to be adventurous and to be creative with it. I could paint the same picture over and over again, but once you've seen that picture I don't think you'd be excited to see me paint it for the 10,000th time. Maybe you'll feel safer with something you recognize, but I don't think, as an artist, you can afford to do that.

"'What I've done is draw heavily from my own background and some of the related background and from the stuff around me and come up with music that I think will be popular. It just so happens that where I am is farther down the road than where everyone else is ready to be. What they're calling world music, or world beat music, I was playing in the '60s and recording in the '70s, but it took a long time before anybody recognized what I was doing, because it was just too far out for people. That doesn't anger me or anything. I'm just glad that the message is getting out there.

"'It seems to me that, in America, we've created a cultural and educational system where heavy-metal guitarists think that the blues came from Europe, through Eric Clapton and The Rolling Stones. Black American kids don't know what the blues is, have never experienced it. When The Rolling Stones came to the United States and were charged with the energy of what black music was all about, they were shocked that people in Chicago – where this stuff was going on – had no idea what was happening.

"'I think that the Stones recognized that we live in a country where people are really divided against each other. There are more misunderstandings between groups of people in America than probably anywhere else in the world.

"'Musicologists can get pretty serious about music. They can intellectualize it too much and forget the physical and spiritual side of it. There's a magic, a visualness to music. You should be able to see and feel it. I had this book called *Ask Your Mama*, which was a series of moods for jazz by Langston Hughes. In it, he asked Louis Armstrong if he could read music. Armstrong answered, "Not enough to spoil my playing."

"'It is all this musical snobbery – I'm a purist at this music, I'm a purist at that music. If you take Vladimir Horowitz, Itzhak Perlman, Stephane Grappelli – they try to learn everything they can about their instrument, and then they throw it all out the window, all that teaching and technology. They try to fly through the music and be able to improvise. The gypsies never learned a note, but they got that sound that the guy who studies violin wants instantly.

"'It's a deal we're talking about here. We're talking about trying to move the energy with what you do, how you sing to create a mood. I've been playing the blues for 35 years. There was a time when I was focused solely on that kind of music, not without listening to what else was happening, but in my playing. I figured that, at some point, I might move off and do some other things, but I'm not going to leave that type of music behind, because it has an awful lot to do with my good feeling from day to day. It's a tone that puts me in contact with a lot of things, culturally, spiritually, cosmically. I really enjoy it, and I'm not going to let it go, because it's that good.

"'There's a tendency for Westerners to look at African music in a sort of monolithic way, because of their own inability to understand the dialects and subtleties of different cultures. There is an incredible ignorance about cultures different from their own, which allows them to misinterpret what the blues is all about. The blues does play off a lot of bad feelings, but it also brings in good feelings, smart-ass questions, and biting satire. It does a lot of different things. It's really more flexible than we allow it to be. Unfortunately, one of the reasons why this is so is because of the kind of pressures we put on people to use the vehicle as that type of expression.

"'If you take calypso, which tends to sound like it's smiling, underneath that smile are some barbs that are so sharp that you can't see them if you're not paying attention, and especially if it's directed at you. The majority of people think it's the happy native style on the islands. Some of them play reggae and the others play calypso. Reggae tends to confront you a little more face to face, head to head, mind to mind. Calypso often does the same thing, but it kinda slides underneath what you're being told. You've already swallowed it and the hook is way down deep. These musics are cousins to one another. There is a similarity that runs through all of them, that makes them "in the family."

"'I champion individuals to develop themselves and develop their potential, to be something and someone and try to create some kind of growth from within and stop whining about what's not there – and, if it's not there, try to supply it. I walk with the energy of music every day. I don't have to turn it on to hear it play.'"

Geoff pauses, clearly awed by Taj's words. "Here's a guy who is so much more than just a musician. He doesn't just show up and play his music; he lives his music every minute of every day."

When the first draft of *Scrapple* was completed, Geoff and Chris met with Taj's tour manager, Carey Williams, in Salt Lake City. Carey liked the script so much that he agreed to be the co-producer, and said that Taj would do the soundtrack. "It's a testimony to Taj that we never had a contract with him," says Geoff. "Taj said that he would do it. That says all you need to know about Taj. He is a man of his word. He's a man of incredible integrity, incredible musical talent. As soon as he committed to doing the music, January 1995, we went around saying, 'We got this film and Taj Mahal is going to do the score.' He was the only talent we had, the only 'name' associated with the project. He was the horse. When we wrote the script, we had one image in our minds: a guy riding a motorcycle with a pig in the sidecar and Taj's song 'Further On Down The Road.' Taj recorded a new version for the soundtrack, and that song became the theme for *Scrapple*. The song is so inspiring, like the line, 'When I look back/your love is like the sun/I don't remember any cold days/just the warm ones.'"

The soundtrack was recorded in the Ultratones Studios – that is, the garage of Johnny Lee Schell, the former guitar player for Taj's Phantom Blues Band. The musicians behind Taj on the soundtrack – jokingly referred to as Garage Mahal – are The Phantom Blues Band, with Jon Cleary on piano and Alvin Youngblood Hart on guitar. Alvin, an up-and-coming blues player, is managed by Carey Williams.

Johnny Lee is a true Texan, who says things like "That guy is lower than a snakeskin in a wagon rut." His Ultratones Studio, next to his house in Studio City (a satellite of Los Angeles), is a 20-by-20-foot room. When you look up, you see the underside of the roofing shingles. The mixing console is in the middle of the room. Guitars and amplifiers lie scattered about. Against one of the wood-sided walls is a piano, and a big couch is against the opposite wall. Pictures of Elvis Presley and of Roy Rogers on his horse, Trigger are the only decorations. The wall is lined with Grammy certificates from the *Señor Blues* album and from Bonnie Raitt's band, in which Johnny Lee played for seven years. In 1999, he played on three Grammy-nominated records, so he's left room to extend the row of certificates.

The Hanson brothers put *Scrapple* on a projector and show the film against one wall. They explain the feel that they wanted to have expressed with music. Johnny Lee and Tony Braunagel (the drummer for The Phantom Blues Band) came up with ideas and Tony found the tempo. When the basics had been worked out, Taj came in and added his special touches. Thirty pieces of original music came out of those sessions, including new versions of Taj's songs 'Lovin' In My Baby's Eyes' and 'Corrina.'

Johnny Lee has collaborated with Taj on several projects, the most recent being the Columbia/Tri-Star made-for-TV film *Outside Ozona*, which is also out on video. (Ozona is a small Texas town near San Antonio.) In the movie, Taj stars as a DJ. "He did really well," says Johnny Lee, sitting on the couch in his studio. "At the end, he has a four-minute close-up speech. Four minutes where your face fills the screen is a good test for someone's acting ability. He pretty much steals the picture."

Johnny reaches down to pet one of his dogs and explains the process of collaborating with Taj on *Ozona*: "I did all the underscore and Taj came over and helped with a few cues. He was very helpful. We wrote 'Slow Blues' and some other stuff and recorded them here in the studio. When we wrote the songs, Taj had a guitar, I played the bass, and there was a drum machine going. We'd watch the picture and come up with ideas off of what we were seeing. When we got something we liked, we had a drummer come in and replace the drum machine. Then we'd add other parts, like the keyboard and horns. It was very spontaneous, but we had a deadline, which tends to spur your spontaneity.

"I remember hearing his *The Natch'l Blues* album when I was a young guitar player, and that made a big impression on me. It was different from what else was going on. Taj has figured out a way to slither through this crack or that crack and keep himself unique among blues artists. Basically, he's a soul singer, because he sings from his soul."

Taj's youngest sister, Carole, agrees. "He has a passion for his music," she says from her home in Paris. "That's what he gives to people, this passion for what he does. He gets off on it, so hopefully everybody else gets off on it. I can't tell you how he does it. People are mesmerized when they see him. That's a gift of his. It's nothing that's tangible – you can't touch it. Basically, you don't want to know what it is. The person who has it doesn't want to know what it is, because that way you don't lose it. To sing the blues the way Taj does can't be explained away."

Carole knows from whence she speaks. She's a top singer in France, where she's lived since 1979. In 1998, she had a Number Three song there with 'Personne Ne Saurait' ('No One Will Know'), and from 1990-96 she was with the trio Fredericks, Goldman And Jones, which garnered two diamond and two platinum albums. In 1995, she put out her first solo album, *Springfield*, on which Taj played harmonica and sang vocals. Her second solo album was released in 1999.

"Bluesmen seem to get recognition later in life," Carole says. "It's Taj's time now. He deserves it. He didn't steal it, not one minute, one second. He has the talent to impress even the youngest, who are into hip-hop and not the blues. When they hear Taj, they pay attention, because they recognize the quality. He's a blues legend, and more and more people are beginning to realize that."

25 Cultural Warrior

We're at the Cello Studio on Sunset Boulevard in LA, where Taj is to cut a track with Jimmy "Papa" Smith, who is credited with giving voice to the jazz organ. Accompanying Smith, Taj will do his song 'Strut,' from the album *Dancing The Blues*. Next week, BB King and Etta James will come in to lend their voices to Smith's CD-in-progress. Taj walks into the lounge, the walls of which are covered in blue- and red-print Indian bedspreads, *de rigeur* home decorations for authentic hippies in the 1960s. Smith playfully greets Taj in a whispery, raspy smoker's voice as "Massage Mahal." Smith wears a pressed striped shirt, gray slacks, and highly shined shoes. He is 71 years old, a slim, small man, without a wrinkle on his boyishly handsome face. His neatly trimmed hair is pure black, without a white hair to be seen. Only the slow walk belies his age, as he moves bent slightly forward from the waist. But one can imagine him always walking like that, a slow cool taking the world in his stride.

Taj sets down his new guitar case and his shoulderbag. Two green wooden yo-yos spill from the bag. Taj was the 1954 Strand Theater yo-yo champion in Springfield, Massachusetts, and can still do tricks like Dog Bite, Spaghetti, Walking The Dog, and making the yo-yo sleep. The other musicians sit on chairs and a sofa watching a college women's basketball game on the color television.

John Porter – who produced Taj's Grammy-winning *Señor Blues* album – steps into the room. "Hello," he says in his English accent. He's dressed for work – red sneakers, black jeans, black T-shirt, scruffy beard and lank, dark hair nearly touching his shoulders. "Are we ready to give it a go?"

Smith pushes himself slowly out of the too-soft sofa. "I was up until 4am playing at home," he says. "That's why I'm a little late. When it's rolling, you've got to stay with it." The other musicians – Harvey Mason, drummer; Russell Malone, lead guitar; and Reggie McBride, bass guitar – follow him into the recording studio. Taj tunes up his guitar while Smith and the musicians lay down a jazz number.

"You don't know how heavy it is for me to play with Jimmy," Taj says. "I listened to him as a boy. He's one of the greats who has never gotten the widespread acclaim he deserves, but he's kept going all these years, doing his music. He's a cultural warrior, a fighter and survivor.

"A point about warriorship is that you have to survive. There is no other option. Failure is not an option. You can't be afraid, even when exposed to people who can do you harm by not supporting you, be it record companies or individuals. You have to stay open and vulnerable, even when you know people have lances pointed at your heart. If you don't continue to grow then those people will misinterpret you. They have their issues, and none of it will have any meaning beyond what they want. If you don't grow, you allow them to overpower you by not doing what you have to get done. You have to do what needs to be done. There's no two ways about it.

"Warriorship is not feeling the need to be bound to security. There is no security. As soon as you get that out of the way, nobody can hold you. You'll never be anybody's slave. I knew that as a boy, but it wasn't my voice saying that; it was the voice of my nearest ancestors, my parents and grandparents. Now, how do you take what you've learned and find your own voice? That's why it was important for me to go out to the blues. I have sounds in my head from so many languages and people, but I know what my sound is in the middle of this whole. It's not something I don't take lightly.

"The warrior spirit seems to have been, and still is, a major part of the male energy on this planet. Warriors have fought the wars, although they're called grunts or GIs or swabbies or whatever. The great warrior kings realized that you have to bring people together and then instill in them the virtues of settling down and dealing with everyone's differences. Battlefield warrioring becomes cultural warrioring when you champion the differences as well as the similarities between people and cultures. That step takes you away from, 'Okay, I'm good with the blade and can move my horse through battle.' That step takes you into being a cultural warrior. Instead of using a battle ax, you find another way to use the energy more toward constructive criticism, win-win situations, people working toward a positive end.

"A warrior takes responsibility for what he or she brings to the table.

This requires you discovering your own motivation. Maybe you are fortunate enough to be anointed by the universe to be a cultural warrior through song, dance, word, art, color, poem, information. Then how do you take that energy and not let somebody from the outside use it against people who really need to have a lightbulb turned on in the darkness around them?

"It's like I'm wandering around in the darkness and all of a sudden somebody grabs my hand and puts it on a string. I pull it down and a light goes on over my head. A warrior gives people something to hold onto so they can see their way out of the darkness. I know from where I'm talking. I can remember the feeling of being way at the bottom, and there is this little pinhole of light at the top. Every now and then it disappears, and I feel the darkness in my mind. Finally, I commit to come out of that. I think, 'That's enough.' But no, that's not enough; something else comes along to keep me from climbing out of the darkness. Well, okay, I'm going to get some cleats on my shoes and get some gloves and start to climb out. Well, that helps, but that ain't enough. Finally, what happens, I start to see that pinhole get a little bigger. That's the first inkling that, if I get out of this goddamn hole, I ain't coming down here again.

"It's possible to climb up to that hole of light and climb out of the darkness and then realize that just getting into the light is it. Being in the light allows more light, information, music, whatever, to come in. Once you get over yourself, you realize that everyone is there in the light. All the ancestors.

"Yes, people in difficult darkness do have their responsibility to get out of it, but it's certainly nice, every now and then, if somebody turns on the light. This is what the cultural warrior does. It is much more subtle and complex than straight-on weapons and battle.

"I know people who, like Jimmy Smith, are really serious troopers, musically. A lot of them have never gotten the recognition for what they have done. Those are the people who have inspired me over the years. They are in communication with the Larger Element that is stepping the light down through them. They're not worried that others don't know what they are doing. They're not worried about their ego.

"Frank Zappa was a cultural warrior. Zappa came along more as a composer, although most people think of him as this crazy rock 'n' roll guy. He was a bit like Duke Ellington, because he composed for orchestration, but he had a little of Groucho Marx and Spike Jones. Zappa was a modern cat, but he was using an older form of communication. He was an incredible satirist of the time. The real artists, the cultural warriors, do what they do because they have to. Do you think Dali or Goya or Picasso did their art to impress you, or to make money? It's incidental that the adoration and money came along.

"Part of warriorship is being tender. Even back in college, I came upon this. I might have been one of the few, or the only, black person some of those people had ever come in contact with. After they got to know me a little, they'd say, 'I was so scared of you when we first met. Here you were, this big black guy.' And I'd think, 'What did I do that they would be afraid of me?' I realized that they had their expectations of what a big black guy was suppose to be. So I let that pass, didn't hang on it, and that made it more comfortable for everyone. I didn't want to perpetuate any bad energy.

"A couple of times, I did lose it to the bad energy. I don't hassle nobody, but on the other hand, seriously, don't try me. If I need to draw on some bad shit, I can find some and whup your butt.

"One time when I lost to bad energy was with the Jessie Davis band. The girlfriend of our road manager, Ron Nehoda, was mad at him. She made the mistake of really insulting all of us, and me. Rude, in my face. Wait a second, hold on. She needed to have the spanking her parents never gave her. Somebody didn't teach her any manners. Everyone was allowing her to act badly and didn't know how to do anything. Finally, enough was enough. I grabbed her around the waist, put her rear end up in the air, and cracked down on her. Left a few handprints. From that point on, she was the nicest person you'd ever want to meet – at least, around me.

"Another time I lost it was in Ibiza. I was dancing in a club and a couple of guys from North Africa were being obnoxious. I was having a good time, dancing with a lot of ladies, and these two guys were unnerved that the women would walk up and ask me to dance, one after another. These two guys did not appreciate me having this much fun. They started with jeering. I let them get by with it. Then they started pushing the women around I had been dancing with. I warned them that it wouldn't happen again. It happened again. And they came physically onto me. I picked one of them by the back of the belt and collar of his shirt and threw him through a door. The other guy came for me. That was a bad thing to do. I was running on pure adrenaline. He went over the bar.

"That type of warrior power has come up in my relationship with record companies. I'm probably one of the most hostile people they know, because I'm smart. They tried to nigger me, and I'm not going for it. I'm in their face. My grandfathers didn't take this shit. My father didn't take this shit. I grew up thinking that I didn't have to take anything from anybody, no matter who they are or what their station in life. I'm just not scared. When Samuel and I worked together, we stepped on toes without even trying, just being that we were trying to do business. He had a different kind of that same energy, in that he organized the business.

"I apply the warrior energy to the blues by tapping into the ancient job of the *griot* class. That wasn't a job you did because someone said you had to do it; you did it because that's what you did. It was your right as a person. In terms of warriorship, you had to stand up and do what was right, what you were born to do. George Clinton did that when he came out with song that said America eats its young. He said, 'I've had enough, and you should, too.'

"In warriorship you have to be very present, very aware of where you are, where you've been, and where you're going. You have to do that inside songs when you're playing. With the blues, I'm really not singing the past; I bring the past with the present and then step on out of line to go further. And when an artist goes further out than most people, then it's their responsibility to bring the information back and articulate it in such a way people can understand. That's what's important.

"I believe that everyone can hear the music. What is available for me is available for you. But part of the hearing is not being bound to security. You have to give up, surrender to that energy. Once you hear the music energy, you've got to let all the other stuff go. Some people don't know what to do when they hear the force of music. They go out but don't know how to get back with the information. They think tripping out is the purpose. The music is coming from very powerful beings. Those beings are from a long time ago, but they are speaking through the time now. You have to feel them and go where they go. It's not any more than that.

"Part of what a warrior does, the compassion and generosity of warriorship, is to get the door open and hold it open for other people to come through. That means the warrior is often out there alone. Sometimes the door closes behind you and you don't know that it happened. Then you have to stop, put the guitar down, go back and get a wedge, and get the door open again so those people can hear the music. You can't be afraid, no matter what's going on. A lot of musicians tell me that my albums *The Natch'l Blues*, *Mo' Roots*, and *Giant Step* were the road maps for them in finding their way through the music. Those albums were wedges holding the door open.

"My thing was that I really loved blues, and I was moving through with that. I realized that a lot of people didn't have a positive take on black American music. When I came back from Ibiza, I knew that I could not compromise my music or my approach to music. If that meant war with the record companies, if that meant staying on the outside, so be it. No more compromise. That is when I began to be conscious, as a cultural warrior. For me, cultural warriorship is heeding the call of the music."

John Porter steps back into the lounge. "All right, we're ready for you, Taj."

Taj walks into the recording studio, which has the atmosphere of a mechanic's shop without the grease, all work and no frills. Extraneous equipment is covered with black quilts to dampen the sound and stop it from bouncing around and muddling the recording. The musicians sit with their instruments in niches, connected by earphones. In the sound booth, on the other side of the large plate-glass window, Porter and his engineer, Eric, sit behind a twelve-foot-long, bright-blue soundboard studded with row upon row upon row of switches and slide bars. The music is blasted into their faces from two speakers perched on either corner of the soundboard. In the booth with them is Ron Goldstein, president of the Verve Music Group, Smith's label. Goldstein – black hair swept back from a widow's peak, black horn-rimmed glasses, black crew-neck T-shirt, black pants, black shoes – flew in from New York, and will catch the late flight back after the session. He was the president of Private Music when Taj recorded for that label.

"In those days, Taj and I would have two-hour shouting matches, from Berlin to Los Angeles, over the phone," Goldstein confided. "He'd demand to know why his records weren't in the shops over there, and I'd try to explain the intricacies of the business. He was difficult."

"We hated each other," Taj confirmed later.

Taj's voice comes in over the speakers: "Give me *blat-blop-blop*," he instructs the musicians. "I can't tell you how to do it, but I'll know when I hear. We need to get the form down."

The drummer taps out the countdown on his sticks. One, two, three, four, one, two – and Taj strikes the first chord. But he's off a half beat. "What beat do you want in front of this?" he asks. "I'm terrible on the count. Give me the count."

One, two, three, four, one, two – and Taj hits the opening chord again. They do eleven takes, making adjustments along the way. Smith says too much bass. Porter wants more Smith on the bridges. Goldstein wants more Smith up front. After all, it's his album. None of the musicians have played together. They've never rehearsed the song. They have no sheet music in front of them. They are out of the line of sight from each other. Then, like mysterious alchemy, it all comes together. Smith pounces on the strut beat perfectly. He plays vigorously, with authority, flawless, letting the music get ahead of his mind so that the organ's voice is heard first. Malone jumps in with a guitar solo that literally knocks Porter back from the soundboard. "Where did that come from?" he asks with a big grin. Taj's voice cuts in right on the beat as the drummer holds the pace, adding cymbal flourishes to a phrase like bookends.

After the song, the musicians gather around the soundboard to hear the playback. By the third chord, they are clapping their hands and dancing. Smith and Mason get in a gyrating groove together. They're on an adrenaline high, like athletes who've just won a game. They know they've hit a home run. No need to take another pass. They can go home early.

In the lounge, Russell Malone says, between grins, "I first heard Taj when I was ten years old and saw the film *Sounder*. Taj's playing stood out in that film. It's an inspiration to play with Jimmy and Taj. It brings my level up."

26 Music Boat Home

Athens, Georgia, is Deep South. Many of the houses have colonnaded porches and expansive lawns, harking back to the plantation mansions of the antebellum South. Broad-leaved shade trees arch over the streets, their bosky shadows offering some relief from the humidity and constant sun. Athens has a genteel, courteous air, much like that of a Southern gentleman who uses manners to disguise his human frailties. Located 60 miles northeast of Atlanta, Athens is on the edge of the booming New South, just far enough away to maintain a leisurely pace but close enough to share the cosmopolitan sheen. It is home to the University of Georgia, the United States' oldest state university, founded in 1801. An academic sophistication caps Athens' rural roots, which show through if you look – or listen – close enough.

On a hot summer's day in 1999, folks in Athens were treated to a sight that they had never seen before, at least not in Athens: tall, regal black men walking down the street in colorful, silk, flowing West African clothes. Pick-ups circled the block twice or three times so that the drivers could take it all in. People on the sidewalk stopped the men and asked, "What are ya'll doing here?", their tone not hostile, just curious.

"These musicians are from Mali, and we're here recording early Southern music and African music," Taj answered for the musicians, who spoke French and Mandinka but not Southern-drawl English.

"Oh. Well, y'all have a nice time."

The Malian musicians and Taj were in town because of Joe Boyd and Lucy Duran, old and persistent friends of Taj's who believe in authentic music. Boyd had been trying for years to get Taj to record for his independent record company, but the hook-up never happened. Then Boyd – who had recorded the Malian virtuoso Toumani Diabate on two albums, playing with gypsies from southern Spain – suggested that Taj and Toumani play together. Flat-out, hands-down go, replied Taj. We'll work out the details later. Toumani had once opened for Taj, and both men were eager to play together.

Taj settles back to tell of the experience that has profoundly affected what he does musically and will continue to do so for the rest of his life: "Working with the musicians from Mali to create the *Kulanjan* album was probably the highest coup I might ever achieve, musically. The next level that could happen would be to immerse myself in the actual instruments in Africa and Mali, to learn and play only those instruments, and guitar, for the rest of my life. The Malian music was like finding the ancestors of my music. The Malian instruments was like my instrument finding its ancestors in itself. This music has been handed down for 71 generations. There is so much to explore and learn. That's a lot of music to hear about – about the musicians who played it, how and when, what they did, what sound they brought to it, what they saw during their time. It's so deep. It's not some sort of fleeting kind of thing that some guy at the university thought would be a good idea to record. *Kulanjan* was recorded by the musicians themselves, and in the real, resonating chamber self-history where those instruments come from.

"For me, *Kulanjan* was very highly personal. It was closing a gap before the year 2000. It's been just about 120 years since my grandfather – who was born in 1881, and whose ancestors came from West Africa – until I've been able to make a musical connection to my roots, like Alex Haley, who wrote *Roots*, was able to make a family connection.

"About 30 years ago, I saw on a record album of kora music the face of Batrou Sekou Kouyate, one of the elder players from Mali, who passed on recently. He looked so much like my uncles and father and grandfather on my father's side that I was shocked. It was like looking at somebody I knew, not just looking at the face of a beautiful person from Africa and having some kind of connection.

"On *Kulanjan* (Hannibal), Toumani Diabate, the six other African musicians, and I explored the roots of American blues guitar expressions found in Mali traditions. I found an ancestral home to the sounds I'd been hearing since a young boy. When I started playing guitar, I discovered that we – that means the Afro-American/Native-American/European-American community – created music based on sound imprints from ancient Africa. We had developed a whole new set of songs off of fragments of great long songs from a long time ago.

"Something kept telling me all of these years that, if I stayed with music long enough, I'd find out the source of these songs. I'd come to a place where the great long songs came from. I knew that, for some reason or other, the source of the music that resonated in me came from Western Africa. The words of the music might be in a different language, but the music has a language sound of its own.

"How the blues is sung, the rhythm of black English, comes from that source. It comes from our ancestors' effort – who came here as slaves – to take their native sounds and learn the English language in the various dialects. The music took on some of the sound of those dialects, combined with the patterns of the African music. That's why, over the years, everyone has thought that anyone who plays the blues well must come from the South and have the Southern experience. They don't understand that the experience comes from beyond the South and goes out of the South.

"When I first started hearing guitar music, and before I wanted to play the guitar, Spanish music rang immediately to me. Any string music. I'm talking about Hawaiian music, Spanish music, blues – all these had a ring as soon as the guitar was played. There was a life there, and it brought something from a farther time. So I started having ideas about how that could have happened. One of the earlier albums I heard in the '60s was *The Guitars Of Africa*. I've always heard strings, like a guitar, as the primary sound. Drums make me move, but when the strings come in I vibrate the way they vibrate. It's always been that way. I never knew why, and I didn't understand why. I said to myself, 'Don't clutter your life up with stuff that keeps you away from responding in a fully inspired way to the way this music is coming back at you.'

"The further you go back into the music, the more you see how it develops. The gypsy music of southern Spain, and the instruments that music is played on, came up from Africa with the Moors, who occupied Spain for more than eight centuries. The guitar and the violin evolved out of the elemental bow strings and lutes of Africa.

"Even further back in history is kora music, which comes from West Africa. The chief kora instrument is either a 19- or 21- or 23-stringed lute harp. The kora is the center of the Mande culture. The Mande speakers established some of the earliest civilizations in Western Africa. There is a long tradition of Mande oral history. One story tells of a ruler who sailed across the Atlantic toward the Americas in 1312. Many musical things that started from the 13th century are executed through musicians who played the kora and its accompanying instruments: the ngoni, the banjo's great, great relative; the balafon, which looks like an ancient xylophone, which is exactly where a xylophone came from; and the bolon, a large calabash instrument, which has seven strings and functions as the bass. The khalam, riti, ngombi, obukano – all these stringed instruments were the predecessors of the modern-day string instruments. The guitar evolved from the ngoni, a gourd outfitted with strings.

"Early on, I knew only one song that led directly back to this music, which has an older sound than, say, the Jimmy Reed type of sound – more of the sound that John Lee Hooker has. He learned his sound from his stepfather, who was from an area of Louisiana where the people descended from Mande speakers [were] brought over as slaves. A certain kind of sound comes out of those folks. An ancient sound.

"When you listen to the way the words are put together in those African dialects, you start realizing that's where the sound of the music comes from. The Mande languages – grouped under the heading Mandingo – include Malinke, Vai, Toma. Lots of them, like Kpelle, are spoken throughout West Africa. They are tonal, in that changes in pitch are used to distinguish words or phrases otherwise constructed exactly alike. It's how you breathe the language, how you sing the speech, that makes you understand it.

"The language the Africans brought to this country influenced the rhythm of the blues. Language and music have a great deal in common. You can hear this in the lilt and rhythm of the speech of the Africans trying to learn this new language spoken by the heads of the plantations, many of them Irish, both in the South and in the West Indies. The overseers spoke a particular kind of brogue on top of the English, so a lot of the bending and rounding-out of sound, like you hear in the West Indies, comes from the blend of the Irish-African English. The rhythm of black talk in this country carries the history.

"Because of the psychological and social climate in the United States, people look down on black people and look down on the blues and look down on Native Americans and look down on people who had anything to do with the ethnic experiences. They say, 'No, if the music, art, whatever, was generated from those peoples, it can't be good.' Yet somehow or other, because of their two-facedness and their constant deception, somebody somewhere along the line hears some things in the original, and as long as they can take it out of the hands of the original purveyors of the music and create something commercial with it, put a different face on it, then it's okay. The poetry of a man with no education who has written something as brilliant as Shelley or Keats or Shakespeare, lyrics that are on par with those works, that uneducated man got nothing – no recognition, no money, no respect, no honor.

"Once things are broken up – as they have been between Africa and the Americas – there's a certain level of communication that you don't know. It's only been in the last 25 years that I've been making a clear connection with the musicians who help me make that connection with the older communication, where the source of my music comes from. What I saw for myself was that this huge music business is really going to blot out people even thinking about playing music for the soul and heart of themselves, humanity, culture, or anything like that. The music business is so huge that it has to hunger for more and more just to stay alive. It's a scale thing. In the enormity of the music industry's appetite, the individual, intimate experiences are lost.

"I really thought that music was something people did devoid of being paid to do music. The music industry, as it continues to develop in the United States, is a commercial industry, in that people play music only if they are paid. Even if they wanted to play it because they loved it, once they got paid, somehow or other that seemed to take over playing music for cultural and spiritual reasons. They couldn't separate the two. But playing music and playing music commercially are only connected when you are surrounded by people who are trying to figure how to exploit your youth, your enthusiasm, your song. When you first join this great big river of the music business, you might think that you're playing music on your own; but if you don't co-operate with the powers that be in the music industry, they send in their people to figure what they can glean off of your ability to make magic with the music.

"In the United States, black people are generally judged by the larger culture on the basis of color, not on the basis of culture. Because of that, you can see why some people won't appreciate a certain type of music, because they don't have any blood that runs in that direction, no cultural ties to it. If blacks have been in the United States long enough, they don't have any ties to the root culture or the ancestors, so we don't understand what any of this is about, either.

"When we have a constitution that says [that blacks] are three-fifths of a human being – says so in the founding constitution of the country – you don't get a second chance to make a first impression. It's institutionalized at such a level that people could do anything they wanted to those three-fifths humans. Well, I was never taught that those things applied to me. You may think they do, but that is your thought; I don't have to accept that. My father gave me the idea of the whole Marcus Garvey thing, that I *do* have a home in this world. Any time I get fed up with what's happening in the United States, and am not being able to do what I need to do here, I can go to Africa and be welcomed.

"I was raised that the Caribbean, Central and South America, and Africa was a homeland. I was connected to humanity in general and to people connected to the experience out of Africa one way or another, because the blood runs in all directions. Besides, it seemed to me that there is a lot that travels on African music.

"It seems to me that the call from the ancient people is still strong from one generation to the next. My quest has been to rediscover the combinations, to find what door to go through, that kept this information musically up at a high level.

"There are certain people whose music I play, music that always goes right up to the sky, like that Ali Farka Toure. What does he do? He spends six months of the year doing his work, doing all his farming, and getting all his business done. Then he plays music for six months of the year with no thought of having to go about his other work. He says that he can't play music if he's got other thoughts in his head. Now he's through with touring. If you want to record with him, you have to go to his village, Niafunke. He took some of his touring earnings to help his village with irrigation and rice farming, to raise the level of agriculture.

"Music out of Africa has always been familial, sort of family, to me. The source really was ancestors. I grew up with that idea. One thing I feel bad about in the United States is the level of communication from generation to generation about the ancestors. You can't make it unless the people before you did what they did to get you to where you are. Now you have to give something up to the universe for them, to them, about them. You have to bring them into your thoughts. The ancestors are so powerful that they can get around all this so-called New World stuff and make the real connection.

"Djelimady Sissoko and Sidiki Diabate, the great kora musicians, recorded years ago an album called *Ancient Strings*. Toumani Diabate – son of Sidiki Diabate – who put out the album *New Ancient Strings*, is prominent in the new generation from the kora tradition. That's how I got to know Toumani. One day I read the liner notes on the *Ancient Strings* album and I see Toumani Diabate's name. Then I realized the connection. I was blown away. Next thing I know, he's coming to the States to play. So I figured there are some bridges to be built.

"The *Kulanjan* project really started with – aside from my own personal interest in finding more about the music – when I heard some music out of from Gambia. I heard some strains that belonged to the greater songs. The way the melody played back to me, I was, like, 'Wait a minute.' I started to hear the way the notes are laid out in the way Elizabeth Cotton plays the music, the way John Hurt plays the music, the way Reverend Gary Davis plays it, or anybody who picks the old, old style of guitar. That old style is closer to the source.

"Whenever I heard music from Western Africa, it really got to me. I tried to figure out where those sounds came from, geographically. More and more sounds that I wanted to play came from Mali. The Mississippi sound that Skip James played, which is that long *bulong-badung-dadung-dabebadong* – that *dong*, that note that goes long before he picks it up – that is straight-up Malian. It's exact.

"With Toumani Diabate and the musicians from Mali, when I'd go *bulong*, everybody was right there. I hardly had to talk to those guys while making *Kulanjan*, in the sense of explaining the blues. When doing the songs, the music spoke. I played some old blues and all these guys had to do was hear it go by one time, and the next time they were playing, and playing all the way to the end of the song, or as long as I wanted to play.

"For them, an 18-minute song that gives the description of a particular family and all the great people in it – that is not something they are unused to doing. They have a tradition of including in a song information about the patron who looks out for them, along with the history of a village or tribe or family. In the old days, the African musicians went from village to village to announce that a notable visitor was coming. They gave the background on that person. When the person arrived, he would be treated according to how the musicians brought the information to the village. These musicians, even now, are used to playing the complete story.

"On *Kulanjan*, we put instruments together that had never played together in their entire existence in Africa. Guys from one group played their music in their territory and guys from another group in another territory played their music over there. The lines were drawn where the hunters played and where the *griots* played. But the younger musicians are connected into a way of putting things together differently. That's what *Kulanjan* did. We put the blues directly back on its African root.

"Now that this summer touring season is over, I'm thinking about some future projects. I have a tremendous amount of ideas about music. I have all this wealth of knowledge, and rather than just commit it to records that are going to sell a minimal amount and still be in somebody's catalog 40 years hence, I think it's more important to just jump over this river going through American music and connect with the Africans who have been reaching out for years through their music. In all these years I've been doing music, I really haven't changed the mind of the music industry to do anything different. It's time for me to consider different projects while I'm at the top of my musical playing.

"I am thinking of taking a steel-drum orchestra and a regular orchestra and having them simultaneously play the *William Tell* overture under the baton of the same conductor. In a traditional orchestra, the musicians read all the notes off a score in front of them, and the conductor also has the score. With a steel-drum orchestra, nobody but the conductor has the score, so all the musicians have to know their parts. They have to be committed to the part they're playing, not like, 'Wham, bam, thank you ma'am, and I'm out of there.'

"Most people know the *William Tell* overture from the build-up – you know, the *Lone Ranger* theme. I want to build up to the trumpet part, that Lone Ranger bit, then take a huge aircraft propeller engine and blow off the music score sheets of the traditional orchestra players and see who could keep playing, the steel-band guys or the orchestra guys. Now, that may be a bit tongue in cheek, but then people might realize that you can't play the jump-up steel-band sound everyone associates with the carnival without having to be able to play real classical music. This is a fact that needs to be brought out, because everybody is able to dip into this so-called Third World music, take what they want, manufacture it the way they want, and rip it off.

"What I'd really love to do is have the opportunity to take the sounds that I know and score some movies that have some cultural and redeeming values. I'm presently involved [with] writing music for a play about Satchel Paige.

"The play *Mule Bone*, which premiered at the Lincoln Center on

February 14, 1991, was the first opportunity I had to take the kind of music that I think of on my own, with nobody telling me what to or not to play. The play was written by the poet Langston Hughes and Zora Neale Hurston, a folklorist and novelist. It was about a love triangle but was never produced, because of a feud – supposedly a lover's spat – between Langston and Hurston. As the musical director and the composer, I put Langston's poetry to music.

"I loved that project. I didn't just sit down and say, 'Okay, now I have to write music.' For me to write music, I have to hear the music coming out of the universe in order for me to say, 'Okay, here we are. This is going to work here.' In *Mule Bone*, there is a song called 'Crossings.' My idea wasn't to try to weld it to jazz or weld it to something that made the poetry and music grate against each other; the words came alive by the tone and voice I used for the music and how it made me feel, into how Hughes was when he was writing at the time. The music played through me. I didn't do it intellectually.

"When *Mule Bone* went on Broadway, at the Ethel Barrymore Theater, it was packed every night. Packed. People crying because they couldn't get in. That was the first time, for me, to stand back offstage and hear my music. I'm always onstage with it. To be a composer and hear my music live, along with the dialogue, was a thrill beyond words.

"One of the great things about doing the play was the acknowledgment of me by people who were aware of me as a musician and had been following my career, people who were also themselves great actors and actresses and playwrights in New York. One other stellar talent that I admire is Judith Jamison, the lead dancer for many years for the Dance Theater of Harlem, which she now heads. During the years she was the principal dancer, under Alvin Ailey, she danced my music. I was really shocked. Alvin Ailey loved my stuff. There was no bigger thrill than to work with these dancers, who could hear the music and get down to their work of setting up the steps. There was no, 'Well, Taj, I don't know what this means.'

"I think I'm called to make music. Music is a major energy from the universe that is stepped down through human consciousness. It's a bigger thing than most people are aware. We're working in a world that tends to try to control nature and surround it in some kind of way. What I'm saying is that the style of the West is to put a corral around lightning. You cannot stop lightning from its own will.

"If you do music long enough, many generations ahead of anybody coming along, your music pops up every now and then. You are an ancestor. It is clear that the musicality of my ancient people is still on me and on us as a society. The rhythm of the music is going out to everybody in the world, because it comes in on a basic, human, tribal kind of thing, which we all are, whether we like it or not. I'm trying to say to people that music exists, whether it's recorded or not. In listening to music, each individual is having an individual – as well as a group – experience.

"My father and my mother really wanted to do their thing as musicians. Neither got the opportunity. I've been able to live a life as an artist on my own cognizance of the way I wanted to. It's been wonderful, because I've gone the way I wanted to go. The gift is that I've been able to be an artist and live the life of an artist.

"As de León would say, you pick the pearl and you pay the price. That means that you have to take whatever consequences come along. I went and did what I've done. I've enjoyed it, and I'm glad I've done it."

Selected Discography

TAJ MAHAL
Taj Mahal (1968)
The Natch'l Blues (1968)
Giant Steps/De Ole Folks At Home (1969)
The Real Thing (1971)
Happy Just To Be Like I Am (1971)
Recycling The Blues And Other Related Stuff (1972)
Sounder (soundtrack, 1973)
Oooh So Good 'n Blues (1973)
Mo' Roots (1974)
Music Keeps Me Together (1975)
Music Fuh Yuh (Musica Para Tu) (1977)
Satisfied 'n' Tickled Too (1976)
Anthology, Volume One (1976)
Evolution (The Most Recent) (1977)
Brothers (soundtrack, 1977)
Best Of Taj Mahal, Volume One (1981)
Taj (1986)
Shake Sugaree (1987)
Live And Direct (1987)
Big Blues, Live At Ronnie Scott's (1988)
The Hot Spot (soundtrack, 1990)
Brer Rabbit And The Wonderful Tar Baby (1990)
Mule Bone (1991)
Like Never Before (1991)
Taj's Blues (1992)
Rising Sons, Featuring Taj Mahal And Ry Cooder (1992)
Smilin' Island Of Song (1992)
World Music (1993)
Dancing The Blues (1993)
Mumtaz Mahal (1995)
An Evening Of Acoustic Music (1996)
Phantom Blues (1996)
Scrapple (soundtrack, 1996)
Follow The Drinking Gourd (1997)
Señor Blues (1997)
Taj Mahal In Progress And In Motion, 1965-1998 (1998)
Kulanjan (1999)
Shoutin' In Key (2000)

TAJ MAHAL AND THE HULA BLUES BAND
Sacred Island (1997)

Bibliography

HERZHAFT, GERARD (translated by Brigitte DeBord): *Encyclopedia Of The Blues* (University of Arkansas Press, 1992)

BICKNELL, JULIAN: *Great Buildings Of The World* (Clarkson Potter, New York, 1995)

COWDERY, CHARLES K: *Blues Legends* (Gibbs-Smith, Salt Lake City, 1995

WRIGHT, ESMOND: *The Dream Machine, From Reconstruction To Reagan, Vol 3* (Blackwell, 1996)

LANG, PETER: *The Lost Decade, A Story Of America In The 1960s* (American University Studies, 1987)

STERN, JANE and MICHAEL: *Encyclopedia Of Pop Culture* (HarperPerennial, 1992)

OLIVER, JAMES and HORTON, LOUIS E (consultant editors): *A History Of The African American People* (Wayne State University Press, Detroit, 1997)

JAMES, STEVE: "Blues Across Borders" (*Acoustic Guitar*, March/April, 1993)

DAVIS, FRANCES: *The History Of The Blues* (Hyperion, New York, 1995)

JONES, LEROI (Amiri Baraka): *Blues People: Negro Music In White America* (Greenwood Press, 1983)

CROUCH, STANLEY: *The All-American Skin Game, Or The Decoy Of Race* (Vintage, 1995)

COYOTE, PETER: *Sleeping Where I Fall* (Counterpoint, 1998)

Like Never Before (record review, *Rolling Stone*, September 19, 1991)

FRINKE, DAVID: *Rising Sons, Featuring Taj Mahal And Ry Cooder* (record review, *Rolling Stone*, March 18, 1993)

NELSON, WALDO E, MD; BEHRMAN, RICHARD E, MD; KLIEGMAN, ROBERT M, MD; and ARVIN, ANN M, MD (editors): Textbook Of Pediatrics (15th edition: WB Saunders Co, 1996)

Index